Political Economy of Reform and Change

First published in 1997, this collection of articles and essays analyses the political economy of reform and change in Eastern Europe during the years of Gorbachev's *perestroika* and the years immediately following the fall of the Berlin wall and the collapse of the Soviet Union.

Written by Polish economist Jan Winiecki, between 1984 and 1996, this work explores the issue of the feasibility of reform and change during the period of decline and collapse of communist economic order and, later, the emergence of the capitalist economic order in the post-communist Eastern Europe. Split into three parts, the work considers firstly the failures of Gorbachev's political economy of reform, secondly the determining factors in the collapse of the Soviet system, and finally the feasibility of the systematic change which began in the wake of its collapse.

T0299958

Political Economy of Reform and Change

A Case of Eastern Europe

Jan Winiecki

Routledge
Taylor & Francis Group

First published in 1997
by Nova Science Publishers, Inc

This edition first published in 2011 by Routledge
2 Park Square, Milton Park, Abingdon, Oxon, OX14 4RN

Simultaneously published in the USA and Canada
by Routledge
711 Third Avenue, New York, NY 10017

Routledge is an imprint of the Taylor & Francis Group, an informa business

© 1997 Nova Science publishers, Inc

Publisher's Note
The publisher has gone to great lengths to ensure the quality of this reprint but points out that some imperfections in the original copies may be apparent.

Disclaimer
The publisher has made every effort to trace copyright holders and welcomes correspondence from those they have been unable to contact.

A Library of Congress record exists under ISBN: 1560724498

ISBN 13: 978-0-415-69993-8 (hbk)
ISBN 13: 978-0-203-12742-1 (ebk)
ISBN 13: 978-0-415-50594-9 (pbk)

POLITICAL ECONOMY OF REFORM AND CHANGE

A CASE OF EASTERN EUROPE

JAN WINIECKI

NOVA SCIENCE PUBLISHERS, INC.
COMMACK, NY

Creative Design: Gavin Aghamore

Editorial Production: Susan Boriotti

Assistant Vice President/Art Director: Maria Ester Hawrys

Office Manager: Annette Hellinger

Graphics: Frank Grucci

Manuscript Coordinator: Phyllis Gaynor

Book Production: Michelle Keller, Ludmila Kwartiroff, Christine Mathosian,
Joanne Metal, Tammy Sauter and Tatiana Shohov

Circulation: Iyatunde Abdullah, Sharon Britton, and Cathy DeGregory

Library of Congress Cataloging-in-Publication Data
available upon request

ISBN 1-56072-449-8

Copyright © 1997 by Nova Science Publishers, Inc.
6080 Jericho Turnpike, Suite 207
Commack, New York 11725
Tele. 516-499-3103   Fax 516-499-3146
E-Mail: Novascience@earthlink.net

Printed in the United States of America

To my Mother who taught me
To see the difference
Between good and evil
- and between good economics
and bad economics

CONTENTS

INTRODUCTION

This book aims at offering the Reader a kind of intellectual guide through the collection of articles and papers that make up 'Political Economy of Reform and Change - and, in this manner, through the general issue of the f e a s i b i l i t y of reform and change. They were written by the present writer over the period of 12 years (1984-1996) and, therefore, should be perceived in the context of both time and place, that is the period of decline and collapse of communist economic order and, later, the emergence of the capitalist economic order in the post-communist Eastern Europe.

To exemplify the idea, it is a different story to have written in 1987 (as this author did) that there is strong probability that Gorbachev's economic *perestroika* is going to be carried much further than both its proponents and opponents (i.e. in the East communist *apparatchiki* - *J.W.*) perceive at the moment than to have written it in, say, 1990. In the former case the author thought it necessary to substantiate the prediction with references to the logic of decline of the Soviet economic system; in the latter the decline would have been clear for all to see.

The intended guide should start with the title. There exists an intellectual muddle in the literature on the subjects in question, where the terms: 'reform' and 'change' are used interchangeably. However, **equating reform and change is an error of a large magnitude**. One 'reforms' something that already exists and is in need of more or less substantial modifications to make it work better. On the other hand 'change' suggests shift from one state of affairs to another. Thus, one reforms an economic system but one changes from one system to another.

In the relevant context 'reforms' mean near-continuous attempts to improve the performance of the communist centrally planned (centrally administered, Soviet-type) economy. These reforms usually tinkered with the structure of incentives, administration of planning and plan implementation, etc., but without breaking decisively with fundamental institutions of the e c o n o m i c system, let alone questioning the fundamentals of communist p o l i t i c a l system.

By contrast 'change' signifies a shift from the communist centrally planned to a capitalist market economy. **Such shift must, however, entail b o t h political and economic change - and in this order.** As political change destroys the symbiotic relationship between political and economic system under communism, it opens up the possibility (but in no way the c e r t a i n t y !) of successful economic change. Without such a decisive break with the political past the economic change is well-nigh impossible. A substantial part of the pre-collapse and post-collapse writings of this author, collected in this book, consistently stress the point.

Furthermore, **there is no necessary continuity between earlier tinkering and later systemic change.** The successful quasi-liberalizations accomplished under the banner of 'reform' were not always beneficial in terms of their contribution to later systemic changes. For among the countries that are widely regarded as success stories there are both perennial tinkerers under communism as well as those that remained close to the Soviet economic orthodoxy.

A 'political economy' term raises fewer questions. Thus, this collection concerns itself not so much with the question how badly the Soviet system performed and how successive modifications failed to improve it but rather with the question why, although badly needed, reforms, let alone fundamental institutional changes, were not implemented. In other words it concerns itself not with 'hows' but with 'whys', or with **the political feasibility of reform**.

The same applies to systemic change. It is not the efficiency and coherence of stabilization, liberalization, and institutional change-related measures that are a prime consideration here but rather political feasibility of their elaboration and implementation. Also, the role of coalition-

_0

building in support of transition from plan to market is repeatedly stressed by this author.

The term 'Eastern Europe' requires some comments as well. Many a Reader would be surprised to learn that it is of a rather recent vintage. It, in fact, came into being after the World-War-II to stress the division of Europe, with 'Eastern Europe' understood as the part under the Soviet communist domination. But in the somewhat more distant past, various parts of what used to be later called 'Eastern Europe' were called 'Northern Europe', and more recently 'Central' or 'East-Central Europe'.

These differences are of interest not only to historians or geographers, though. They have also important connotations for the subjects covered in this book because **'Eastern Europe' covers countries with sharply differing political histories and these differences may, in turn, strongly affect the systemic change**. The 'East-Central Europe' is, thus, a narrower term covering most often the countries historically belonging to the Western Christendom. A look at the map of Eastern Europe and the dividing line between the East-Central Europe and the rest may also look like a dividing line between success and failure of systemic change [see Winiecki, 1996].

But let us turn to the reform failure, first, as it makes up the first part of this book. The Soviet economic system could be characterized as one, where initiative was limited by and large to the center (central planners and their political masters), thus missing the benefits of entrepreneurship and innovation of autonomous economic agents. System's ability to utilize information available throughout the economy was by its centralized nature extremely poor. Finally, incentives to perform well were either non-existent or heavily distorted. The system was also unstable over time. As economic structure became increasingly distorted and complexity increased [see, *i.a.,* Winiecki, 1987a, 1988, and Winiecki & Winiecki, 1992], as external shocks began to exert growing influence on performance, the initially low capacity of the system to perform began to decline, slowly at first and precipitously at some point.

The foregoing has given an impulse to the search for performance-improving measures - the search that began already in mid-1950s [see, *i.a.* Kornai, 1959, and Berend, 1990] and continued throughout the system's existence, until its collapse at the threshold of 1990s. These **continuous attempts at economic reforms were unsuccessful, marginal improvements notwithstanding**. Therefore, over time, the literature on the subject of reform began to be increasingly interspersed with questions concerning not the e c o n o m i c s of Soviet system's reform but the p o l i t i c a l e c o n o m y of reform.

The present writer began asking **the question: 'why reform fail in the Soviet economic system?'** in terms of political economy, rather than economics from mid-1980s [see i.a. Winiecki 1984, 1986, and 1987b]. He pointed at the apparent irrationality of the resistance to performance-enhancing reforms. After all, as Mancur Olson once remarked, 'even in dictatorial systems, the dictator has an incentive to make an economy of the country he controls work better, since this will generate more tax receipts he can use as he pleases and usually also reduces dissent' [1984, p.637].

The 'New Economic History' school, led by Douglass North, underlines the benefits from the institutional arrangements, primarily the existing property rights' structure as a reason why high-cost institutions survive. **If the shift to low-cost institutions is detrimental to powerful elites who draw benefits from the existing arrangements, such shift will be abandoned, distorted, or reversed** [North, 1979].

Following this property rights-based approach, this author identified **fundamental system-specific forms of rent-seeking** that exist only under the particular political-economic system of communism *cum* centrally planned economy. Also, he identified **those who were primarily interested in maintaining institutional** *status quo* and, given their position in the ruling stratum, were able successfully to block the shift to low-cost institutions.

Of the two system-specific forms, the principle of *nomenklatura* is a better known one. It entails the privilege of the communist party apparatus to recommend (read: nominate) candidates to all high and middle level managerial positions in the economy and in state administration. These appointments were made primarily on the basis of loyalty to a given *coterie* rather than competence. Unsurprisingly, *apparatchiki* appointed to these best paid positions their card-carrying cronies from the party organizations and bureaucracy.

Another form was benefits from the privileged, non-market access to goods and services in short supply at below market clearing prices - a very important feature in shortage-plagued economies. These came often in the form of kickbacks from the very same managers appointed to *nomenklatura*-covered positions, supplying those who appointed them, as well as other superiors and collegues (who could help them in their careers).

These peculiar methods of rent-seeking could be maintained o n l y thanks to the existence of the communist political system. The domination of the communist party apparatus and the bureaucracy, that is main beneficiaries of system-specific appropriation of income and wealth, insured that no change took place in th economic system that would eliminate these opportunities for enrichment.

It was abundantly clear that *apparatchiki* and bureacrats were keen not to allow the economic system to be transformed into the private property-based market economy. For in the latter there would be no *nomenklatura*. Morover, a 'normal' capitalist market economy tends toward equilibrium, and et equilibrium it is market prices that allocate goods. Thus, there would be no apartments, cars, TV-sets, etc. to be distributed at below market prices to the privileged minority.

The whole Part One is devoted to answering the basic: 'why reforms fail?' question. The texts contained therein point to options available to the ruling stratum in communist countries at the time of decline, explain why some segments of that stratum resist the performance-enhancing reforms and change, describe *techniques* of resistance, dispel ambiguites concerning the attitudes of enterprise managers toward reforms and change and even consider how much it would cost to 'buy out' the resisting *apparatchiki* and bureaucrats so as to remove the obstacles to institutional change.

Although all these texts were written b e f o r e the communist system's collapse, *i.e.* before the verdict of history was delivered, the present writer regarded the prospects for reforms, i.e. of successful performance-enhancing modifications w i t h i n the system, as non-existent. Therefore, I stressed that 'until those pillars of the system that benefit most [...]

withdraw their opposition, are forced to withdraw it, or are forced out of power, things will get from bad to worse' and warned than 'things will get worse, may be much worse,' before systemic change may take place [Winiecki, 1984 and 1987b]. Incidentally, this author's predictions as to the probable timing of such a change were not very wide off the mark since he did not expect 'such fundamental economic change to come about earlier than in the next five to ten years' [*ibid.*]. And the first, *mimeographed* version of the 1987 book quoted above had been written in 1984.

The t i m i n g of successful systemic change inevitably raises the question as to **why the communist system's collapse happened when it did** - and not earlier or later. As an answer to the question, **the determinants of the collapse, are dealt with in the Part Two of this book.** This author thought it advisable to include his earlier considerations on the issue since there has been a lot of misunderstanding - or even outright nonsense - surrounding the issue. Sometimes one might have surmised from reading the pundits that it was Mr. Gorbachev who, singlehandedly, accomplished the change (one is tempted to add: including his own political demise).

The 'Spring of Nations' that came in the autumn of 1989 to East-Central Europe, as well as the disappearance of the Soviet Union in 1991, were **the phenomena to which Mr. Gorbachev contributed mightily, although for the most part inadvertently**. Except for the apparent abandonment of the doctrine of intervention in the 'outer empire' (i.e. East-Central Europe), whatever Mr. Gorbachev did, it turned out into something contrary to what he intended to do. He tried to improve, not to dismantle the system, both political and economic, but by trying s i m u l t a n e o u s l y *perestroika* (restructuring) and *uskorenye* (acceleration) he pushed the already declining Soviet economy over the brink. He tried to install in East Berlin and Prague more reformist (but communist) regimes but his inefficient fumblings accelerated the political change and brought communism to an end in both countries more quickly than would have happened otherwise.

The texts in the Part Two try to explain precisely w h y **it would have happened otherwise, Gorbachev or no Gorbachev.** The major contribution to Part Two is an essay that lists major economic determinants of Soviet economic system's decline, underlines that they were inherent in the economic system in question, and tries to establish the period, when the Soviet-type economies passed the point of no return on the path to terminal decline [*text no.6*]. The text was published in 1991, i.e. *ex post*, but the story has already been told in greater detail in earlier publications of this author [1984, 1986, 1987b]

One learns from the text that **most of the determinants of decline became, for internal or external reasons, more painful in the 1970s.** This is revealed also in the analysis of performance indicators of the countries in question. Thus, *Mane, Thekel, Fares* has been on the walls of the communist edifice for quite some time before system's collapse. **The collapse has been the outcome of 'long processes rather than spasmodic events',** as it often seemed to outsiders [see, the the text in question].

One more acknowledgement should be made here, when the timing of system's collapse is considered, namely that for Mr. Reagan. Reagan's policy has been well-thought-of and based on better perception of Soviet reality than that of Mr. Gorbachev. Consequently, the Soviet response to the new U.S. technological challenge was an, already quoted, 'acceleration' program that, indeed, accelerated but only the process of unraveling of the Soviet economy and, consequently, of the communist system .

As the Soviet communist system collapsed in East Central-Europe, and two years later in the Soviet Union itself, the political change became a fact - and, with it, the o p p o r t u n i t i e s for the decisive shift to a capitalist market economy. **The political economy of the shift, or transition, or transformation,** as the systemic change is often called, **forms the core of Part Three of this book.**

To begin with, almost everywhere standard IMF/World Bank 'package' of measures have been accepted (even if not always consistently followed, while in some cases not followed at all). Again, almost everywhere, the knowledge of the Soviet-type economy has been largely neglected [see, specifically Winiecki, 1993, 1995]. Therefore, **a higher economic price was paid than if decision makers were prepared for what was to happen, given the legacy of the past**. This, in turn, made the p o l i t i c a l price of systemic change higher, because the usual disillusionment (or the

'reform fatigue', as the phenomenon was called by Michael Bruno [1992])
set in earlier.

Nontheless, economic fundamentals of the 'package' have been sufficiently sound to ensure that countries staying on course progressed toward
stability faster than those doing it hesitantly and with zig-zags (let alone
those doing little or nothing). Liberalization has been even more successful than stabilization. Usually a greater degree of stabilization discipline
went together with a greater degree of liberalization - and both went together with the already stressed decisiveness of the preceding political
change.

Underappreciated in a l l cases - more and less successful alike - was,
however, the fact that **costs of systemic change are front-loaded**, *i.e.*
borne in the early transition period, while benefits begin to be felt with a
considerable time lag. As this author wrote in 1989, at the start of transition, 'Polish economy is abandoning the Soviet-type economy, a creation
of historically unparalleled wastefulness. **The costs of bidding utopia
farewell are less than the costs of forty years of utopia, but unfortunately they are still high** [Beksiak, Gruszecki, Jedraszczyk, Winiecki,
1989 and 1990]

Indeed, output fell steeply in the early transition, when Soviet system-
specific sources of demand (excessive inventories, overinvestment, etc.)
disappear, while new demands for old output of state enterprises are not
yet found and new output from the emerging private sector is not sufficiently large to compensate for the fall in output of state enterprises [see
Winiecki, 1990 and 1991].

Moreover, the large gap between the demand for and supply of market-type institutions makes the performance of the emerging market
economies inevitably unsatisfactory. The institution-building and its political economy-type implications take a lot of space in two important texts
included in Part Three [*see texts no. 9 and 10*].

The first stresses the priorities forced upon the politicians by the need
to create the institutional rudiments of stabilization policies. It also points
to the role of **the time factor**. For regardless of policy makers' performance the supply of institutions will be for the time being insufficient to
create a platform for healthy economic growth.

The second tries to approach the issue of **policy responses to the build-up of disillusionment and pressure to slow down the process of systemic change**. It addresses the issue of rapid change (called sometime a 'big bang') *versus* gradualism, as well as the tactics of change in the face of strong political resistance, *i.e.* Hirschman's [1963] 'roundabout strategy'. With respect to the latter it suggests measures strengthening the constituencies in favour of change rather than tackling head-on powerful interest groups benefiting most from the inefficient past institutional arrangements.

A next batch of texts deals with the privatization issues. Among the many hotly debated - and politically sensitive - issues, two in particular seem crucial from the political economy vantage point. The first is the way policy makers deal with the privatization. It is, of course, first of all an e c o n o m i c phenomenon stemming from the need to transform state ownership into private ownership because private economic agents on the whole act in a more efficient manner.

However, as there is no clear-cut path of 'getting from here to there', it may be pursued in a manner that p o l i t i c a l l y enhances or, on the contrary, handicaps the overall process of systemic change. **If privatization is seen as a 'fair deal', then the political capital spills over beyond privatization itself; if it is not, then it may become an albatross around the transition's neck** (a contrasting experience of the Czech Republic and Poland is most telling in this respect [*see text no.14*]).

The point has repeatedly been stressed by this author since the start of transition, as the excerpts from the program of stabilization and systemic change written in August-September 1989, at the time of creating the first non-communist government in Poland (and f o r that government) testify . His later articles and papers included in Part Three also underline the political economy aspects of privatization.

The second issue concerns **the difference between the privatization of state enterprises and that of the national economy**. For in the latter case, the private sector emerges from both 'privatization from above', i.e. ownership transformation or privatization proper, and 'privatization from below', i.e. the creation and expansion of the generic private sector [on this point see Gruszecki and Winiecki, 1991, Winiecki 1992]. The latter is no less important, as underlined by the present writer in the text concerning the superiority of eliminating barriers to entrepreneurship *vis-a-vis* the privatization activism of the state [*text no.13*].

The elimination of barriers to initiative, entrepreneurship, and innovation may be more rewarding than privatization in economic terms, as **the resultant expansion of the generic private sector creates firms where the structure of incentives and employers-employees relations are geared from the start to the competitive conditions of the market economy**. On the other hand, privatized firms largely carry over the distorted employers-employees relations from the communist past. Furthermore, the impact of the structure of incentives is weakened by the legacy of corroded work ethics, more harmful in the, largely unchanged, personal setting in the long established firms. Herein, *nota bene*, lies an explanation of a superior growth performance of the Polish economy, where the generic private sector is larger than in other countries of the region under consideration

The foregoing development has, additionally, an important longer term political economy advantage. As the number of people working in the generic private sector increase, so does, over time, the number of those who understand the linkage between individual effort and reward, between firms success and reward, and - through the latter - between the environment conducive for business (inclusive of the regulatory regime of the economy) and reward.

Capitalism and the role of a capitalist are better understood in private firms, and even more in relatively s m a l l private firms. After having worked in such a firm for some years, few would declare, as Lenin did, that a management of a firm is 'within reach of anybody who can read and write and knows the first four rules of arithmetic', a view that Mises rightly dubbed 'the mentality of the filing clerk' [Mises, 1972, pp. 24-25].

With better understanding of the 'rules of the game' comes greater acceptance of the system based upon those rules, and, consequently, political support for the parties standing for the capitalist market economy. Thus, the proportions of those in favour of systemic change to those *de facto* against it will be changing in post-communist so-

cieties in the longer run, increasing the numbers of the former and, therefore, reinforcing the emerging system.

Last two texts in Part Three tackle the underpinnings of the strong
support - unexpected for many pundits - for the political forces of the
communist past. The earlier stresses **moral degradation** resulting from
communist ideology and, even more, from its actual 'rules of the game'.
The latter links that up with the respective political influence of the state
sector *vis-a-vis* the emerging private sector. Also, the text in question pin-
points **two major social groupings that are definitely hostile to systemic change**.

The first, the present writer calls *industrial lumpenproletariat*, under-
lining the fact that what in capitalist societies lingered on the margins of
society, under socialism could be found in large, industrial state enterprises, where economic performance was the worst, waste was staggering,
while rewards were at their highest. The outcome was the greatest extent
of demoralization among the labour force. Now, as the inefficient socialist
mastodonts are theatened with extinction in competitive market conditions,
or at least require a major downsizing [see Winiecki and Winiecki, 1992] ,
their labour force is in the forefront of resistance to change.

In the same camp, however, one finds educated people, largely from
what is called in the West: 'public services'. They got their education, including university education, in communist times, often being the first in
their families to do so. Under more normal circumstances they would
adapt to professional and moral codes of their peers and respective professional associations. But under communism middle class, or *bourgeois*, morality was most viciously attacked, as well as adherence to it penalized,
and all independence of professional (and all other) associations was almost completely destroyed. Consequently, these people, once employed,
entered the moral and professional void - and increasingly so, as the older
generations retired and passed away. The outcome was the emergence of
the class of semi-professional, shifty, immoral (or amoral) *lumpenintelligentsia*. Although dissatisfied with their pay, they are against any rise in
the professional and any other standards of their work. **They, too, like
workers from large state enterprises are happy to have capitalist**

plenty in the shops, but prefer to keep sloppy socialist work practices
in factories, schools, hospitals, etc.

The influence of these two groups upon the course of the transition
process is all the greater as they work in the best organized segments of
the economy. **'Big battalions' of large state enterprises and public sector trade unions are strongly overrepresented politically,** *vis-a-vis* the
thriving, but fragmented generic private sector. Although, the last text in
this collection concerns the situation in Poland, the situation, apart from
some Poland-specific developments, is not drastically different elsewhere.
Both the existence of the two social groups described here as *industrial
lumpenproletariat* and *lumpenintelligentsia* are present everywhere, in
greater or smaller numbers, and their political overrepresentation through
labour unions are characteristic of a l l post-communist societies.

Now,, a plea of understanding seems in order here. The Readers are
asked for understanding that some of the texts presented in this book may
lack the necessary distance to the subject of reform and change. However,
**the articles and papers are not concerned with a subject of historical
interest only.** Nor the present writer has been an ivory-tower type of an
academic. A dissident economist at first, an adviser and critic later, he has
been more than present at the demise of the old system and the creation of
a new one. Some texts were written in the heat of debates that had more
than only intellectual issues to settle. A *sine irae et studio* approach has
been sometimes all but impossible.

Next, acknowledgements are in order here. The author would like to
thank editors and publishers of various texts included in this collection.
Thus, the thanks go, in the order of the texts, to editors and publishers of
*Soviet Studies, Intereconomics, Economic Inquiry, Routledge, Interna-
tional Journal of Law and Economics & Elsevier Science Publishers,
Springer Verlag, The World Today and Royal Institute of International
Affairs,* London, *Banca Nazionale del Lavoro Quarterly Review, Centre
for Research into Communist Economies,* London, *Basil Blackwell, Com-
munist Economies and Economic Transformation*, and, finally, *Adam
Smith Research Centre,* Warsaw. Of course, proper references are found at
the bottom of the first page of each text.

Finally, some technicalities in the presentation of the collection should be indicated. Thus, a sign: '(...)' marks each abbreviation made in the texts. Often, these abbreviations eliminate repetions. In such cases references are made of other texts where the issue has been considered. Texts are presented in the original form, except for corrections of discovered lingustic errors. Wherever earlier abbreviations required additional word(s) to be added later on, such additions were clearly marked '[ ]'. There were only two types of changes *vis-a-vis* original texts. First, the present writer stressed some parts of texts differently to suit the new context within which they were presented. Second, references in the text were changed where necessary to ensure the same format of references throughout the whole book.

REFERENCES

Beksiak, J., Gruszecki, T., Jedraszczyk, A., and J.Winiecki, 1989, Program stabilizacji i zmian systemowych {English version: Outline of a Programme of Stabilization and Systemic Change, in: *The Polish transformation: Programme and Progress*, Centre for Research into Communist Economies, London, 1990]

Berend, I.T., 1990, *The Hungarian Economic Reform*, Cambridge University Press, Cambridge.

Bruno, M., 1992, Stabilization and Reform in Eastern Europe: A Preliminary Evaluation, *IMF Staff papers*, Vol.39, No.4.

Gruszecki, T., and J.Winiecki, 1991, Privatization in East-Central Europe: A Comparative Perspective, *Aussenwirtschaft*, No.1

Hirschman, A.O., 1963, Journeys toward Progress: Studies in Economic Policy-making in Latin America, Twentieth Century Fund, New York

Kornai, J., 1959, *Overcentralization in Economic Administration*, Oxford University Press, Oxford.

Mises, L. von, 1972, *The Anti-Capitalist Mentality*, Libertarian Press, Spring Mills, Penn.

North, D.C., 1979, A Framework for Analyzing the State in EConomic History, *Explorations in Economic History*, July

Olson, M., 1984, Microeconomic Incentives and Macroeconomic Decline, *Weltwirtschaftliches Archiv*, Vol.120, No.4

Winiecki, E.D. and J.Winiecki, 1992, *Structural Legacy of the Soviet-Type Economy*, Centre for Research on Communist Economies, London.

Winiecki, J., 1984, Economic Trends and Prospects: East, Warsaw, mimeo.

Winiecki, J., 1986, Are Soviet-Type Economies Entering an Era of Long-term Decline?, *Soviet Studies*, Vol.38, No.3.

Winiecki, J., 1987a, The Overgrown Industrial Sector in Soviet-Type Economies: Explanations, Evidence, Consequences, *Comparative Economic Studies*, Vol.28, No.4.

Winiecki, J., 1987b, Economic Prospects: East and West, Centre for Research into Communist Economies, London

Winiecki, J., 1988, *The Distorted World of Soviet-Type Economies*, Routledge, London.

Winiecki, J., 1990, Post-Soviet-Type Economies in Transition: What Have We Learned from the Polish Transition Programme in Its First Year? *Weltwirtschaftliches Archiv*, Vol.126, No.4.

Winiecki, J., 1991, The Inevitability of the Fall of Output in the Easrly stages of Transition to the market: Theoretical underpinnings, *Soviet Studies*, Vol.43, 1991, No.4.

Winiecki, J., 1992, Privatisation in Poland: A Comparative Perspective, *J.C.B.Mohr*, Tubingen,

Winiecki, J., 1993, Knowledge of Soviet-Type Economies and 'Heterodox' Stabilization-Based Outcomes in Eastern Europe, *Weltwirtschaftliches Archiv*, Vol.129, No.2

Winiecki, J., 1995, The Applicability of Standard Reform Packages to Eastern Europe, *Journal of Comparative Economics*, Vol.20, No.3

Winiecki, J., 1996, Transforming to Economic Freedom: At High Cost, Often with Long Lags, and not without Question Marks. A paper presented at the Mont Pelerin Society General Meeting, Vienna, September 9-13, 1996, mimeo.

PART I

POLITICAL ECONOMY OF REFORM: FAILURES AND THEIR CAUSES

CHAPTER 1

POSSIBLE SCENARIOS FOR EASTERN EUROPE*

On the one hand, continuation of the old wasteful, 'extensive' growth is impossible because of constraints on quantities of production factors and material inputs. On the other hand, qualitative changes in East European economies (innovation, quality improvement, structural change, greater international division of labour) are impeded by system's inherent constraints.

It is this perception of **the lack of any prospects for the continuation of the traditional Soviet-type growth model**, coupled with sharply curtailed possibilities of its prolongation by means of Western credits, which led some scholars, both in the East and in the West, to believe that reforms are inevitable. This view is very optimistic, however, as it does not take into consideration certain vital determinants of any remedial action (...)

FROM OBVIOUS TO LESS OBVIOUS NON-SOLUTIONS

Something which is quite often not appreciated is **the low learning capacity of the Soviet-type system**. If by learning we mean change in reactions to unchanged actions (stimuli), then learning by a system in which all

---

* These excerpts are a part of a book 'Economic Prospects - East and West', published in 1987 by **Centre for Research in Communist Economies**, London. The book itself had been written in 1983-84 period.

dissent has been eliminated (or its outward signs suppressed) has been shown to be agonizingly slow. Overvaluation of the ruling elites' collective memories and corresponding undervaluation of incoming current information adversely affect the capacity to recognise the problem, while the narrowing of information inflow decreases the capacity to select a solution.

All this affects the system adversely, quite apart from the fact that proposed solutions may run contrary to the ruling elite's interest in maintaining the *status quo* - a question to which we return in the next section.

The signs of the exhaustion of expansion possibilities began to appear in Eastern Europe in the early 1960s. Attempts at partial economic reforms in late 1960s, even if limited, did inject some new vigour into these economies and, with production factors still available in large quantities and natural resources relatively inexpensive, a renewed acceleration of the traditional, wasteful type of growth occurred.

In the early 1970s Western technology and credits were substituted for economic reforms. The fact that the exhaustion of expansion possibilities has since reappeared with much stronger symptoms, due both to the decreasing rate of growth of availability of factors of production and much dearer natural resources, does not guarantee that some obvious non-solutions will not be proposed and attempts at their implementation not undertaken. Such developments have actually been taking place for some time in certain East European countries.

'DOWN PERISCOPE' SCENARIO

Two scenarios of this sort can be envisaged, in fact. The first we would call the 'down periscope' scenario. Both the frame of mind of the ruling elites and their reactions to the stimuli can be deduced from its title. Overvaluation of the elites' memory of the 'good old days' and undervaluation of unpleasant current information degenerates, in extreme cases, into a kind of withdrawal symptom. The facts indicate that things are bad and getting worse. If we disregard them, problems may go away. And even if they do not, let us enjoy both the power and the wealth we still have. Moreover, let us eradicate any statements reminding us of the unpleasant problems in question, for if nobody states openly that the emperor has no clothes, then, by convention, the emperor is well clad. And let us repeat on all possible occasions the litany of advantages the system possesses in comparison with any competing one.

In such a scenario grotesque propaganda reigns supreme while nothing really changes in the economic system (the sphere from which the hard data on the deterioration come). The late Gierek era in Poland is a good example of **a 'do nothing, pretend the problems do not exist' attitude**. This complacency could last, however, as long as Poland 's borrowing ability and ceased abruptly in 1980. In this scenario at least some measures are taken, but they are mainly non-economic in character. Exhortations become more and more frequent, campaigns against absenteeism, shoddy goods and black market activities become more shrill, as symptoms are treated (often in all seriousness) as causes of the decline. New layers of control are created and enmeshed with the existing ones and *ad hoc* shock therapies applied, like searches in public places to find people who ought to have been at their respective workplaces (these were instituted in Poland during the early martial law period and then in the Soviet Union at the beginning of Andropov's period of power).

In the management of the economy 'more of the same' still seems to be a frequent resort. Czechoslovakia, for example, carried out another unsuccessful drive to make enterprises adopt more 'taut' plans in the late 1970s and a phony reform that changed nothing in the early 1980s. Everywhere, except in Hungary, one hears about the need to strengthen the role of medium-term plans, as if repeated investment cycles had not shown their untenability. Learning capacity is indeed very low and Pavlovian reflexes dominate the way the system reacts to repeated, although increasingly strong, stimuli.

Even some partial reforms aimed at improving the performance of the increasingly inflexible multi-level hierarchical organization of the economy may be cautiously undertaken, modifying (usually not very consistently) certain less decisive elements of the traditional Soviet-type model. But given the preponderance of the elements of the traditional model they are unable to bring about any discernible and lasting improvement. On the contrary, they may even become a source of new disturbances.

Under the circumstances of the 'down periscope' scenario, performance has nowhere to go but down. All the causes that have been contributing to its deterioration so far are still present, while the cynicism and accompanying corruption spread further. The elites have nothing to offer to the population at large: consumption is falling or stagnant, the conditions of acquiring goods and services are getting worse as disequilibria increase.

Moreover, the population is not willing to 'swallow' the ideology any more. Neither the ruled nor the rulers believe it any more. A.J. Toynbee, tracing the sources of the breakdown of civilizations, found that failure voluntarily to imitate the behavioural patterns demonstrated or suggested by the ruling elites usually preceded failure to obey.

In the Soviet-type system the control and repression are so strong that failure to obey may appear only after a relatively long lag. But when the demonstrated behavioural patterns of the ruling elite deviate consistently from the suggested ones a 'reverse mimesis' begins to take place. The population adapts itself to the existing conditions and imitates the demonstrated behavioural patterns of the elite only too well, with corroding effects on the system (and on itself).

Thus, whether one begins with the repeated disappointments due to the inferior and deteriorating performance of the economic system, or with the deteriorating integrity of the elites, the outcome is predictable and the same: cynicism and corruption. A second order but lasting and self-reinforcing cause of the economic decline has taken root in the body social. There is no need to outline here the step-by-step development under this scenario. Both causes-symptoms-effects linkages and the constraints on the 'more of the same' type of response allow us to predict in sufficient detail the dynamics of slow decline.

'RECENTRALIZATION-CUM-REPRESSION' SCENARIO

But what if the decision makers decide to apply a large dose of the old medicine to decentralize decisions and repress those who protest or only dissent? **The 'recentralization-cum-repression' scenario would lead, in my opinion, after a short acceleration due more to imaginative reporting from below than increased effort, to faster decline.** As in the previous scenario, all the causes contributing to the decline would be present, but their impact, or at least the impact of some of them, on economic performance would become stronger.

Let us begin with the feasibility of the recentralisation part of this scenario. With gross national product now many times greater than in the earlier period of extreme centralization, during the forced industrialization in the 1950s, and with a more sophisticated structure of production, the earlier level of centralization simply cannot be repeated. To give an example, the Czechoslovak economy produces over 5 million products, finished and intermediate. The number of decisions concerning production factors and material inputs to produce each product is far beyond what can be decided consistently at the top of the hierarchical pyramid with the speed necessary to achieve planned production targets (leaving aside the allocational efficiency of such decisions). Nor is it possible at intermediate levels of the hierarchy. It is worth remembering that recentralization reactions historically have followed the failure of attempts at partial decentralization of decision-making to the middle levels of the hierarchy (but not to the enterprises). Under these circumstances the decision-making process would slow down to a snail space.

The next issue to be considered is the non-economic consequences of the 'great (investment) leap forward' that would become a key component of this scenario. Rapid growth in the share of investment would result, under the existing circumstances, in an absolute fall in consumption, or an accelerated fall if consumption were falling already. Would such a fall generate Toynbee's 'failure to obey', open eruption of discontent? It is difficult to answer this question with a high degree of probability. Polish and Romanian experience so far suggest different answers. The limitation to the present is legitimate. For in both cases the fall in living standard has occurred in spite of cuts in investment (...). Thus the negative consumption effects of any large-scale investment expansion would come on living standards which were already falling.

If an open eruption of discontent is a probable, but not a certain outcome of the 'recentralisation-cum-repression' scenario (given the efficiency of the repression), there are other outcomes well known from past and present, that would certainly contribute to the accelerated decline. **The reactions of producers-consumers would, however, be more accentuated** than in the earlier case of slow decline and would result in a precipitous fall in the quality of manufactured products. Under the double impact of sharply reduced import possibilities and falling quality, exports of manufactures to world markets would suffer disproportionately.

The export structure would resemble that of less entrepreneurial developing countries due to the more than usually dominant role of commodities. Given the fact that commodities would become scarcer and their production more costly, the limits would quickly be reached in the external sphere too. An alternative to exporting more manufactures would be to increase exports of certain commodities (food, fuels) to an even greater extent at the cost of further cuts in consumption, but here, again, the question of possible eruption of discontent has to be taken into account, for it is assumed that there are limits to cuts in living standard below which the fear of repression ceases to be a deterrent (although the threshold may be different in each country).

All in all, the above scenario may be regarded as a short- to medium-run one. It is doubtful whether the kind of developments described could last, in the face of much stronger constraints than before, beyond one investment cycle without a serious break-down (economic, social or both). And even if the 'down periscope' scenario could be envisaged as a longer lasting one, it is obvious that both are non-solutions to the problem of decline.

THE HUNGARIAN SCENARIO

Yet another scenario is the Hungarian one, that is a more serious attempt at economic reform of the Soviet-type model without relevant changes in the political and social environment in which a reformed model has to function. With respect to the Hungarian scenario, held up sometimes as an example of the reformability of a STE, we have to consider two questions instead of one, as was the case with the previous scenarios. Before ascertaining whether it is possible to repeat it, it is worthwhile considering whether it is desirable, that is, whether it is a clear enough success to be worth emulation.

In my opinion the Hungarian economy since 1968 cannot be regarded as an unqualified success, in spite of the good press it has enjoyed both in the West (due to brilliant salesmanship by Hungarian officials and experts) and (to an extent) in the East. It is true that in macroeconomic terms the level of disequilibrium in the consumer goods market has been smaller than elsewhere. It is also true that its input-output characteristics, like the material intensity of the national economy, are somewhat better than those of other East European countries. Another point in favour of Hungary is its agricultural sector, which since the 1960s has been a significant exporter - and this without simultaneously impoverishing the domestic market (as other food exporters in Eastern Europe do). Yet another difference, since 1980, has been an enhanced entrepreneurial (and, to a much lesser extent, also innovative) vigour on the part of Hungarians, mainly visible in the development of intra-enterprise production initiatives by employees and, to a smaller extent, in new small business establishments, both cooperative and private.

On the other hand, system-specific features continue to affect adversely Hungarian economic performance. Disequilibria, although smaller, still add discomfort to constraints on the level of consumption. Input-output characteristics, better, as we have stressed, than in other STEs, are nevertheless very much higher than in most market economies (MEs). A substantial number of large industrial enterprises, inflexible and shunning innovation, are chronically unprofitable. The enterprises that needed relief in 1972 were found in the same situation in 1982, receiving large subsidies, tax reductions and other forms of assistance [see, e.g., Csaba, 1983]. It comes as no surprise then that export performance on world markets is not at all impressive as far as manufactures are concerned and small surpluses on trade with the West have been achieved mainly by the familiar method of import cuts. Actually, if it had not been for the favourable view of Hungarian economic reforms taken by Western governments and banks, Hungary might have followed the path of other STEs that asked for debt repayment relief (just as, at the other end of the reform continuum, the West German 'umbrella' helped the GDR to avoid a similar necessity at the peak of the latter's debt repayment burden).

In consequence the Hungarian economy is not reducing the gap in development between itself and the West. On the contrary, in comparison with countries like Austria, Italy and France, or medium-developed Spain, the distance seems to have increased since the late 1920s. Also, the newly industrialising countries (NICs) have been performing much more impressively in the last 15-20 years.

The Hungarian economy is therefore a qualified success, the most important qualification being its geopolitical limitation: **it is a success relative to other STEs only**. This precariousness of the Hungarian position is best understood by those Hungarian economists who know what makes their economy tick. They are concerned that without keeping up the momentum of far-reaching economic reforms, and extending reforms beyond the purely economic area, the gap in development between Hungary and the medium-developed and developed market economies may increase. Very often they voice their concern, even if more obliquely, about all East European countries.(...)

Obviously, in Hungary the market has not been substituted for the traditional central planning and the institutional and procedural void has been filled by many auxiliary and guiding indicators (generally in conflict with one another), by bargaining *ex ante* between managers and their superiors for the expected values of these indicators, by participation of economic bureaucrats and party apparatchiks in the preparation of allegedly 'autonomous' plans of enterprises, as well as by an amalgam of disguised and undisguised, formal and informal, persistent or *ad hoc* interventions in enterprise activities. Inevitable contradictions of such a process reinforced by the prevalent loyalty-based rather than efficiency-based choices sharply limit efficiency gains of Hungarian reforms. Consequently, patterns of economic growth, structural change and foreign trade have not been significantly better than those in other STEs [see, e.g. Bauer, 1984]. (...)

[Furthermore] it is doubtful how much even the unimpressive improvements achieved outside agriculture owe to economic reforms. It should also be noted that in the 1961-80 period Hungary was the only STE in which the growth rate of consumer goods was higher than that of producers goods during each five-year plan (while the opposite was the case in all the other STEs). This was so before, during and after the introduction of the 1968 reforms. One may hypothesise that it was rather the ruling elite's collective memory of the year 1956, when communists, for once, found themselves, albeit briefly, on the receiving end of repression, that made them later more cautious in undertaking 'taut', 'mobilising', welfare-reducing, plans, as well as in avoiding other drastic excesses of arrogant *extravaganza*. In other words, they learned the lesson that if there is an outbreak of discontent Soviet assistance may come in time to save the system, but not necessarily to save them personally.

The experience of Hungarian communists is unique in Eastern Europe and without this moderation attempts to emulate Hungary may fail. Thus **the replication of the Hungarian economic reforms, minus the Hungarian ruling elite's unique experience and minus its limited political concessions to society, would not bring even those relative successes** that are the lure of this particular scenario. Moreover, Hungarian economic reforms are clearly an unfinished business and, without meeting some important political requirements, may be not only unfinished but unfinishable. Clouds over the horizon are already visible in Hungary itself and they are not absent elsewhere. Thus, if one adds to the above both less time and a less conducive environment for trial-and-error policies one may be justifiably doubtful about the effects of attempts to solve problems of strategies and decline of Soviet-type economies through the emulation of the Hungarian economic reforms.

NECESSARY POLITICAL INPUTS TO ASSURE SUCCESS OF ECONOMIC REFORMS

We have so far looked at probable scenarios of economic change for East European STEs without reference to the third and most important determinant of the choice of remedial action, namely the interests of the ruling elites in maintaining the *status quo*. Awareness of the deteriorating performance and of alternative solutions is a necessary but not a sufficient condition for selection of a possible solution. It is the various interests involved, economic and non-economic, that narrow the list of possible solutions down to a few (if any) desirable ones.

Any analysis of the interests of various groups in democracies would have to be much wider in scope, encompassing, among others, political parties, trade unions, business organisations and professional associations. Here, I shall limit myself to those organised groups which, taken together, constitute the four pillars of the communist system of government. As the political and economic components of the system are all but inseparable, far-reaching reforms in the economic area strongly affect the interests of all these groups. But are the pillars of the system, or even their top eche-lons, which make up the elite, as monolithic as sometimes portrayed? Are their interests identical? And, in consequence, would they all go to the same (extreme) extent in defending the status quo?

DIFFERING INTERESTS OF SYSTEM-SUPPORTING GROUPS

The issues have not received the attention they merited in the analysis of possible solutions to the stagnation and decline of STEs. It is obvious that, given their limited or non-existent legitimacy, the pillars of the system pre-fer the *status quo* that gives them more than they could have obtained un-der the democratic alternative. But this does not mean that all those pillars of support - the communist party apparatchiks, the bureaucrats from the multi-level management hierarchies, the police and the military - would have the same interest in maintaining the political *status quo* if important political changes were necessary to reverse the deterioration of economic performance, that is threatening to decrease (or is already decreasing) the economic benefits those groups derive from their dominant political posi-tion.

The participation of these four groups in power sharing has been exten-sively researched, but little attention has been devoted to their role in **wealth sharing**. It is the latter, however, that in my opinion is the key to understanding their potentially divergent attitudes to economic reforms coupled with political change that would be able to reverse the decline.

Let us put the question of wealth sharing in the communist system in a more systematic, and comparative, perspective. First of all, **two modes of benefiting from the dominant position in the political system ought to be distinguished**. One is a traditional, long recognized way of benefiting in non-democratic systems, that is through the appropriation of a larger share of the newly created wealth (national product) than would have been possible under the democratic alternative. In dictatorships the police and/or the military simply get better paid and enjoy more perquisites relative to the rest of society. Also, their professional needs (and desire for status symbols, like modern military equipment) have a priority claim on the state budget. The police and the military in the communist system do not differ much in this respect. The salaries may be relatively higher, the 'perks' may be relatively more important in terms of privileged access to goods in short supply, yet their mode of wealth sharing is much the same.

This cannot be said about the party apparatchiks and the bureaucracy, though. Traditional dictatorships do not know ruling parties of that sort. Nor do they know multi-level economic management hierarchies that spawn the ever-growing bureaucracies trying to manage STEs. These two pillars of the system may also help themselves to a larger slice of the economic pie, relative to the rest of society, but for them this is not the only, or even the most important, way of benefiting from the system. Political control of the economy, an important communist *credo*, allows those two groups to benefit not only by appropriating more of the newly created wealth, but also continuously to appropriate benefits by interfering in the process of wealth creation itself. It is the latter feature that sets the STEs apart from others.

There are two ways of benefiting from the system, over and above the way characteristic of 'ordinary' dictatorships. The first and most important is, of course, the **nomenklatura** system of party control over all important appointments, and especially those of enterprise managers. Party apparatchiks have traditionally taken advantage of this to appoint themselves and their cronies to well paid bureaucratic and managerial jobs. Once appointed, enterprise managers may (and do) return the favour by selling products in short supply directly to their colleagues in the party apparatus and/or selling them at discount prices, using phony excuses of lower quality (lower quality goods do reach the market, but those that are a form of **kickback** are carefully selected!). Managers themselves, their families and friends, benefit handsomely in a similar way.

If and when the modes of participation in wealth sharing are systematized in this manner, the differences between the party apparatchiks and the bureaucracy on the one hand and the police and the military on the other become clearer. **Both subsets prefer the *status quo* to the democratic alternative** because shared power permits them to draw bigger economic benefits than would have been possible otherwise. **However, only the latter subset, party apparatchiks and the economic bureaucracy, are interested in the mode in which wealth is created**. This explains why economic reforms fail in a communist system, or at least why they do not go far enough to make a decisive impact (in the Hungarian case). For their success depends on the two pillars of the system that stand to loose most from successful reforms!

There exists no theory of reforming a centrally planned economy but, in a nutshell, it may be said that such an economy shows greater distortions than other economies and, in consequence, reforms have to remove, or substantially reduce, distortions in three broad areas: the institutional setting, product and factor prices, and external linkages.

In my opinion the removal of institutional distortions should precede everything else for it is the middle levels of the organizational hierarchy, whose jobs are threatened with extinction (industrial branch ministries, associations of enterprises), that offer the strongest resistance to reforms. Any serious reform has to make them superfluous and, if the hierarchy is left intact, that part of the economic bureaucracy concentrates on throwing sand into the machinery of reforms.

In this they are supported by the rest of the bureaucracy and by the party apparatchiks who tend to lose not so much their relatively well paid jobs, but the economic benefits they derive from interfering in the process of wealth creation. The more indirect policy measures supersede direct commands and the more autonomy enterprises possess in reacting to parameters (interest rates, exchange rates etc.), the less time and effort managers would be willing to spend on 'kickback' activities.

Also, the more far-reaching the reforms are, the clearer it becomes that enterprise managers cannot be appointed by bureaucrats from above (and the party apparatchiks behind them), if they are not to be less interested in efficiency than in the whims and wishes of their superiors and the apparatchiks who control appointments through the *nomenklatura* system. This is why two aspects of economic reforms, self-management (which would hold managers accountable for kickbacks) and appointment of managers on the basis of merit, with the abolition of the *nomenklatura* system (which would end the reservation of lucrative managerial positions for the dominant minority), have hitherto been successfully resisted.

Actually, those who benefit economically from the system in a totalitarian rather than authoritarian way would resist changes in other areas as well.

They would, for instance, be hostile to price reforms, because equilibrium prices would tend to reduce their welfare. In a shortage economy privileged access to otherwise rationed goods is a source of wealth gains, either in the form of a higher level of consumption than would be possible at equilibrium prices or in the form of higher income if goods acquired at below equilibrium prices are resold later at equilibrium (i.e. black market) ones. When, for example, car prices in Poland are equal to about 40% of the equilibrium price the gains from privileged buying are indeed significant. The same goes for other goods in short supply.

Thus it is obvious that the apparatchiks and the economic bureaucracy have more to lose because they benefit economically from the existing system both in the traditional way (in this way they do not differ from the police and the military) and in a non-traditional system-specific way (particularly through the *nomenklatura* system). They can therefore be expected to resist change in the economic component of the system more strongly.

MILITARY/POLICE REGIME ALTERNATIVE

This distinction may not have meant much in a period when in spite of the waste of resources , production and - at a lower rate - consumption were still growing. But with production increasing slowly or stagnating and consumption stagnating or falling the situation may become different. **With less to gain from the petrified economic system**, increasingly unable to cope with the problems of modern industrial society, and more to lose because of the shrinking their own wealth (in absolute terms), **the other two pillars of the system may come into conflict with the party and the bureaucracy.**

Judged in terms of successful economic reforms, the advantages of a scenario in which the communist party is pushed into the background, reduced to a largely ornamental role or dissolved altogether, and the military, with or without the police, take over the leading role in the country are considerable. The latter groups are not so attached to the model of central planning because they do not draw totalitarian material benefits from it. Consequently, they could be willing to discard it when returns to the system began to diminish or become negative.

Almost as important in the success of economic reforms would be the elimination of the obnoxious politicization of everyday life. The foundations of a military (or a military-police) regime would be those of an 'ordinary' rather than a totalitarian dictatorship and they would need neither Byzantine symbolic politics nor an unceasing barrage of mendacious propaganda to create a *quasi*-legitimacy for themselves. In other words the system would then rely on authoritarian 'don'ts', rather than on totalitarian 'do's'. The economy could then be freed from many of the constraints analyzed above, while society, assured of the opportunity to realise its aspirations in the economic (even if not in the political) sphere and freed from a major irritant (politicization) could turn its energies to entrepreneurship, innovativeness, and simply better work, all of which would become more profitable.

The scenario need not stop at this point. It is obvious that, with the main obstacle to economic reforms neutralised or removed, the 'ordinary' dictatorship need not become a permanent feature of the political landscape. The example of Spain clearly shows that greater reliance on the market and the concomitant opening up of the economy to external influences result in both rapidly rising incomes and an incomparably more complex set of economic and non-economic domestic and transnational interactions. As a result, the ruling elite may find clinging to power both less important, owing to the increased level of wealth, and more costly, owing to the inordinate amount of effort necessary to control an open society dictatorially.

We return to this case later, since its lessons are important for yet another scenario. At this point I would like to add one, rather obvious, comment. In outlining the above scenario I have not differentiated between the Soviet Union and the smaller countries of Eastern Europe under Soviet influence. If this scenario of military (or military-police) dominance and shift to an 'ordinary' dictatorship were to take place in any of the latter countries, the new ruling elite would also take over from the respective communist party the role of guarantor of the Soviet Union's strategic interests in the country concerned. It is worth noting that the martial law period [in Poland] gave rise to some speculation that Poland would become an early case of such a scenario, combining some decentralization and marketization with a degree of 'militarisation' and that the system would evolve toward that prevailing in. Spain under Franco and similar regimes [see, e.g. Gomulka, 1982]. Subsequent developments, however, have made the Polish case look more and more like the 'normalisation' of post-1968 Czechoslovakia. As there are no resources to support an increase in consumption to mitigate political repression, the failure of attempts to enforce such a scenario is certain and a new shock all but inevitable.

At times it looks as if the present communist leadership in Poland were of two minds as to which aim to pursue, vacillating between the Czechoslovak-like 'normalization' and Hungarian 'goulash communism' but - for obvious reasons - without goulash...

SELF-LIMITATION BY THE COMMUNIST PARTY

Yet another scenario that would have a reasonable chance of economic success, is self-limitation by the communist party itself. It ought to be stressed from the outset that its probability of success is markedly higher than the probability of its occurrence. I have explained why the communist party has the strongest interest in resisting any change in the traditional Soviet-type model and its political ramifications. But the scenario, even if not highly probable, is not impossible. Havrylyshyn, in the report to the *Club of Rome* on the roads leading towards more effective societies [Havrylyshyn, 1980], gives some pointers with respect to the USSR as to why the ruling communist parties might, after all, be interested in limiting their role both in the economy and in politics and putting the economy on a path of economic efficiency and growing wealth (rather than growing production that feeds upon itself).

Beside the increased pressures stemming from economic decline, Havrylyshyn rightly underlines the increased costs of 'keeping the lid on' the population when the contradictions between theory and reality cannot be camouflaged much longer. Also, there is the cost of party dominance in managing an ever more complex system like the Soviet Union, which 'absorbs a disproportionate amount of energy, which could be used otherwise for production of useful economic and social goods and services' [*Ibid.*, p.43].

This can best be explained in terms of Deutsch's distinction between gross and net power [Deutsch, 1966]. *Gross* power is understood to be the amount of change imposed by the application of power, while *net* power is the amount of change that would have been accepted without the application of power. The greater the difference between gross and net power the greater the amount of effort and resources necessary to achieve certain ends (whether related to change or to maintaining the *status quo*).

This difference is very great in the communist system. In economic terms it may be said that to achieve economic growth the difference between the total uses of resources (gross production) and the amount of new material wealth created (net material product) is strikingly higher than in MEs. One may assume, judging by the size of the respective party, economic control, police and propaganda apparatuses, that it is very costly in terms of human effort as well.

When the total wealth begins to decrease and so does the volume of benefits drawn by the ruling elite, the apportioning of a greater share of the shrinking pie to themselves to maintain their absolute level of welfare may be a short term solution. But it is one which is likely to boomerang, either in the form of falling production quality and quantity or open discontent. The late nineteenth century black educator, Booker T. Washington, stressed the futility of slavery by pointing to the amount of power that would have to be expended, saying that 'the only way the white man in the South can keep the Negro in the ditch is to stay in the ditch with him' [quoted in Deutsch, 1966, p.115]. With falling living standards and ever more discontented societies, ruling elites may find it so effort-consuming to control the sullen or rebellious societies, while getting less and less in terms of their own welfare, that, after some time, they may find it convenient to enlarge the power base and gradually or radically relinquish the system-specific controls.

The withdrawal of the [communist] party from interference in the wealth creation process, as well as the dismantling of the petrified structure of central planning, is a key ingredient of success. The experience of Yugoslavia clearly shows that the dismantling of the latter by itself is not enough. Given its total political control, the Yugoslav communist party retains the ability to interfere in the selection of managers and to lean on regional and local administrations and banks, with the resultant strongly negative outcomes. Investment cycles in Yugoslavia have not followed the time pattern of STEs; the interaction between central planners and enterprises within the five-year planning framework has been absent in Yugoslavia. But cycles and over-investment have continued and nonviable 'political factories', products of interference, have been lavishly sprinkled all over the country. Efficiency has not been markedly higher than under central planning.

IN PLACE OF CONCLUSIONS

There is not much new that can be added. Conclusions concerning both the present deterioration and the future prospects of STEs, as well as their determinants, are to be found throughout the pages, and summarising them now would be both uninteresting and superfluous. In consequence, I will add only four brief remarks constituting comments on my earlier discussion.

First, **the outlook for Eastern Europe is gloomy**. Even if one takes into account differences in economic performance between countries, the system-specific causes of stagnation and decline show rather clearly what would come next. The picture is even more depressing because of the clear recognition that **the system of central planning has been unable to cope with problems that have long ago been solved by the market system.** STEs are not yet anywhere near the economic, social, psychological and other problems MEs are coping with at their higher levels of development. Nor will they reach such levels, given their inability to solve problems, the elimination of which is absolutely crucial, if those higher levels are ever to be attained.

Second, it is not surprising that **the only scenarios that offer a reasonable chance of success are those envisaging the transformation of
the whole communist system, not only of its economic component**.
Without such a transformation the lasting reversal of the long-term deterioration is clearly impossible. The Hungarian scenario may improve the
situation slightly and temporarily, the West German 'umbrella' may make
the strain in the GDR economy somewhat less visible (and less painful for
the 'other' Germans), the plentiful resources of the Soviet Union may permit the elite to prolong the yesterday a little longer - but none of these is
much more than a temporary reprieve.

Third, I have discussed the STEs of Eastern Europe. That does not
mean, however, that economies in other parts of the world, that opted for
central planning economically and resembled East European countries in
their political arrangements have fared any better. Elsewhere I have ana-
lysed, the performance in the 1970s of a group of developing countries
(LDCs) that chose to a smaller or larger extent the Soviet path to development, and compared it with the average growth performance of low income and middle income LDCs and, particularly, with the group of newly
industrializing countries (NICs) that chose the opposite path, namely
greater marketization and export orientation of their economies. The results were highly significant. The growth rate of a group of 9 countries that
chose central planning as a dominant form of organization and for which
the data were available was 1% annually (unweighted), with big variations
between countries, compared with 3% for all low income and 5.1%% for
all middle income LDCs and 8.9%% annually (unweighted) for Asian
NICs. In the last group variations between countries were much smaller.
No less significantly, on a case-by-case basis, a regime change in an LDC
toward greater centralization of economic management resulted in a
marked fall in economic growth rate, while the reverse change toward
greater market orientation resulted in acceleration of the growth rate. An-
gola, Ethiopia, Mozambique, Madagascar, Peru and Jamaica all experienced a drop in growth rate after their regime changed, if the 1970s are
compared with the 1960s, while the opposite was the case with Egypt, In-
donesia, Somalia and the Sudan, where growth accelerated in the 1970s in

spite of the more difficult international economic environment. **Evidently the decline is system-wide and not confined to Eastern Europe.**

Fourth, and last, **the decline is not confined to economics** and narrowly interpreted living standards, i.e. current consumption. The scars of pollution are much uglier and pollution itself greater when generated by **the 'civilization of poverty and stupidity'** as a Cracow columnist wrote about Poland's environmental degradation. This view can be easily extended to other STEs where the same problems are created by the same system-specific features. Also, a combination of high socio-psychological pressure upon those living under totalitarianism, bad working conditions, the above-mentioned pollution and unhealthy food due to unsanitary conditions has resulted in what another, better known columnist, Alain Besançon, aptly called 'the return of death' [*L'Express*, 1985, September 6]. Various demographic time series began to reverse themselves in STEs (with the Soviet Union in the lead) showing increasing mortality and decreasing life expectancy.

All walks of life tend to coalesce to paint a bleaker future than the one derived from economic analysis only. No surprise then that many people shudder at the thought of what the future holds should the system remain basically the same. Fortunately for East European societies, the system's ability to survive intact is weakening fast and this may be the only ray of hope in the otherwise discouraging picture outlined in this part of the book.

REFERENCES

Bauer, T., 1984, The Second Economic Reform and Ownership Relations, *East European Economics*

Csaba, L., 1983, New Features of the Hungarian Economic Mechanism in the Mid-Eighties, *New Hungarian Quarterly*, Vol.24, No.90, Summer

Havrylyshyn, B., 1980, *Road Maps to the Future. Towards More Effective Societies*. A report to the Club of Rome, Pergamon Press, London

Deutsch, K., 1966, *The Nerves of Government. Models of Political Communication and Control*. The Free Press, New York

CHAPTER 2

A TOUCH OF SOCIALIST MIDAS: HUNGARIAN AND POLISH REFORM FAILURES*

Various market-type reforms have been introduced into the economies of Eastern Europe in recent years. These have often been warmly applauded in the West, but their success so far has been at best marginal. Without radical changes in the fundamentals of the Soviet-type economic system such reforms can have no lasting impact.

'A half-formed country. An unfinished society. It seems we have neither the time, nor the stamina, nor the decisiveness, to finish anything...or to put anything in order. Our houses are without plaster, our investment projects half-finished, our reforms - unfinished... A conviction is quite widespread that it is not worth-while doing anything, no matter how important it might have been, since our attempts are doomed anyway.'

Is this a report from Poland, where the feeling of hopelessness is running high after five years of dashed hopes passing in the midst of continuing decay? No, it is a Hungarian sociologist [E.Hankiss]'s portrait of Hungary, a Soviet-type economy so often acclaimed in the West as a reformers' paradise. Hungary, a country of relative success, i.e. which works marginally more efficiently and makes life somewhat more bearable than elsewhere in the Soviet bloc, is facing an uncertain future. Unsolved funda-

---

* *Excerpts from an article:* Soviet-Type Economies and Reform Failures: A Touch of Socialist Midas, *published in bi-monthly* **Intereconomics**, *Vol.22, 1987, No.4 (a publication of HWWA, an economic research institute in Hamburg).*

mental problems with regard to economic reforms are exerting increasingly strong pressure upon the prospects of that country.

If fundamentals have been avoided in Hungary then the same situation exists to an even greater extent elsewhere in the Soviet bloc, i.e. in Poland or in the *Johnny-come-late lies* of economic reforms in Eastern Europe. **With fundamentals left unsolved, difficulties are intensifying everywhere.** And these fundamentals are not tantamount simply to introducing some market-like measures, which would be widely applauded by Western journalists, economists and bankers.

The reason for such applause would seem natural enough. Since these measures work well in the market system, they are believed to be good for market-type reforms in the Soviet-type economies. However, **isolated bits and pieces fitted into a fundamentally unchanged Soviet-type economy cannot work.** There is a phenomenon that this author calls 'a touch of the socialist Midas'. Just as everything that the legendary king Midas touched turned into gold, so any promising market-like measure 'touched' by the fundamentally unchanged system becomes perverted, loses most of its impact or turns into an ornament. It may generate Western goodwill (if skillfully advertised) but will not push the economy further toward the market type [one].(..)

This author has maintained elsewhere that analysis of the Soviet-type economy has centered excessively upon power distribution within the ruling stratum to the detriment of wealth distribution within it.[*see texts 1 & 3*] This type of analysis is best applied within the increasingly popular institutional framework. Thus, Douglass North described the typical conflict in a society with a pre-representative type of government as a conflict between the efficient property rights structure designed to lower transaction costs, i.e. those that facilitate an increase in wealth, and the property rights structure designed to maximize rent to the ruling stratum [North, 1979]. Accordingly, political rulers tend to avoid offending powerful segments of the ruling stratum who benefit most from the inefficient property rights structure.

This approach suits ideally the analysis of Soviet-type states, where the inefficient property rights structure bringing substantial benefits to certain powerful segments of the ruling stratum is the main obstacle to successful market-type reforms.(...)

A DISTORTIVE TOUCH

The author has already used the term 'a touch of socialist Midas' above to describe the impact of unchanged fundamentals upon market-type measures introduced into the Soviet-type economy during numerous attempted reforms. No other term seems precise enough to reflect the process through which the gold promised by market-type measures turns into the trash of wasted efforts, or through which something that works efficiently in a normal environment brings about perverse or at best negligible effects in Soviet-type economies.

The socialist Midas, i.e. Midas in reverse, is able to affect the process of economic reforms or - more precisely - to ensure the failure of these reforms for two general reasons. The first is that it is precisely those two segments of the ruling stratum with the strongest incentives to maintain the economic status quo that are entrusted with designing, introducing and managing the reforms. Consequently they are able to design reforms in such a way as to ensure their internal inconsistency, which later allows party apparatchiks and economic bureaucrats cither to return to old central planning-type commands and control or to fill new market-type measures with old central planning-type content.

The second reason is that the loyalty-based *nomenklatura* has been able to pervert market-type measures in practice without the necessity of re-designing given reforms. Since nominations, appraisals and demotions depend primarily upon loyalty, managers' performance becomes an amalgam of actions undertaken for the sake of satisfying the particular wishes of their superiors and of those aimed at improving bottom-line results. The unholy mix mostly results in gross distortions of efficiency especially as the former generally take precedence over the latter.

In the following we refer mostly to the Hungarian and Polish reforms as these are deemed to be the farthest-reaching in Eastern Europe. The former especially have enjoyed an almost continuously good press in the West in the 1980's. But the realities have been much less positive and even

Hungarian reforms are not very far from being a failure. (Their success is limited to being the least of the failures among reforms in Soviet economies.)

We begin with the Polish reforms of 1982, where commands as to plan targets were abolished but the rationing of inputs was to a large extent maintained by the economic bureaucracy above the enterprise level. Given the loyalty-based *nomenklatura* system, managers now follow 'suggestions' rather than commands by their superiors. They know that if they do not follow these 'suggestions' they will not obtain scarce inputs rationed by the economic bureaucracy, will not achieve the desired results and will be punished financially (will not receive bonuses from their superiors) and may even be demoted, ostensibly for not reaching allegedly autonomously established performance targets. Thus, caught in the dilemma of whether to follow 'suggestions' or pursue other options more rewarding in terms of the bottom-line results, **they usually follow 'suggestions' first and ask for subsidies afterwards**. Old central planning wine is poured into new market-type bottles.

Another typical defensive action by economic bureaucrats and party apparatchiks is to shift to (some) market-type measures but retain the central planning institutional framework. While the ruler, or the ruling group, does not need the institutional framework for his rule, those upon whom he depends to a large extent in maintaining that rule draw considerable benefits from the existence of such arrangements in terms of well-paid *nomenklatura*-covered jobs in all those industrial ministries, unions, enterprises and/or trusts and the associated return flow of goods and services from enterprise managers.

Accordingly, both Hungarian 1968 and Polish 1982 reforms reduced to a greater or lesser extent the arsenal of typical central planning-type command, rationing and control measures but retained the multilevel economic bureaucracy - with predictable results.

Retained bureaucracies had to find roles for themselves and, beside 'suggestions', flooded enterprises with the myriad of 'orientating' and 'auxiliary' targets, guiding principles and some specific goal-oriented campaigns that all had - in practice - binding character for enterprise managers due to their superiors' right to evaluate, reward and demote. As these (formally non-binding) indicators were internally inconsistent, they gave rise to bargaining between bureaucrats and managers for the level of and priority among the allegedly autonomously established performance targets, giving the former yet another measure of control over the latter [for an excellent overview see Laky, 1980]. Under the circumstances, **a touch of the socialist Midas transformed the otherwise efficient contractual (i.e. horizontal) relations between enterprises into a near empty shell behind which old style subordinate-superior (i.e. vertical) relations have been by and large maintained**. It does not need to be added that the old inefficiency of 'suggested' and bargained-for targets has also been maintained.

HUNGARIAN REFORMS

Little was changed in this respect in Hungary in the second phase of reforms that began in 1980 and included the dismantling of the multilevel economic bureaucracy, for two reasons. Firstly, the remaining Ministry of Industry transformed itself along old industry lines, with each department, division or group overseeing one particular industry. Thus, the old vertical relationship was retained to a considerable extent, with all its associated efficiency-reducing 'suggestions', orientating targets, guiding principles and bargaining. Secondly, allegedly autonomously established performance targets are concocted with the active help of bureaucrats from various ministries and party apparatchiks both directly through their 'voluntary' participation in the preparation of the 'autonomous' plans of enterprises and indirectly through the continuous stream of 'suggestions', orientations and priorities sent by phone, telex, and letter that narrowly circumscribe enterprises' search for better (profit-measured) performance. The Midas in reverse continues, then, to transform the gold of managerial initiative into the trash of indirectly enforced, and as such inefficient, options.

The socialist Midas has also been at work perverting the practice of all more or less unreformed Soviet-type economies. Everybody knows that the persistent excess demand of enterprises in all Soviet-type economies is caused first of all by their 'soft' budget constraint [see Kornai, 1980]. They display insatiable demand since incentives for enterprises are positively correlated to the volume and/or value of output but are not negatively correlated to the cost of inputs (factors of production and material inputs). Since their superiors put more stress on targets of particular importance at a given moment, they are willing to cover the cost overruns or outright financial losses through a variety of subsidies.

Intermediate causes of such basically accommodative behaviour by the higher levels of the economic bureaucracy have been well described in the literature. But the root causes have been barely broached and these are twofold. The first is the already analyzed loyalty-based *nomenklatura*. The stress on loyalty, understood as the execution of particular commands, 'suggestions', etc. that are of primary importance at a given moment (or at least apparently favourable reports on their execution), usually adversely affects bottom-line results.

Thus, to increase the probability of compliance, economic bureaucrats and party apparatchiks have to give tacit or open assurance that managers will not be left in the lurch and - if things go wrong - they will be helped one way or another. **'You follow our whims and wishes and we shall help you if something goes wrong with respect to bottom-line results' is the unwritten rule.** A *de facto* reciprocity in loyalty is established this way. Besides, since almost all *nomenklatura* appointments are 'in the family', a today's higher level bureaucrat or apparatchik may be appointed tomorrow to a very well-paid managerial job and then may in turn need a subsidy for 'his' enterprise. Reciprocity in loyalty is, consequently, reinforced, just as it is reinforced by the return flow of goods and services from enterprises to bureaucrats and apparatchiks.

ON UNREAL REFORMS

The second root cause is the type of the indicators of success deemed to be important by the ruler or the ruling group, their great number and the shifting of priorities over time. **The rejection of the universal yardstick, i.e. money, puts Soviet-type economic policy not so much in the category of early Keynesian accommodating economic policy but in the category of pre-Phoenician economic policy.**

Thus, various indicators are applied in increasing numbers as national economies become more and more complex. Also, besides the universally worshipped industrial production indicator, the priority changes constantly as decision-makers react to different signals of shortage in a persistently disequilibrated economy. With priorities shifting, often within a year, from, say, decreasing steel use, to increasing output of intermediate inputs, to saving energy, to increasing exports to convertible currency areas and what not, bottom-line results become a low priority indicator and are bound to suffer. Various subsidies flow to enterprises to support the implementation of 'priority' targets and 'soft' budget constraint reigns supreme. The bigger the enterprise, the softer the constraint.

Bankruptcy under the circumstances continues to be a very distant threat. In Hungary the same enterprises were on the list of the biggest losers before the start of the 1968 reforms in Hungary and after the second phase of reforms in the early 1980's. In the opinion of this writer nothing is going to change in the future either without changes in the fundamentals described above. Laws on bankruptcy, so well-received in the West, that were introduced in 1986 in Poland and Hungary are going to remain toothless in the face of a touch of the socialist Midas. After having passed the bankruptcy law, Hungarian authorities wrote off outstanding debts of metallurgical enterprises to the tune of 22 billion forints, i.e. a sum equal to about two years' output of that industry!

No surprise, then, that **some Hungarian economists began distinguishing between real reforms and those that change the means of control but not the extent of control** [see, i.e., Bauer, 1985 and Salgo, 1986]. They also, like the already quoted Tamas Bauer, point to **the need for political reforms** that would leave managers their sphere of authority, i.e. they hint at the need to solve the problems created by *nomenklatura*.

The question may arise as to how important, if at all, various new market-type measures are, both those already introduced and those envisaged, if the Midas in reverse always stands ready to turn gold into trash with a touch of his hand. Are they really bits and pieces of the emerging market-type economy? Very often they are regarded as such in the West. The reasoning behind such an assessment is simple. Since they work well in the West, they should also improve the performance of reforming economies in the East. But do they? Given the political-economic interface of a very special kind - here figuratively called 'touch of the socialist Midas' - the results are not encouraging, to say the least.

This being so, a couple of provocative questions are in order. Are the ruling groups and strata in the Soviet-type states ready to introduce real market-type reforms? If they are not, have they any shorter-term gains in mind that could be realized through proceeding with market-type measures that change little of substance? And, finally, what preconditions would be needed for real market-type reforms to begin?

The answer to the first question is the simplest. They are not. Nowhere are there signs that the ruling stratum is ready to relinquish the benefits stemming from parasiting upon the economic system. On the contrary, in Poland for example the number of *nomenklatura*-covered jobs increased under the Jaruzelski regime from 100 to 250 thousand. In the Soviet Union editors of a leading daily were sharply reprimanded just for having published a letter from a reader inquiring about shops with restricted access and how they fit into the much-lauded openness of the present era.

The above is not intended to mean that the ruling groups are not ready to do *something*. After all, even with the doctored information they get, they see multiplying signs of decay. The typical conflicts described by North between the competitive constraint that deters the ruling group from changing the inefficient property rights structure, which favours powerful segments of the ruling stratum, and the transaction cost constraint, where the inefficient property rights structure results in decreasing wealth and may generate internal dissatisfaction and unrest is very real in Soviet-type economies. **Finding itself between the devil and the deep blue sea, here and there a ruling group undertakes various half-measures - or even quarter-measures!** - in the hope that, in spite of unchanged fundamentals, these will somehow reverse the continuing decay. The fact that the Hungarian ruling group has been ready to go further than any other ruling group in Eastern Europe is irrelevant for the general analysis.

THE CASES OF 'BOND' SALES

But the reversal is not going to occur even if measures are unquestionably of the market-type variety. Let us point to a few of the most recent examples. Much has been written in Poland and Hungary about the lack of a financial market. Consequently, some market-type instruments were introduced by the authorities, with approving nods in the West. However, not unexpectedly the socialist Midas touched these measures as well.

Take, for example, obligations, which were introduced in Poland recently Although potential bond-holders were restricted by law to enterprises and institutions, it is not this limitation that matters but the perverse effects of unchanged fundamentals upon the law in question. When, after a long period of inaction, one enterprise in the printing industry issued obligations it guaranteed their buyers priority in printing services! Thus, it is not the interest earned on bonds that mattered for bond-holders but the guarantee of services that - like most goods and services - are in short supply. With a touch of the socialist Midas **a classical market-type measure redistributed shortage just like any central-planning type measure**, without increasing the efficiency of the economy. In this respect it is worth keeping in mind that the bond-issuing enterprise will not be able to do much with the money generated by bonds, since under formal and/or informal rationing its ability to re-equip or set up new printing shops depends to a very large extent on factors other than money.

Hungarians went even further and made certain bonds saleable to individuals but they, too, were unable to avoid a touch of Midas in reverse. The Hungarian Post Office issued low-interest bonds saleable to individuals, who obtained the guarantee (whatever it is worth) of obtaining a telephone connection in 3 years rather than in the usual 5-10 years. Thus, again, not the interest to be earned on the bonds (set below the inflation rate) but access to services in short supply was the main motive of those buying bonds. This time shortages typical for central planning were redistributed among households. The same happened in the case of bonds saleable to individuals by the oil and natural gas trust.

Moreover, bonds sold to individuals are guaranteed by the state with respect to both interest and principal, which takes any risk off the bond-issuing enterprise. Thus, 'soft' budget constraint reappears in new market-type guise. It need not be added that such a guarantee is not needed in the case of bonds bought by enterprises. Traditional 'soft' budget constraint-related measures (various subsidies) are more than sufficient there.

Yet another measure in Hungary, also warmly welcomed in the West, is a promise to separate the central bank activities and the commercial bank activities of the national bank and, prospectively, to split it and create several commercial banks that would compete among themselves. But also in the case of this - undoubtedly market-type - change the promise carries with it the certainty of perverted effects. The presidents of those prospective commercial banks would also be appointed, evaluated, rewarded and demoted through *nomenklatura*. Accordingly they would, just like enterprise managers, be highly accommodating with respect to 'suggestions', guiding principles, etc., coming from economic bureaucrats and party apparatchiks with respect to commercial credit policies pursued by their banks.

Indirect support for the expectations of certain failure comes from Yugoslavia, where unchanged political monopoly and the specific political-economic interface with respect to personnel policy resulted in precisely such failure. When the multilevel economic bureaucracy was dismantled in that country, bureaucracy and party apparatus found alternative (market-type!) channels of influence, i.e. banks whose appointed presidents were sensitive to pressure for credits coming from these directions. The Yugoslav crisis of the 1980's is, *inter alia*, the result of such 'soft' credit constraint that showered the country with unviable 'political' factories unable to sustain themselves, as well as with unfinished and often unfinishable investment projects.

CONCLUSIONS

This author is tempted to guess that those introducing such measures - if they are able to understand at all implications of such measures - do not themselves believe in their efficiency under unchanged fundamentals. Consequently, **'doing something' that entails measures warmly applauded in the West is, rather aimed at earning the goodwill of West-**

ern bankers and governments through the much-more-apparent-than-real marketization. Short-term gains resultant from such measures may consist of a flow of credits that helps the authorities to carry yesterday on somewhat longer. There is, however, a difference between Hungary and Poland in this respect. Hungarian authorities do their part with good grace and even better marketing skills, while Polish ones are unwilling and incompetent with respect to both reforms and advertising quasi-marketization.

An answer to the question as to what preconditions would be needed for real market-type reforms to begin has already been given, explicitly through the posited requirement of detotalitarianization of the economy at the beginning of this article and implicitly through the long survey of cases showing the purposelessness of alternatives pursued without success by some Soviet-type states. The success of the latter alternatives is precluded by the political-economic interface typical for these states, whose perverse effects this author called 'a touch of the socialist Midas'.(...)

REFERENCES

Bauer, T., 1985, Reform Policy in the Complexity of Economic Policy, *Acta Oeconomica*, Vol.34, Nos.3-4.

Csaba, L., 1983, New Features of the Hungarian Economic Quarterly in the Mid-Eighties, *New Hungarian Quarterly*, Vol.24, No.90.

Kornai, J., 1979, Resource-Constrained Versus Demand-Constrained Systems, *Econometrica*, No.4, July.

Laky, T., 1980, The Hidden Mechanisms of Recentralization in Hungary, *Acta Oeconomica*, Vol.24, 1980, Nos.1-2.

Salgo, I., 1986, Ouverture, competition et monetarisation du commerce exterieur, *Revue d'Etudes comparatives Est-Ouest*, Vol.17, No.2.

CHAPTER 3

WHY ECONOMIC REFORMS FAIL IN THE SOVIET SYSTEM: A PROPERTY RIGHTS-BASED APPROACH[*]

Why do economic reforms fail in Soviet-type systems despite the obvious interest of ruling groups in improving the performance of their ailing economies? The author applies a property rights-based analysis stressing modes of rent-maximization by ruling groups as a crucial explanatory variable. Party apparatchiks and economic bureaucrats particularly benefit from persistent interference in the economic sphere and consequently are most interested in maintaining *status quo*. The author surveys the impact of these motivations on the content of economic reforms, outlines the strategies of counterreformers and predicts the future of reforms in Soviet-type economies.

INTRODUCTION

In analyzing the disequilibrium characteristics of contemporary Western economies, Mancur Olson [1982; 1984a; 1984b] agrees with the neoclassical macroeconomists in finding that, given the tendencies of markets to clear and given the rational expectations of economic agents, any disequi-

[*] *This is a slightly abbreviated version of the article* 'Why Economic Reforms Fail in the Soviet System - A Property Rights-Based Approach, **Economic Inquiry,** *Vol. XXVIII, 1990, No.2. The first version of this article appeared in mimeo form in January 1987 as a Seminar Paper No.374 of the Institute for International Economic Studies, Stockholm.*

librium indicates that all mutually advantageous transactions have not been consummated. Having made this point, however, he asks what can make agents ignore the potential gains from unconsummated transactions and turns his attention toward the structure of incentives, and thus of institutions and policies. Olson insists, and rightly so, that a satisfactory static and dynamic macroeconomic theory has to explain who, among key actors, has the incentive to generate economic growth and equilibrate the economy and who does not. Furthermore, no government, even an authoritarian one, has an incentive to generate serious recessions or disequilibria. Olson [1984a, 637] writes that 'even in dictatorial systems, the dictator has an incentive to make the economy of the country he controls work better, since this will generate more tax receipts he can use as he pleases and usually also reduce dissent.'

Olson's arguments about incentives, institutions, and disequilibria offer an ideal basis for **an inquiry into why reforms fail in Soviet-type economies** (STEs). In Olson's theory of incentives, the old Roman principle of criminal law *cui prodest* (who gained) is applied to modern economies, and the results suggest that, contrary to widespread opinion, it is not necessarily the 'small but powerful group of high and highest leaders' that stands to gain most in terms of power and privilege from the preservation of the existing order' [Thalheim, 1986, p.40].

A powerful political elite could satisfy its desires for both power and privilege through an alternative undemocratic system, one which involves authoritarian "dont's" rather than totalitarian "do's." In that perspective, the inefficient system of economic control typical in STEs, involving centrally planned production goals and input rationing, would not be a *conditio sine qua non* of an authoritarian solution. Since totalitarian command and control systems persist, however, **one must seek groups other than the powerful and privileged few which have incentives to resist reforms and keep the economy inefficient**.

The following sections identify the membership and motives of groups having strong incentives to keep the STEs inefficient and prevent successful (i.e.market-oriented) reforms. We show how these groups operate, and analyze their effects on the economic performance of their countries. First, the incentives of these groups to prevent decentralized management in the state sector are spelled out. Then, their incentives to prevent the expansion of the more efficient private sector are outlined. Third, having identified who benefits from the *status quo* and why, the paper discusses when and how market-oriented reforms are aborted, limited or reversed by those who stand to gain from reforms' failure. (...)

WHO GAINS FROM *STATUS QUO* AND WHY

DISINCENTIVES TO DECENTRALIZED MANAGEMENT IN THE STATE SECTOR

Most analyses of Soviet-style systems focus excessively upon the distribution of power and neglect the distribution of wealth across the ruling stratum. By contrast, in an incentives-oriented analysis the distribution of wealth becomes a focus of attention. Power and privilege are viewed as means of acquiring wealth, and the desire to acquire wealth motivates the actions of the ruling stratum.

This shift of analytical emphasis does not mean that power and its distribution does not matter. On the contrary, the rulers of an STE may regard control over the working population as satisfying their need for power, either as an end in itself or as a means to attain some long-run goal, such as the creation of 'true communism'. It is important, however, to realize that **the means by which wealth is distributed is crucially important in determining the attitudes of elements in the ruling stratum toward decentralizing, market-oriented reforms**. Without considering this issue, it is difficult to explain why economic reforms-badly needed by the rulers themselves to correct flagging economic performance-did not materialize or, if they did, why they failed or at best brought about very little improvement in economic circumstances.

At this point, Douglass North's explanatory framework for the structure and enforcement of property rights, as well as their changes over time, should be brought into the picture. Applying what North [1979] calls a predatory theory of the state to the Soviet-type state, two, sometimes conflicting, objectives of such a state are identified:

1. to provide a set of public goods and services designed to lower transaction costs and increase the efficiency upon which the growth of wealth is predicated. (In non-STEs economic growth is synonymous with the growth of wealth, but in the STEs the two are distinct. For this argument see Winiecki [1986a]);

and

2. to specify the fundamental rules of the property rights structure, i.e., the ownership structure in factor and product markets, in a way that maximizes the rent flowing to the ruler and the ruling stratum. The fact that this structure is extremely muddled in STEs is irrelevant, since such muddle, i.e., the dominance of non-exclusively owned resources in the state sector, actually facilitates the expropriation of rent.

At this stage also two of North's [1979] reservations about *predatory states* must be addressed. First, he saw complications arising for such states from the advent of representative government. Soviet-type states, however, despite their coexistence with states having representative government, clearly have pre-representative governments and, accordingly, can be easily analyzed within the basic predatory state framework.

Second, North [1971] also pointed out that his model, predicated upon profit-maximization, does not hold if social reformers change institutions so as to benefit groups other than the rulers and profit-makers. However, contemporary Soviet-type states lack profit-maximizing institutions, and the existence or non-existence of social reformers at the beginning of such states is irrelevant. Indeed, any impulse for social reform in the founders of the Soviet-type states quickly degenerated, and the ruling stratum established property rights that maximized their rent. The process has been criticized by insiders such as Trotsky [1937] and Djilas [1956].

The following hypotheses now arise from these considerations:

i. In STEs the fundamental conflict described by North [1979], i.e., the conflict between efficient property rights designed to lower transaction costs and increase wealth and inefficient property rights designed to maximize rent to the ruling stratum, is strongly in evidence;

and

ii. in such states the nominal ruler will avoid offending powerful groups in the ruling stratum, i.e., the apparatchiks and economic bureaucrats, who benefit most from the institutional and economic *status quo*.

In STEs the rulers agree to maintain a property rights structure favorable to those groups, regardless of the effect upon efficiency. In fact, modes of wealth distribution resulting from the STE structure of property rights differ so much from those in other pre-representative government states (i.e., traditional and 'modern' autocracies), that institutional change leading to lower transaction costs and increased wealth is much more difficult to achieve. No STE, for example, has replicated the successful, efficiency-enhancing institutional changes of 'authoritarian' South Korea or Taiwan.

In 'old' autocracies the ruling stratum consists of either the traditional hierarchies or elites based on the military and the police. These appropriate to themselves a larger share of created wealth than they would obtain under a representative government. They get higher salaries and more 'perks', while their status symbols (articles of conspicuous consumption or modern professional equipment) have a priority claim upon the state budget. According to Winiecki [1986a] however, the rulers of an STE preside over a ruling stratum consisting of the four pillars of the system: communist party apparatchiks, economic bureaucrats, the police, and the military. All may (and do) receive a larger share of the created wealth than is true in representative states. Their salaries may be relatively higher and their 'perks' relatively more important in the STE shortage economy. So far, the mode of wealth distribution appears to be the same as in 'ordinary' autocracies.

In the STE, however, another mode of wealth distribution exists that maximizes the rent of two particular segments of the ruling stratum: party apparatchiks and members of the economic bureaucracy. This mode, unknown in other systems, enables these groups to benefit from their protracted interference in the process of wealth creation itself. There are two interconnected ways in which this is done.

The first is through **the principle of** *nomenklatura*, i.e., the right of the communist party apparatus, from the central party committee down to the enterprise committee, to 'recommend' and 'approve' appointments for all managerial positions in the economic (and public) administration and all managerial positions in enterprises. These appointments are made primarily on the basis of loyalty rather than managerial competence, and apparatchiks usually appoint themselves and their friends in the party to those well-paid jobs, *Nomenklatura* has adverse effects for at least two reasons.

i. it signifies a severe limitation on the pool of talent from which managers are drawn;

and,

ii. given the well-known negative selection process under totalitarianism, the pool of *nomenklatura*-included talents is not only smaller but also of lower competence relative to any other pool in the society with similar occupational, age, sex, and other characteristics.

Since loyalty is the foremost concern, managers, once appointed, are evaluated on the basis of their loyalty as measured by their compliance with commands (e.g., achieving planned targets or meeting *ad hoc* commands) rather than their efficiency (e.g., producing desired outputs at least cost). Of course, loyalty to one's own superiors is not necessarily perceived by subordinates as involving an obligation to fulfill commands to the letter. Winiecki [1988a] reports that falsified reports on economic performance are the rule rather than the exception in STEs. Falsification continues, *perestroika* or no *perestroika*.

Does the preference for loyalty to one's superiors over real performance signify the dominance of power or ideology over wealth considerations? Since the power of the party and the ruling stratum has rarely been threatened, while a relative neglect of real performance *vis-à-vis* loyalty has been a constant in STEs, the answer appears to be in the negative. Bureaucrats and apparatchiks learned long ago that their wealth does not depend primarily upon ideology or upon creating social wealth but upon the rents they extract through their control of the wealth creation process. Thus, loyalty to superiors is important in struggles between various coteries within the ruling stratum who position themselves to extract more benefits from the inefficient economic system [Hillman and Schnytzer, 1986]. Power or ideology considerations alone, i.e., the attempts of any one group to set an ideologically different course for the party, rarely dominate. A **major mode of rent extraction involves the system of side payments, or kickbacks,** from managers of (primarily industrial) enterprises. In a shortage economy these kickbacks are mostly of a non-pecuniary nature. Enterprise managers offer to those who appointed them, and to other superiors and colleagues who may advance their careers a variety of goods and services, and have the opportunity to benefit in the same way. (...) The relative unimportance of efficiency allows managers to absorb, without being held accountable, the costs of these kickback activities. Leakage of wealth thus takes place not only through the losses incurred and gains foregone by incompetent managers but also because of the time and effort spent on rent seeking activities.

Both types of rent extraction exist because of the muddled structure of STE property rights. Since the means of production are in theory, but not in fact, socialized, since workers are 'the hegemonic class' in a socialist society and the communist party is 'the leading force of the working class', any appointment through the *nomenklatura*, or any other decision process for that matter, can be justified. It does not matter whether or not STE property rights were originally devised to achieve a socialist purpose or to maximize rents for the ruling stratum. What matters is that muddled property rights allowing protracted interference in wealth creation serve the latter purpose very well.(...).

The different methods of rent maximization used by groups in the ruling stratum are of primary importance for the prospects of reform in the Soviet system. All segments of the ruling stratum prefer the *status quo* to the alternative of representative government. But **two segments only -**

party apparatchiks and economic bureaucrats - have, in addition, a strong incentive to maintain the (...) centralized institutional *status quo* **in the economic sphere.**

To see why this is so, consider that decentralization assumes, as a first step, the substitution of parameters for commands. Since parameters (in contrast to plan targets), such as the interest rate, need not be input- or output-specific, intermediate levels of economic bureaucracy become superfluous. A look at Figure 1 shows clearly that the liquidation of the intermediate levels of economic bureaucracy (the dashed-line rectangular area) makes redundant not only the bureaucrats employed in industrial ministries and unions, but also reduces the pool of well-paid jobs to which apparatchiks may be appointed through the *nomenklatura*. It is only to be expected that such changes will be strongly resisted by the powerful groups most strongly affected.

FIGURE 1

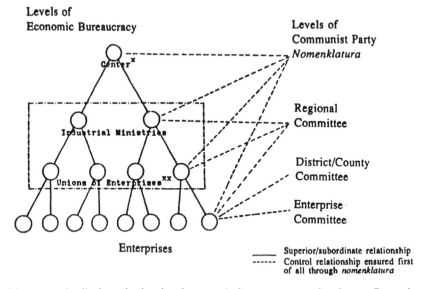

The rectangle displays the levels of economic bureaucracy rendered superfluous by real decentralizing, market-type economic reforms. Dotted lines show also which levels of party apparatus lose the chance to get themselves appointed to the well paid jobs covered by the *nomenklatura* in industrial ministries and unions of enterprises.

*Center also includes certain functional ministries (finance, labor, technology and others).

**Also called central boards or associations. Trusts and combines belong to the Union level as well

Similar resistance appears at the enterprise level. For example, strengthening enterprise's budget constraint by holding it financially accountable for the effects of management decisions will be resisted, since the costs of kickback-related activities would begin to affect the enterprise's balance sheet, as well as rewards and penalties for managers and workers. The effects would also be felt by every actual and potential receiver of kickbacks who would spread resistance even wider. Financial accountability could, in fact, affect the whole system of dependence based on loyalty. Conflict resulting from a divergence between the requirements of loyalty and those of financially sound performance is an everyday occurrence in modified STEs like Poland and Hungary, where financial indicators matter to some extent. That conflict's outcome, however, is predetermined in favor of loyalty because of the operation of the *nomenklatura*. Simply put, **managers caught between whether to follow the 'suggestions' of their superiors or pursue other, more financially appropriate goals for their firm choose the former and ask for subsidies afterwards**. Otherwise they might lose their jobs. That is why even in Hungary, the most reformed STE, the budget constraint continues to be 'soft' (...).

Predictably, apparatchiks and economic bureaucrats would most strongly resist attempts to replace *nomenklatura* by selections based on merit. As a result, *nomenklatura* has never been abolished for managerial posts in the economic sphere, the sphere where efficiency gains are most important for the rulers.

While it is true that apparatchik and bureaucratic resistance is found throughout the STE, its intensity differs among sectors of the economy. Since the best paying managerial jobs under the *nomenklatura* (i.e., those enjoying best opportunities for kickbacks) are in industry, it is in industry that reform faces the strongest resistance and, correspondingly, the highest probability of failure. The economic history of STEs shows some partly successful reforms of state agriculture, a sector in which opportunities for rent extraction are less frequent and the benefits smaller. To date, no reforms of state industry, based on general parameters, accountability, or merit, have been successful.

The wealth-maximizing interests of apparatchiks and bureaucrats in maintaining the inefficient economic *status quo* is in sharp contrast with that of the current ruling groups in the Soviet-type states. On the other hand, while a 'small but powerful group at the top', to employ Thalheim's phrase, does not necessarily need central planning in its system of rule and wealth-maximization, those upon whom it depends for maintaining that rule - those who control the STE - draw considerable benefits from the existing economic arrangements.

Before proceeding with the argument, the term 'control of economic activity' by the economic bureaucracy and party apparatus requires some further definition. In an STE this function has little in common with guidance toward efficient achievement of desired economic outcomes, at least those desired by the public or even by the ruler. Rather, the goal most often sought is to maximize rent for the ruling stratum. Control is process-oriented, rather than outcome-oriented, and is based on detailed prescriptions of how, when, and with what means to produce what outputs. The obedience of subordinates is all-important, since this gives superiors a sense of control and of an ability to protect their rents.

Ironically, control of the process does not confer control of the outcome because the consequences of following such detailed prescriptions are far from the expected ones: part of output exists only on paper; products are shoddy and obsolescent; deliveries are late; efficiency indicators miss plan targets and the managers are obviously unable to do anything to correct the situation [see, Winiecki, 1986a]. Another irony is that this style of control may impede realization of the ruler's own objectives, yet the ruler(s) are also powerless because the apparatchiks and economic bureaucrats are essential for his (their) political control of the whole system. Controlling economic activity means simply that the apparatchiks and economic bureaucrats are able to issue commands ('suggestions' at the very least) affecting process or product.

These commands are superficially, in form but not in substance, obeyed by enterprises. The amount of effort expended on control by the economic bureaucracy and party apparatchiks will be lower with a simpler control procedure. For example, commands are preferred to suggestions, since the latter require bargaining. Commands may be, and are, often changed, but changes later need less arguing, since the disparity between targets and reality becomes more visible over time. The fact that making changes later is also more costly does not bother bureaucrats and apparatchiks in the least. Thus, even if systemic modifications or reforms do not actually threaten maximum rent extraction, such changes may increase the effort needed to maintain (superficial) control of economic activity. Therefore, the apparatchiks and bureaucrats have incentives to resist change, however modest it may be.

The ruler-ruling stratum relationship clearly is crucial to understanding reform failure in the Soviet system. The juxtaposition of these two groups in this article should not be confused, however, with the oft-encountered 'good czar, bad officials' approach to Russian politics. The rulers (or 'ruling group') is actually representative of all the ruling stratum and reflects all the moral, intellectual and professional consequences of decades of system-specific negative selection. Thus, the czar is not any better than his officials. Nonetheless a great difference exists between the rulers and other groups in the ruling stratum. **The ruler, alone within the ruling stratum, is interested not only in seeing reports that commands are fulfilled, but also, and more importantly, in seeing that the commands were actually fulfilled!** No other group bears that ultimate responsibility. He (they) will be blamed for any failure of the system by competing groups within the ruling stratum, and his interest in real performance makes the ruler more sensitive to falling efficiency and consequently more ready to reform the economy than is the average representative of the ruling stratum.

As a result, **if rulers try to change the economic system significantly, they may face a revolt by functionaries who have the strongest incentives to maintain the *status quo*,** placing their political dominance in jeopardy. Thus, rulers face both the rent-maximizing and the transaction cost constraints stressed by North [1979]. In periods of declining performance, the ruler feels the transaction cost constraint. Inefficient property rights do not generate the increased wealth needed, for example, to sustain the superpower status of the Soviet Union, or to avert consumer dissatisfaction in all Soviet-type states.

On the other hand, if the ruler attempts a significant revision of the existing property rights structure, he risks loss of support from important members of the ruling stratum who will turn to competitors for political power. It is, moreover, a special feature of STEs that even if competitive constraint on the ruler diminishes and reforms begin, their implementation is in the hands of party apparatchiks and economic bureaucrats. Reforms, if not aborted or weakened from the start, may then be sabotaged, distorted or finally reversed. Clearly and unequivocally **it is the apparatchiks and bureaucrats of STEs who gain most from maintaining the institutional *status quo*, and they are the groups which resist change most strongly**. Given the key positions of these groups in the STE system, we may predict a very high probability of failure of decentralizing, market-oriented, efficiency-increasing reforms.

DISINCENTIVES TO EXPANDING THE PRIVATE SECTOR

Expanding the role of the private sector in an STE usually has the same objectives as decentralizing, market-oriented, efficiency-enhancing reforms in the state sector. Theoretically, private sector expansion could serve as a substitute for state sector reforms, and could provide the means to circumvent strong resistance to market-oriented change in the state sector. In actuality, attempts to reform the state sector have complemented simultaneous private sector expansion, Changes in policy toward the private sector have been numerous, however, since often the private sector has had to contend with various forced concentration drives in the state sector. In the course of these drives, large state enterprises often gobbled up small state and private enterprises alike.

Analysts invariably cite ideology as the cause for the limited role of the private sector (except in agriculture) in Soviet type economies. The same ideological argument comes to the fore in two other circumstances:

i. when Western experts and journalists seek the sources of vilification campaigns and other obstacles to change that follow each official policy shift favoring the private sector,

and

ii when rulers must explain the unsatisfactory results of pro-private sector policy changes. In the latter case, the rulers usually produce some type of circular memorandum aimed at the economic bureaucracy or party committees and lecturing them on the need to overcome the 'old style', 'dogmatic' approach with respect to the role of the private sector under socialism. These memoranda are usually ineffectual.

An ideological explanation for the failure to harness private enterprise to improve performance in a persistently disequilibrated and structurally distorted STE fails for two reasons. First, ideological fervor has generally subsided, although admittedly to differing degrees, since the imposition of the STE system. This subsidence has occurred in all spheres of the society and suggests that ideology is not a good explanation for unabated hostility towards the private sector. Second, and more important, any ideological reservations have had to be overcome first and foremost at the top. When a policy to promote the private sector is announced, it is actually the ruler who has to 'eat the toad', i.e. to confess directly or indirectly, that the state sector cannot do what the private sector is expected to do. Even policy changes announcing the most limited expansion of the private sector amounts to precisely such a confession. It would seem, then, that few lower level bureaucrats or party apparatchiks, whose position depends not on performance but on loyalty, will dare to sabotage the latest twist of the party line and remain ideologically hostile (...).

On the other hand, the ancient principle of *cui prodest* suggests that there must be strong disincentives for certain groups to follow the rulers' privatization lines. The two avenues of rent distribution, i.e., *nomenklatura* and kickbacks, operate simultaneously in a STE. However, in interactions between segments of the ruling stratum and the private sector, both are conspicuously absent, or extremely rare. There are no well-paid posts to be filled by *nomenklatura* appointments in small private enterprises, nor is there a 'soft' budget constraint, so permissive to a variety of rent-maximizing kickbacks even under reform. **A shift of activity from the state to the private sector reduces, therefore, the possibilities for party apparatchiks and economic bureaucrats to extract rent.** Hostility towards the private sector is, therefore, based not on ideology or even actual rent losses, but on gains foregone when expansion of the state sector is curbed in favor of the private sector. The story does not end here. A bureaucrat, or even an apparatchik who can indirectly influence each decision, may extract rent by taking a bribe for a concession to set up a private industrial firm, or to open a restaurant or a repair shop. But this way of extracting benefits violates private sector property rights, where resources are clearly exclusive, and is consequently much more dangerous. In plain words, taking bribes is a criminal act.

By contrast, in an STE rent extraction from the state sector is either fully legitimized, i.e., through the *nomenklatura* and the rationing of goods at the center's order, or, as with system-specific kickbacks, belongs to the 'grey area' between the improper and the criminal. Therefore, since negative selection assures that moral scruples are rare among ruling stratum rent-takers in an STE, something akin to a political earthquake, like the 'Solidarity' period in Poland [in 1980-81], is needed to threaten all who predatorily extract rent from an STE system. Otherwise, only a few luckless individuals whose punishment was decided upon by higher-ups will be the show pieces in trumpeted, but deceptive, anti-corruption campaigns.

It should be stressed that only so-called 'secondary' corruption - that not legitimized within the ruling stratum - is the type usually punished in an unreformed STE. Such secondary corruption arises from conflicts between the utility function of the ruler and that of his agents. This is readily understandable in light of North [1979]'s property rights approach. The inability of the ruler to constrain his agents perfectly would result in the diffusion of some of the ruler's monopoly rent and would, therefore, call down sanctions on the head of the offenders. Barzel [1974] and Cheung [1974] note the ruler's problem is rendered more difficult, and the rent diffusion is greater, when the measurement of output is more difficult and more costly. Since in STEs this measurement is most difficult in industry, one would expect diffusion is greatest precisely in that sector; Winiecki [1982; 1986a] has confirmed this. Diffusion is so great in fact that it trickles down to some of the ruled as well, through widespread falsification of performance reports by enterprises. *Nomenklatura*-covered managers and, to a smaller extent, but in larger numbers, all employees of affected enterprises may all benefit from these falsifications.

WHEN AND HOW REFORMS FAIL: THE STRATEGIES AND TACTICS OF 'COUNTERREFORMATION'

Because decentralizing market-type reforms of the state sector and expansions of the private sector adversely affect rent extraction possibilities, the apparatchiks and bureaucrats who benefit from the existing STE arrangements embrace what may be termed a multifaceted 'counterreformation' course. To understand how reforms may thus be reversed or aborted one must consider again the relations between the ruler (or ruling group) and key elements in the ruling stratum, especially the apparatchiks and economic bureaucrats.

In analyzing those relationships and the 'counterreformation', however, it is necessary to consider the ability of the members of large groups to act in concert. Olson [1965; 1982] stresses that large groups are not always able to act as if guided by their collective interest, yet for STEs this generally valid point does not apply so fully to actions by the apparatchiks and economic bureaucrats. A large difference exists between, on the one hand, a large, perhaps opposition, group struggling to bring organized pressure on a government or a ruling party to affect certain outcomes and, on the other hand, a large group that consists for all practical purposes of the government and/or its ruling political party.

'Counterreformers' in STEs, indeed, usually are in the party and often coalesce around members of the ruling group itself. There are always one or few top party figures who think that cracking the whip, tightening discipline and increasing control are enough to solve the problem of falling efficiency. The hostile group's capability to act collectively is much greater in such situations for the simple reason that theirs is a very unusual, often majority, interest faction with access to mechanisms of political and economic control. If such a group sets itself to thwarting reforms outlined by the rulers and their advisers, the organizational and destructive capacity of the 'counterreformers' may turn out to be markedly greater than that of politically powerful elements who are outside the mainstream of economic control.

Even if they do not act collectively but only individually, the 'counter reformers' unusual position in the party and the bureaucracy will help them throw sand into the machinery of reforms. Although they may not be members of a strong trade union or an influential professional association, they effectively govern and control the STE. Individual decisions of a minister, a regional party secretary, or a city administrator, all *nomenkla-tura*-linked functionaries, have serious consequences. For example, they can twist and distort decentralizing reforms pertaining to all state enterprises in a given industry or region, or they may forbid establishment of private enterprises in a given industry or region. These actions symbolize **an Olsonian 'free rider' situation in reverse**: everyone outside the informally organized group of 'counterreformers' brings his valuable individual contribution to the common cause of resisting reform.

The preceding considerations suggest that (1) aborting reforms costs less effort by the interested parties than reversing reforms later, and (2) reversing less consistent reforms (with inconsistency deliberately built into the systemic modifications) costs less effort than reversing more consistent reforms. Although the 'counterreformers' are very effective in adjusting their obstructive actions to different circumstances, they probably cannot always implement their first-best (i.e., completely reform-suppressing) solutions and may try to abort reforms, at least in part.

Aborting reforms neither means that no changes whatsoever are introduced nor that all changes are repudiated. It means, rather, that the reforms actually introduced do not threaten the property rights structure in the state sector through which apparatchiks and economic bureaucrats maximize their rent. Abortive reforms also do not alter either the institutions or the procedures of central planning. Examples of such abortive or sham reforms abounded in the 1980s in such STEs as Bulgaria, Czechoslovakia, and the German Democratic Republic. The 1980s Soviet reforms likewise belong to the category of abortive reforms.

The second-best solution for the apparatchiks/bureaucrats is to introduce internally inconsistent *quasi*-reforms, which modify the system so inconsistently that they are doomed to fail. To the category of *quasi*-reforms belong the Polish reforms of 1956-1958 and 1973, and most of the East European reforms of the 1960s (excluding the Hungarian reforms to be discussed later). *Quasi*-reforms may increase the effort apparatchiks and economic bureaucrats must expend in controlling economic activity, but that increase is only temporary, since reversal of the quasi-reforms is assured because of problems created by the inevitable reform and system contradictions. In any case, the structure of property rights remains intact. With inconsistencies often obvious from the start, beneficiaries of the traditional STE model need only to wait until the first problems appear to begin their campaign for reform reversal. Usually they do not need to wait for long, since STEs always enter reform periods in a state of larger or smaller disequilibrium, and reforms can thus be blamed for the persistence of disequilibrium even if no other reform-related adverse consequences have appeared. Actually, major adverse consequences will, in any event, likely arise because of *quasi*-reform and system inconsistencies. To be sure, small efficiency gains may be registered, but they are temporary and disappear over time under the impact of the process of reform reversals. To the dismay of the ruling stratum, some crises are so severe, however, that neither no reform nor abortive or *quasi*-reforms are possible. For example, in Poland in 1981-82 popular pressure combined with economic disaster prevented the abortion of reforms and forced the ruling group to appear to permit fundamental economic reforms, largely in order to deflect pressure for political reforms. A genuine attempt to improve Polish economic conditions was needed, since the rulers realized that the people understood that not all of the problems were the outcome of Gierek's mistakes or of Solidarity-organized strikes (despite attempts to convince the general public otherwise). The pressure for political reform did not abate, however, and martial law was introduced [in 1981] to stave off fundamental political system changes. Ironically, as Winiecki [1986c] has explained real economic reforms are impossible in the Soviet-type systems without political reforms, at the very least without the shift from totalitarian to 'ordinary' dictatorship. (...)

The examples of Poland and Hungary suggest that economic reforms in the STEs, even those with strong popular support do not bring about systemic modifications seriously limiting the ability of the party apparatchiks and economic bureaucrats to extract rent. Reforms at most reduce the number of well-paid jobs in intermediate levels of the bureaucratic hierarchy and increase the effort required to control economic activity. Both 'defects',` however, largely disappear in the inevitable process of reform reversal.

As shown above, the timing of the 'counterreformation' depends on circumstances such as the degree of deterioration of economic performance, the existence of popular pressure for reforms, and the strength of that pressure. Consequently, the most effective time to act cannot be selected *a priori* by the interested parties, since the timing depends on the dynamics of a given reform process. 'Counterreformers' enjoy greater latitude, however, in the choice of measures that will allow them to retain control over economic activity and to ensure that reforms will not succeed. With each failed attempt at economic reform, the apparatchiks and bureaucrats become more effective in applying their reactive measures, largely because of learning curve effects. Some of the most successful strategies to thwart reform are analyzed below.

(1) *Pseudo-reorganization.* This classically Parkinsonian measure makes it possible to maintain the institutional structure basically intact by shedding a few middle levels of the multilevel hierarchy. At the same time, it is preferable to add some functional institutions in order to keep the pool of well-paid *nomenklatura*-covered jobs as large as possible. Pseudo-reorganization was a typical maneuver of 'counterreformers' in the Czechoslovak reforms of 1967, the Hungarian reforms of 1968, all Polish reforms of 1956-1958,1973 and 1982, and the Soviet reforms of the 1980s.

(2) *Limiting the number of obligatory plan indicators for enterprises.* This typical substitute for the abolition of commands has been widely used in most economic reforms under the rubric of simplifying enterprise management. However, with the STE's institutional structure intact and with government campaigns aimed at assuring the implementation of successive partial targets, many obligatory plan indicators are sooner or later reestablished while new ones were added in the process. An example of this in the Polish engineering industries from 1946 to 1981 is shown in Figure 2. The number of obligatory indicators has risen, fallen, and then risen again in a recurrent pattern.

An additional 'counterreformer' device is to shift obligatory plan indicators to other categories instead of simply reducing their numbers. For example, in Czechoslovakia the number of obligatory plan indicators in

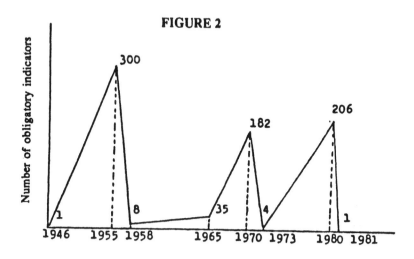

FIGURE 2

Changes in a number of obligatory indicators in engineering industries in Poland in the 1946–1981 period associated with the imposition of central planning and subsequent attempt at economic reforms and reform reversals. Source: [Jermakowicz 1983]

industry was reduced from 1120 in 1965, to 66 in 1966, but at the same time 510 other items were added in two new classes of 'orientating' and 'auxiliary' indicators. The same happened in the Soviet reforms of the 1980s. A large number of indicators were shifted to a new category of 'controlling figures', broken down to the enterprise level and then passed on the enterprises to 'guide' them in their activities.

(3) *Abolishing commands but retaining the rationing of inputs.* Even if most production targets are formally abolished (which rarely occurs), allocation of scarce inputs by superiors in the multilevel economic bureaucracy constrains the pursuit of more profitable output mixes by enterprise managers. Managers understand that any output mix other than that 'suggested' by their superiors will reduce their prospects for obtaining scarce materials, since those materials will be shifted to other enterprises producing 'priority' outputs, i.e., those desired by the economic bureaucracy or party apparatchiks. This pattern was typical of the Polish reforms of 1982,

same was also true in the Soviet Union, even with the USSR's smaller, less ambitious program of command abolition. The modest room for maneuver secured by Soviet industrial enterprises has in the 1980s been reduced to virtually zero due to continuing rationing of almost all inputs.

(4) *Abolishing commands and rationing but retaining the right to appoint and dismiss enterprise managers.* This 'revolutionary' change - one at least hailed as such - has happened to date only in Hungary. However, as was pointed out above, the Hungarian command/rationing system of central planning was not transformed into a decentralized, market-type economy, since the property rights structure in the state sector did not change [*see also text no.2*]. Even without production targets and input rationing, enterprise managers continued to be dependent on their superiors for periodic evaluations based on loyalty first and foremost. In such an environment the strength of their superiors' 'suggestions' was not much weaker than that of commands.

With their position, salary, and bonuses dependent upon the economic bureaucracy above them, managers in STE enterprises analyze performance in terms of efficiency and in terms of the specific suggestions of their superiors. When these conflict, 'suggestions' prevail. (...) Consequently, according to Bauer [1984], patterns of economic development and foreign trade did not significantly differ from those in STEs not formally following the Hungarian reform model.

Counterreform measures designed to maintain an unchanged degree of control over economic activities can be supplemented or reinforced by other measures. These may include expressions of various policy preferences or *ad hoc* regulations that contravene the thrust of reforms and, if implemented, reduce the ability of enterprises to react to profitable opportunities. These measures also raise costs, reduce quality, increase obsolescence of outputs, and otherwise make firms less efficient. Ironically, counterreformers use the adverse results arising from their interference as evidence of the failure of the reforms themselves during the next campaign for reversal. (...)

PROSPECTIVE FAILURES - IMAGINABLE SOLUTIONS

This analysis based on property rights, with special emphasis on the structure of incentives facing the ruling stratum in the Soviet system, not only explains the repeated failures of economic reforms in the STEs but also, given the argument's theoretical underpinnings, enables analysts to predict outcomes of ongoing reforms. This analysis has been applied to three industrial reform programs: the Soviet, Polish [*see text no.2*], and Chinese.

THE SOVIET UNION

In the Soviet case the structure of STE property rights remains intact, retaining both modes of wealth distribution among the ruling stratum - the *nomenklatura* and kickbacks - despite exemplary punishments for 'secondary corruption' handed out to a few improperly constrained agents of the ruler. As to the reforms themselves, Soviet responses display almost all the devices to ensure that reforms fail right from the start.

In the USSR, pseudo-reorganization and illusory limitations on obligatory plan indicators are the most common 'counterreforms' in the measures promulgated so far. Changes at the top, ranging from traditional industrial ministries to committees playing the role of superministries, belong to the category of pseudo-reorganization, aimed nominally at decreasing uncertainty and shortages by integrating certain suppliers and purchasers under the same bureaucratic umbrella. However, this type of reform has never worked anywhere; the only thing it can do is redistribute shortages across enterprises. A given committee's 'own' purchasers are relatively better supplied, while the plight of those under the *aegis* of another committee is ignored or worsened.

A shift of emphasis within the multilevel hierarchy from ministries to unions of enterprises (a measure that has failed many times elsewhere in STEs) is a similar non-performer. Ministries and unions are not interested in increasing efficiency but in showing improved average results from one year to another. Many analysts have shown that these bodies redistribute scarce resources for both current production and capacity expansion with the main intention of improving these average results. Therefore they shift resources from relatively more efficient to relatively less efficient enterprises. Soviet architects of reform in the 1970s and 1980s showed an understanding of this point by early 1988.

In the case of exports, emphasis has shifted from the Soviet Foreign Trade Ministry to industrial ministries, associations, and, in a very limited number of cases, to enterprises. Again, this measure has not succeeded because it is mainly redistributive, not corrective, and it cannot succeed in the future in an unchanged economic environment. Overall, in an STE shortage economy having strong disincentives to innovate and operating with low quality requirements, the costs incurred to turn out manufactures saleable on the word market far outweigh any possible trade benefits accruing to manufacturers.

The STE experiment with limiting obligatory plan targets also has a long history of failure. The Polish reforms of 1956-1973, the Czech reform of 1967, and pseudo-reforms in other Soviet-type economies, support this proposition. The much touted Soviet brigade system, which seeks to reduce inefficiencies by making contracts with small teams ready to implement specific tasks for specified remuneration, may improve the performance of some Soviet enterprises but only to a limited extent and not for long. The extent of improvement cannot be large because enterprises in the STEs are constrained, first of all, by system-specific excess demand, shortages and uncertainty, i.e., by the external environment of the enterprise; worker negligence and inefficiency is only a secondary source of enterprise inefficiency. Therefore, even if brigade workers were to exert themselves somewhat more, their efforts at the team level may not translate into effects at the enterprise level. This failure will raise costs without generating any compensating benefits and will bring conflict with higher levels of the economic bureaucracy. Workers will also have to be paid for their readiness to fulfill the contract even when, as frequently occurs, inputs fail to arrive, which again will increase costs. These problems lead to reservations being written into contracts or *ad hoc* interventions to reduce specified remuneration, actions which subvert incentives for workers to exert themselves.

The whole brigade approach, then becomes another useless institutional fixture under which gains will first decrease and later disappear altogether. Ultimately, even cracking the whip over brigades through tightening labor discipline and more thoroughly checking plan implementation reports will cease to yield even paper gains.

Finally, otherwise laudable Soviet attempts to reestablish some incentives for non-manual workers as means of eliminating plan targets, will have as little, or less, effect on the enterprises' performance as will the brigade system. Both implemented and planned increases in wage differentials between white and blue collar workers in favor of the former are going to disappear rather fast. Winiecki [1988b] shows that STEs tend not only to generate excess demand for labor but also much stronger excess demand for manual labor. Such excess demand combines with a common industrial economy pattern of relatively reduced manual labor supply to decrease wage differentials between non-manual and manual workers. Actually, in some countries these differentials were already reversed in favor of the latter. Even *ad hoc* Polish and Czech interventions similar to those in the Soviet Union did not reverse wage convergence; they only delayed further narrowing of differentials by some two to three years. (...)

CHINA

Ongoing reforms in China sparked the most excitement in the West until the beginning of similar Soviet developments. It appears, however, that the optimism of both Western observers and Chinese reformers reflects wishful thinking more than anything else. Deng Xiaoping, the prime mover of Chinese reforms, may have hoped that 'if the reforms in the countryside worked out very well in three years...it will take five years for the reforms in the city,' but as shown in [earlier] sections (..), the assumption of a causal relation between rural-agricultural and urban-industrial reforms has no foundations whatever. The amount and variety of benefits extractable by the ruling stratum through protracted interference in production are infinitely greater in industry than in agriculture; hence the prospects for successful reform in industry are much dimmer.

Jan Winiecki

The partial success of agricultural reforms in China hence has no bearing on the possibilities for the success of industrial reforms. Hungary is a case in point. The success of Hungarian agriculture (relative to that in other STEs) was not followed by successful reforms in industry. Over two decades have passed since 1968, and Hungarian industry remains by and large unreformed. Whatever marginally greater efficiency it has enjoyed resulted not from a shift to a decentralized market-type economy but from a more cautious policy that alleviates some of the worst effects of the traditional Soviet system.

Reasons why the Hungarian ruling stratum has behaved as it did are clear. By contrast, there was no popular revolution and Soviet intervention in communist China and hence no ruling stratum victims to exert a moderating influence on the conflict between reforms and reactions. On the other hand, the domestic Maoist convulsions may have had a similar effect on party apparatchiks and the economic bureaucracy. Mao Zedong was a social reformer who, in his quest for a coercive utopia, also subjected many apparatchiks and economic bureaucrats (but not the military or the police) to often cruel and humiliating persecutions.

Consequently, these functionaries, mindful of the not too distant past of the 'Cultural Revolution', may have preferred a period of stability. They may have settled for gains in their own wealth proportional to those in the country as a whole, even if they experience a fall in relative position compared to, say, the new entrepreneurs. Attitudes may change, however, as memories of the 'Cultural Revolution' fade. The maintenance of reforms requires further limitations on ruling stratum benefits, including ultimately the abolition of *nomenklatura* in industry. In any case, the situation in a predatory STE state such as China, in which important segments of the ruling stratum are deprived of the power to extract rent through the structure of existing property rights, is inherently unstable.(...)

CONCLUSIONS

Despite the pessimistic analyses offered in this article, one should not conclude that economic reforms in STEs will inevitably fail. Reforms, it is true, are much more difficult to achieve there than in other *predatory states*, largely because of the unique interface between the political and economic spheres in STEs. However, under certain conditions of long-term economic decline, such as apparently affected all East European STEs in the 1980s, political changes may positively affect the chances for the success of economic changes.(...)

REFERENCES

Antal, L., 1976, Development with Some Digression, *Acta Oeconomica*, Vol.23.

- , 1982, Thoughts on the Further Development of the Hungarian Economic Reform, *Acta Oeconomica*, Vol.29, Nos.3-4.

Barzel, Y., 1974, A Theory of Rationing by Waiting. *Journal of Law and Economics*.

Bauer, T., 1984, The Second Economic Reform and Ownership Relations, *East European Economics*, Spring-Summer.

Beksiak, J., 1984, Change in the Economy, Warsaw: PWN Publishers (in Polish).

Cheung, S. N. S., 1974, A Theory of Price Control, *Journal of Law and Economics,* April.

Crosnier, M. A., 1987, L'economie sovietique en 1986: une image brouillee, *Le Courrier des pays de l'Est*, 318.

Djilas, M., 1956, *The New Class*. Praeger, New York.

Hillman, A. L. and A. Schnytzer.,1986, Illegal Economic Activities and Purges in a Soviet-Type Economy: A Rent-Seeking Perspective, *International Review of Law and Economics*.

Jermakowicz, W., 1983, Systemic Determinants of Organizational Structures, Parts I-II. Polish Economic Association, Warsaw, 1983, mimeographed (in Polish).

Kornai, J., 1979, "Resource-Constrained Versus Demand-Constrained System, *Econometrica*, vol. 47, No.4.

-, *Economics of Shortage*, 1980, North-Holland, Amsterdam.

Laky, T, 1980, The Hidden Mechanisms of Recentralization in Hungary, *Acta Oeconomica*, vol.24, Nos.1-2.

North, D. C., 1971, Institutional Change and Economic Growth, *Journal of Economic History*, March.

-, 1979, A Framework for Analyzing the State in Economic History, *Explorations in Economic History*, Academic Press, New York, July.

Olson, M., 1965, *The Logic of Collective Action*, Harvard University Press, Cambridge, Mass.

-, 1982, *The Rise and Decline of Nations*, Yale University Press, New Haven: Yale University Press.

-, 1984a, "Microeconomic Incentives and Macroeconomic Decline, *Weltwirtschaftlicher Archiv*, Vol.120, No.4.

-, 1984b, Beyond Keynesianism and Monetarism, *Economic Inquiry*, July.

Soos, K. A., 1985, Planification Imperative, Regulation Financiere, 'Grandes Orientations' et Campagnes, *Revue d'Etudes comparatives Est-Ouest*, No.2.

Thalheim, K. C., 1986, *Stagnation or Change in Communists Economies*. Center for Research into Communist Economies, London.

Smolar, A., 1983, The Rich and the Powerful in Poland, in: *Genesis of a Revolution*, edited by A Brumberg, Random House, New York.

Trotsky, L., 1937, *The Revolution Betrayed*, Pathfinder, New York. (1972 edition).

Winiecki, J., 1982, Investment Cycles and an Excess-Demand Inflation in Planned Economies: Sources and Processes, *Acta Oeconomica*, Vol. 28, Nos.1-2.

-, 1986a, Distorted Macroeconomics of Central Planning, *Banca Nazionale del Lavoro Quarterly Review*, Vol.157.

-, 1986b, Are Soviet-Type Economies Entering an Era of Long-Term Decline? *Soviet Studies*, July.

-, 1986c, Soviet-Type Economies: Considerations for the Future, *Soviet Studies*, October.

-, 1987, The Overgrown Industrial Sector in the STEs Evidence, Explanations, Consequences, *Comparative Economic Studies*, Vol.28, No.4.

-, 1988a, *The Distorted World of Soviet-Type Economies*, Routledge-Pittsburgh University Press, London-Pittsburgh.

-, 1988b, Narrow Non-Manual/Manual Wage Differentials and Excess Demand for Manual Labor in the CPEs: Causally Linked System-Specific Phenomena, *Osteuropa Wirtschaft*.

Winiecki, E. D. and J. Winiecki, 1987, Manufacturing Structures in Centrally-Planned Economics, *Jahrbuch der Wirtschaft Osteuropas*, Vol.12, No.I.

.

CHAPTER 4

MANAGERS AND REFORMS[*]

The preceding section presented enough evidence on differences between managers in STEs and owner-entrepreneurs or professional managers in market-type economies from the property rights perspective. There are similarities, of course. Informational assymmetry is present in both systems (in fact, it is much greater in the world of doctored reports characteristic for STEs). But the consequences of this assymmetry are strikingly different, given the differences in property rights structure.

Differing consequences for managers and owner-entrepreneurs are more obvious. Since the former have no claim on the residual profit, they are not constrained in rent-seeking activities. Therefore they cheat their superiors through the manipulation of plan fulfillment reports to obtain bonuses, clamour for more resources for current production and take risks in the knowledge that it is not they who will pay the price of failure.

Differing consequences for STE and MTE managers have already been stressed. Economic forces in the market system (i.e. competition) sharply reduce measurement costs and, consequently, the costs of monitoring managers as owners' agents. Also, as Jensen and Meckling [1976] rightly pointed out, the stock market, the market for corporate control and the market for managers - all signaling managerial performance - put self-imposed constraints on managers in the market system, while these constraints on rent-seeking plainly do not exist in the case of STE managers.

---

[*] *The text in question comes from Chapter II of my book:* Resistance to Change in the Soviet Economic System. A Property Rights Approach, **Routledge**, *London, 1991, pp.37-44.*

It may be stressed, however, that STE managers face constraints on rent-seeking of a different type. They are appointed through the system of *nomenklatura*, which is a loyalty-based rather than merit-based system.

CHEATING IN THE LOYALTY-BASED SYSTEM

Under the circumstances, why are managers appointed on such a basis not loyal to those who appoint them and why do they persistently cheat them while reporting about their enterprises' performance particularly since they can be dismissed at any moment without due administrative procedure?

This question brings us to the little considered issue of **the content of loyalty in the Soviet economic system** (and the Soviet system in general). The experience of STEs suggests that submitting truthful reports by managers about the performance of their enterprises is not a part of what is regarded as loyalty to one's superiors. Since these superiors formally base their own decisions upon the aggregated results of subordinated enterprises, this seems to be, on the surface, a surprising thesis.

There are, however, many reasons that make managers behave in the way they do. To begin with the less important reasons, managers feel absolved from the sin of doctoring reports because quite often targets set for their enterprises are unfulfillable. The unfulfillability stems from two sources. First, superiors suspect that enterprises can do better than their managers say but do not know either how or by how much. Thus, by giving so-called 'mobilizing' plans they may overshoot by a large margin. And, second, central planning demands 'balancing' the economy. Now, if there is a perceived problem somewhere, all other enterprises are given correspondingly higher output targets to balance the loss of output there. In this surrealistic way plans become 'balanced'. As revealed by central planners themselves such 'balancing' activities may hide discrepancies as large as a couple of percentage points of the national product.

Faced with such unfulfillable targets, managers see in doctoring reports the only way of getting bonuses. Additionally, they are strongly encouraged to behave in the way they do by their knowledge of the relatively low probability of being caught.

Another economic system-related reason for doctoring reports is that plan targets are contradictory. It should be remembered that STE enterprises are not just minding the balance sheet (actually, this is their least important problem). They are also faced with the myriad of success indicators that are handed down to them as plan targets or are 'recommended' by higher-level bureaucrats or party apparatchiks as a part of some campaign to correct the inefficient workings of the system (and actually making things worse).

If, for example, one target obliges a given enterprise to reduce labour input (apparently to help to relieve excess demand for labour), while another commands it to increase exports in convertible currencies (in order to help to close the trade deficit), these two important plan targets are in conflict with one another because the input selection, assembly, finishing, packaging, etc., of exportables to the West are much more labour-intensive than producing for the domestic (seller's) market. Enterprise managers are perfectly aware of the contradictory character of these (and many other) success indicators and know that they cannot fulfill all of them simultaneously. Doctoring reports is a way to reduce some of the effects of these contradictions.

The foregoing are reasons that, *ex ante*, tempt managers to cheat. But in spite of all the planning - or rather as a result of it! - a high degree of uncertainty, especially on the input side, is the norm in STEs. With a strong probability that supplies will not be forthcoming in expected quantity, quality, type (grade, size), etc., as well as the fact that they will not be at the right time and place, plan fulfillment becomes problematic at best. The temptation is strong, then, to make up for system-generated chaos by manipulating output structure.

POLITICS-ECONOMICS INTERFACE
AND SYSTEM'S REFORMS

Much more important, however, are links between economics and politics in the Soviet system. **The type of management system** still in force everywhere in STEs (whether reformed or not) **is a spillover from the politi-**

cal system. As stressed by Szymanderski [1978], in the loyalty-based political system there are no formal administrative procedures, and no fixed
rules of evaluating and rewarding that constrain the ruling group in deal-
ings with subordinates. The same situation exists with respect to any supe-
rior-subordinate relationship within the system.

Under the circumstances, **loyalty is understood as being the subordinate's unconditional support for any position taken by his or her superior, and there is a rules-unconstrained reward for such loyalty**. It is
worth noting that o n l y in a rules-unconstrained (i.e. in fact lawless) system can loyalty be rewarded better than other attributes. For if some rules
exist and are observed by superiors, then, for example, an efficient but
critical subordinate could be better rewarded than an inefficient but loyal
one. But **it is l o y a l subordinates that matter most for heads of various coteries in their intra-bureaucratic and intra-party manoeuvres
aimed at attaining better positions**, i.e. those allowing appropriation of
higher rent and disposal at will of larger chunks of the aggregate product.

Now, it should be kept in mind that managers are part and parcel of the
ruling stratum. Being appointed mostly from among the party apparatus
and the bureaucracy they are well versed in the loyalty game. They learned
long ago that rewards within the *nomenklatura* system do not depend upon
improvements of the balance sheet or some spectacular entrepreneurial
ventures. With the rules-unconstrained system of rewards and punishments
they are first of all oriented towards the wishes of their superiors. **Whatever their superiors wish will be undertaken with apparent enthusiasm.** Again, they learned long ago that they have much to lose by arguing
with their superiors about target unachievability or contradictions in the
plan, but much to gain by enthusiastically accepting the task first and asking for a downward revision of a plan or doctoring the plan fulfillment
report later. It is Say's Law in reverse, where the demand for declarations
of loyalty creates its own supply.

DECENTRALIZATION - YES,
FINANCIAL RESPONSIBILITY - NO!

There is, however, an internal contradiction in the system. **Managers are appointed within the framework of loyalty criteria, while the enterprises they manage are units which operate (or at least *should* operate) within the framework of efficiency criteria** [Szperkowicz 1986]. At the height of Maoist frenzy, pilots of Chinese supersonic fighters were forced to substitute little red books of Mao Zedong's thoughts for routine check-ups of their aircraft by skilled mechanics. The results of the said contradiction have not been as dramatically evident as those of the Maoist experiment with pilots' loyalty but have been much more costly in the long run.

The foregoing considerations on the content of loyalty supply a missing link between theories of incentives and their STE applications on the one hand and repeated failures of these applications on the other. Without exclusive owners' rights in theory and with rulers of Soviet- type states being unable to constrain their agents properly under such a property rights structure, **the only real incentives for managers are those of being on good terms with those who appoint them and may recall them at their whim**. In other words, managers look towards leaders of various coteries within the party apparatus and upper bureaucracy who have the decisive voice in *nomenklatura* appointments, as well as in politically (i.e. loyalty) motivated allocation of resources.(...)

The more important the enterprise is or the higher the 'priority' it is accorded (to use STE parlance), the greater is the probability that, no matter what its actual performance, managers and workers will be paid respective premiums for plan fulfillment. (...) However, the term 'priority' should be defined at this point. 'Priority' has little (if anything) to do with technological sophistication, quality of output or competitiveness on the world market. 'Priority' enterprise is, first, large in terms of employment and, second, belongs to heavy industry.

Both criteria reflect Marxist dogmas of long standing, namely that the bigger the enterprise the better, and that heavy industry is decisive for the economic development of a country. The former criterion, in particular, has had important effects on the politics-economics link and, consequently, also on the workability of various incentive schemes.

Thus, the larger the enterprise is, the greater is the number of managerial posts covered by the *nomenklatura* system. Since these are the best paid posts, bureaucrats and apparatchiks appoint themselves and their card-carrying cronies to managerial positions. With a large enterprise, those who decide are stronger politically and, accordingly, the managers appointed in that manner have greater political clout. As a result, the quantity of *nomenklatura*-covered posts and their political calibre combine to make large heavy industrial enterprises important in terms of their political clout. Again, these issues will be considered in the next chapter. Loyalty of managers to their superiors as defined above is usually rewarded regardless of actual performance of their enterprises.(...)

There is no market for managerial services in STEs, as rightly stated by John Moore [1981], with the stock market reflecting - through share prices - the market's evaluation of managers' performance. The personnel policy of the party, the surrogate of such a market, is deliberately informal to leave room for a n y appointment, however surprising in the light of past decisions.(...)

The previous discussion explains the environment in which managers operate in the Soviet system. Coming mostly from the ruling stratum and being well versed in the loyalty game (usually much better than in the efficiency game!), **they accept such rules of the game as exist in the loyalty-based system, or rather the lack of binding rules, and adjust accordingly**. The adjustment is facilitated by the extreme high costs of discovering these manipulations.

The previously mentioned problem of the tolerance of plan manipulations by managers' superiors in the bureaucracy and the party should also be considered at this point. At least some of these manipulations are known to or suspected by managers' superiors. It is they who accept changes in the monthly, quarterly and annual plan targets applied for by enterprises. It is also they who cover up, actively encourage or even doctor plan fulfillment reports aggregated at the level of a region or industry.

Thus they not only tolerate being fed with distorted figures but actually do the same thing at the higher levels of aggregation.

What should be stressed here is the similarity of their position to that of managers. Bureaucrats from the middle levels of the central planning hierarchy and middle-level party apparatchiks are both improperly constrained agents of the ruling group. They are responsible for results of 'their' enterprises at an industrial branch or a regional level.

Success indicators for them are average results of subordinated enterprises. Thus, they try to ensure average improvements. This usually means reallocating resources from better performing to worse performing enterprises at the cost of reducing the aggregate output. Lowering plan targets is also a part of averaging; a regional or territorial report looks better if it can be reported that plans were fulfilled, on average, by 99.5 per cent of enterprises.

The fact that plan targets of many enterprises were lowered during the plan fulfillment period is not mentioned and it can be revealed by a special audit only. Bureaucrats and apparatchiks may suspect that even those lowered plan targets are realized partly on paper only (due to output structure manipulations and *pripiski*) but they have little possibility and no interest whatsoever in having enterprises audited.

Their utility is a function of income and effort. Even partial and fragmentary audits would increase their effort and reduce formal income directly or indirectly. Income is presumed to depend on results of subordinated enterprises. In a loyalty-based system they may expect to obtain related premiums anyway (given the unchanged balance of power between various coteries). Thus, direct income consequences of revealing bad results of subordinated enterprises can be minimized. But with the ever threatening prospect of change in the balance of power, the same bad results can be used against them as evidence of their low performance. Although a stronger coterie's candidate would eventually prevail, ready-made evidence would speed up the replacement process, reducing formal income indirectly.

The emphasis above has been on formal income (basic salary, premiums, bonuses and scarce goods rationed by the centre). But it should be remembered that the Soviet system produces a special mode of rent extraction of which *nomenklatura* is only a part. Enterprise managers not only enrich themselves but also those above them in the bureaucratic and party hierarchies. Various scarce goods delivered at below market price as well as even scarcer construction and other services at a fraction of their real costs all flow from enterprises to the ruling stratum (...). Delving too deeply into the 'imaginative' reporting of enterprises would strain relations with managers, i.e. those who dispense the goodies.

This **you scratch my back, I'll scratch yours** principle affects relations between managers and their intermediate bureaucratic and political superiors in yet another manner. Thanks to the *nomenklatura* procedure, managerial positions are distributed by and large 'within the family', i.e. within the ruling stratum. An important consequence is that a present-day bureaucrat or apparatchik is also well disposed toward managers' request for more inputs, lower planned outputs, additional subsidies, etc. After all, in a while he may in turn become enterprise manager and find one of to-day's managers in his present bureaucratic or party position. It is thus better to be well disposed now in order to [ensure] reciprocity when roles are reversed.

The analysis so far explains rather well why managers everywhere in STEs are not in the forefront of systemic change. Even excluding the rent-seeking aspects of their activities, the very fact of performing in the loyalty-based environment **without observed rules** makes them extremely cautious in expressing their real views on the subject. For obvious reasons they reflect the views of their superiors.

The inclusion of rent-seeking aspects turns this cautiousness into well-understood resistance to changes leading to the market system. After all, the managers were appointed to their posts through the *nomenklatura* procedure, i.e. on the basis of loyalty rather than merit. In any merit-based competition they would be at a strong disadvantage. Entrepreneurship, risk-taking and flexibility are not their *forte*. What they do know - for example, how to cultivate political links, bargain for plan change, apply for larger and earlier input supplies, manipulate output structure and doctor reports sent to their superiors - is useless in the market-type environment.

Herein lie the sources of the real - though not always apparent - adverse attitudes of managers to systemic change. But **resistance to a change of**

the system does not entail resistance to a reform of the system, understood here as more or less extensive tinkering with the system. Managers in STEs are always strongly in favour of decentralization, which is a
change in form without the change in substance. The reason of that often
voiced postulate is clear.

**Decentralizing, for example, the price setting to the enterprise
level, increases managers' room for manoeuvre in fulfilling plan targets.** So does the decentralization of, for example, output target setting.
Since, in a loyalty-based system, managers are by and large shielded from
adverse consequences of failure, anything that increases the probability of
obtaining reward or reduces the effort needed to obtain it is welcome.

REFERENCES

Jensen, M., and W. Meckling, 1976, Theory of the Firm: Managerial Behaviour, Agency Costs and Ownership Structure, *Journal of Financial
Economics*, Vol.3.

Moore, J., 1981, Agency Costs, Technological Change, and Soviet Central
planning, *Journal of Law and Economics*, Vol.24, No.2.

Szperkowicz, J., 1986, The Needs-Based Economy (Part II), *Przeglad Or-
ganizacji*, No.3, in Polish.

Szymanderski, J., 1978, Determinants of the Centralization of Power in the
Communist Parties, Polish Academy of Science, Institute of History,
manuscript, in Polish.

CHAPTER 5

BUYING OUT PROPERTY RIGHTS TO THE ECONOMY FROM THE RULING STRATUM[*]

INTRODUCTION

An American economist of an institutionalist persuasion, Steve N. S. Cheung [1986], in assessing the prospects of transforming the Chinese economy into a capitalist system, observed (too optimistically, in this author's opinion) that 'all the officials who would otherwise resist the adoption of private enterprise could perhaps be compensated and put into comfortable retirement with plenty of social gain left over'. However, he regarded the negotiation, enforcement, and other costs as prohibitively high. In this author's view, the proposal is worth pursuing somewhat further. To begin with, two assumptions should be formulated.

The first assumption involves the existence of a system-specific mode of rent-seeking, which makes two segments of the ruling stratum - party apparatchiks and bureaucrats - particularly interested in maintaining a patently inefficient economic system. (...) [see texts 1 and 3 to look at the problems indicated here].

The second assumption concerns the relationship between the rent extracted from the economy by the parasitic ruling stratum by means of this typical system-specific mode and the aggregate economic losses imposed

---

[*] *This article has originally been published under the title:* Buying Property Rights to the Economy from the Ruling Stratum: The Case of Soviet-type States, **International Review of Law and Economics,** *vol.9, 1989.*

by the maintenance of the system itself. The present writer assumes that **the rent extracted is of a much smaller order of magnitude**. In the circumstances, property rights theory suggests that to lower the transaction costs of changing the system, compensation should be offered to those who both are in a position effectively to resist change and have a vested interest in maintaining the present system.

On the above assumptions - plus an implied one about the irreversibility of the decline of the Soviet system - Cheung's proposal seems to be a step in the right direction, that is, a step facilitating change. What follows is an exercise in systematized thinking on the subject.

THE BUY-OUT PROPOSAL: WHAT? FROM WHOM? HOW MUCH?

The first issue in need of clarification is the object of such a transaction. What would apparatchiks and bureaucrats be compensated for? This author's view is that it cannot be anything less than the creation of the autonomous sphere of human activity. Consequently, **compensation would be paid for [their] withdrawal from the economy as a whole**.

All vertical and horizontal channels of political influence at the micro level, typical of the Soviet system, should be eliminated. With respect to vertical channels, it would have to entail the liquidation of *nomenklatura*, the political loyalty- based system of appointment of managers. As regards horizontal channels, the communist party organizations in enterprises and institutions in the economy and intertwined spheres would have to be dissolved. The same would apply to communist front organizations (satellite parties, youth organizations, etc.).

It is obvious that to make a market economy function, much more than **the severing of the totalitarian umbilical cord between the political and economic systems** at the micro level would be necessary. That is, however, a *conditio sine qua non*; without such a severing, only a pseudo-market economy can exist [Winiecki, 1989]. Subsequent changes, such as the liquidation of the multi-level command and rationing hierarchy and turning the state-owned into privately owned (or, where impossible, employee-owned) enterprises, should be regarded as modifications for a later stage.

Next arises the question, from whom the economy would be bought out, or, more precisely, who in the ruling stratum would have to be compensated for not being able to maximize rent through various interventions in the wealth creation process? Would they all be pensioned, as Cheung suggests in his proposal? The first among these to be compensated would be party apparatchiks. Sharp cuts in personnel would be necessary, since macro-level policies do not require 'labor intensive' individualized command and control activities. This would affect all levels of party hierarchy from central- to regional- to enterprise-level apparatchiks. Then would come bureaucratic positions covered by *nomenklatura* in the economic and related spheres: ministers (with their deputies); directors of various departments and bureaus within ministries; directors of enterprise associations; presidents of boards supervising cooperatives; heads of input-allocating and output-purchasing bodies (with all their deputies).

The number of managers in state-owned enterprises who would have to be pensioned would be much larger. At least some of them might have the necessary qualities to compete for managerial positions in the market system. Given, however, the difference in desirable qualities needed to manage enterprises in the market (efficiency-based) and Soviet (loyalty-based) economic systems respectively, competitive leftovers from the Soviet system would be a distinct minority. Finally, the detotalitarianization of the system (and the buy-out proposal amounts precisely to that) would make a part of the security police also superfluous. To maintain a 'traditional' system, as contrasted with the present dictatorship, the ruling group would not need, for example, security police supervisors of enterprises listening to what is going on there and ordering managers to withdraw promotions or dismiss 'politically undesirable' employees. Also, the detotalitarianization would generally reduce the ruling group's demand for invigilation, misinformation, provocation, and so forth. In aggregate it would probably reduce the security apparatus by about two-thirds.

This account is conservative in the sense that it points to a lower, rather than an upper, range of the estimated number of beneficiaries of the system. But it is otherwise realistic if society is ready to buy out property rights to the economy from the ruling stratum. **The price (that is, compensation) should be paid not to all who benefit but to those who really rule.** Thus, compensation would not be justified for the following three (often large) groups of beneficiaries.

1. Small fries of the communist party: These include various lower-level managers in enterprises and bureaucracies. They were appointed to their positions through the *nomenklatura* procedure as a result of their 'proper' political attitudes rather than their qualifications, but their ability to insert a spoke in the wheels of change is, at their level, very limited.

2. Apparatchiks from the satellite organizations of the communist front: All these organizations have no power of their own. Like the moon that only shines with reflected light, whatever power they have is a power reflected upon them by a given communist party. Their own apparatchiks undoubtedly draw (often not inconsiderable) benefits from the existing property rights structure, including some *nomenklatura* - covered positions, but they do not wield power over anything.

3. Economic 'fellow travelers': The term 'fellow travelers' has long been used in political science to describe the various naive left-wingers who helped communists to destroy the existing system only to be later eliminated (often physically) or turned into political puppets of a newly established communist regime. Economic 'fellow travelers' never belonged to the ruling stratum, but, given the properties of the Soviet system, they are its permanent, rather than ephemeral, feature. Corruption, waste, disorder, and the general climate of shortage allow them to obtain incomes often many times higher than those of members of the ruling stratum. Corrupt butcher shop managers cheating on meat grades and selling the best parts under the counter, warehousemen in construction firms selling building materials in short supply, state enterprise employed plumbers and other craftsmen offering their services during working hours, using factory equipment and stolen spare parts, as well as many others belong to this category. In terms of property rights theory, they constitute examples of a rent dissipation problem

related to the difficulties of measuring output [see Cheung, 1974]. They can neither delay nor prevent change of the system. Their ability to draw substantial benefits would gradually disappear with the return to normalcy.

Thus, of the three groups described above, two would be excluded from compensation on formal grounds and one, the first, on *realpolitik* grounds. Now, let us turn to the last of the three questions posed in the title to this section. In theory, the answer to the question 'how much?' is simple. In the case of each representative of the ruling stratum, compensation ought to amount to the capitalized value of his future stream of net income under the present property rights structure, less the expected net income stream under the changed property rights structure. In practice, as Cheung [1986] rightly stressed, the problems are enormous.

Obviously, salaries are only a part - and in the case of party appa-ratchiks and higher bureaucrats, including enterprise managers, often the smaller part - of their total income. We may assume an average age of some 50 years for pensioned and compensated representatives of the ruling stratum (the average age of managers in Poland was 48 at the beginning of the 1980s). This means that compensation should include the capitalized value of 15 years' net salary in the same occupation, with the same level of qualifications for a position not covered by *nomenklatura*.

Nevertheless, even for this, by far the easiest, part of the estimate, there exist complicating factors. How, for example, should account be taken of the anticorruption campaigns waged from time to time in Soviet-type states and intended to demonstrate that a fundamentally honest communist party can eliminate the few corrupt individuals from its midst? These cam-paigns affect that part of the stream of goods and services which flow to the ruling stratum and which have not been distributed by or from the center. They definitely raise the probability of an earlier end to rent-maximizing behavior than the statutory retirement age. Anticorruption campaigns should somehow be included, by means of an appropriate dis-count, in the calculation of the compensation-related future stream of net income.

Next, centrally approved benefits other than *nomenklatura* should be taken into account. The data are hard to locate, but, for example, it has been estimated that in 1983, in Poland, 40 percent of the cars in the domestic market were allocated through the system of coupons (*asygnata*), enabling cars to be bought at the listed price without waiting for years, as is usual in that country. Also, listed prices are usually much lower than market prices; for example, in Poland at that time the former were some 40 percent of the latter.

The really intractable problems begin with some of the less costly consumer durables and other nondurable goods, as well as with services distributed through nonmarket channels. More often than not, these are distributed without approval from the center. For obvious reasons, there are no permanent files on these matters and whatever distribution lists exist temporarily at a given time and place are quickly destroyed once the spoils are divided among the local groups of the ruling stratum. Moreover, the ever-changing phenomenon of shortages in Soviet-type states creates possibilities of extracting rent through privileged access at some periods and eliminates them at other periods.

VARIABLES AFFECTING THE SIZE OF RENT: A SURVEY

More generally in Soviet-type states, the differentials between the income of the ruling stratum, *per* representative of that stratum, and the average income in the national economy are affected primarily by three variables:

1. the level of economic development;
2. the degree of control of the ruling stratum over the economy; and
3. the tradition of governance.

The lower the level of development, the greater the control and the tradition of corruption in the government, the larger would be the differential in question. Therefore, for example, in China where these variables affect the outcome in the same way, 'you have to be a government official to live at all well' [Cheung, 1986, p.27]

Cheung then proceeds to show the range of privileges available to various representatives of the ruling stratum from food without queueing and lower-than-listed prices to chauffeured cars and air-conditioned offices. It is worth noting that such privileges all belong to that part of rent that we have attributed to centrally approved corruption. Elsewhere Cheung mentions various payments in return for favors (assistance in obtaining goods and services) that fall into the category of centrally disapproved corruption. In the People's Republic of China, the difference in income between the 'owners of the system' and the masses was enormous. Only in the 1980s has the expansion of quasi-private and private entrepreneurship created a legal alternative road to (relative) well-being.

However, both speculation and evidence about corruption in the USSR point to the differential there being not much smaller than in China [see, e.g., Simis, 1982, and Hillman and Schnytzer, 1986]. The main reasons seem to be the preserved Byzantine tradition associating the ruling stratum with costly splendor and the no less traditional Russian association of public administration and private enrichment, dating from tsarist times. The same forms of rent appropriation exist in the Soviet Union as in China, notably the shops available only for the chosen and supplied with better goods and/or at lower prices. The privileges belonging to the category of officially approved corruption also abound in the USSR. If one compares the number of chauffeured cars and the number of *nomenklatura*-covered positions (600,000 and 750,000 respectively), one is immediately aware of the much greater possibility of making a large profit since the majority of those appointed through the *nomenklatura* procedure have a chauffeured car and consequently can easily sell a new car obtained through the coupon system.

Benefits from centrally disapproved corruption are probably no smaller. A simple example should suffice. If food is subsidized, those able to acquire above average quantities are subsidized by the rest of society. Thus, if 30 percent of all meat were distributed in Kazakstan through the illegally established shops within various offices, this means that about 2 percent of the population (representatives of the ruling stratum and their families) gain 15 times the average subsidy *per capita* on meat.

At the other end of the continuum representing the level of economic development variable are Czechoslovakia and East Germany. With the population accustomed to higher living standards, a sharp redistribution of wealth toward the ruling stratum and attendant absolute deprivation would be an invitation to a social explosion. Not unexpectedly, it was in East Berlin that the first such explosion took place in Soviet-type states, in 1953. An intellectual revolt from the top, as the 'Prague Spring' may be described, although suppressed by Soviet intervention, probably mitigated the ruling stratum's acquisitiveness, since the latter understood the dangers of simultaneous political oppression and economic deprivation. The tradition of relatively efficient governance in both countries may also have contributed to smaller differentials in aggregate income between the ruling stratum and the rest of society. However, the third determining variable, the degree of control, strongly affects the differential in the opposite direction.

For some time and for country-specific reasons, the degree of totalitarian control in Hungary and Poland has been lower than elsewhere. Accordingly, at least after 1956, the ruling strata in these countries have been to a somewhat greater extent constrained in their rent-extracting pursuits by collective memories of past tensions - such constraint being much stronger in Hungary. Also, it is in these countries that alternative routes to material well-being have been made more available to a part of the population. More powerful constraints on the ruling stratum in its rent-maximizing pursuits and the greater possibility of improving material well-being in some sectors of the economy have reinforced one another in narrowing the differential under consideration.

To generalize, under the Soviet system, wide disparities among countries in the income differentials between the ruling stratum and the rest of society are to be predicted. In consequence, **the amount of compensation in buy - out contracts would vary between states**. Whether the buy out burden would be greater or smaller, the present writer is deeply convinced that **there would be very large social gains for these societies after compensating for the withdrawal of the communist ruling stratum from the economy**. This conviction stems from the empirical evidence on the enormous costs of the functioning of Soviet-type economies [see, for

example, Winiecki, 1986], given the fact that the misallocation of resources, the persistently high level of waste embedded in the structure of
incentives, institutional setting and pursued strategy are of a much higher
order of magnitude that the rents that the ruling strata are able to appropriate even in the most corrupt Soviet-type state.

PRECISION IN ESTIMATES OF COMPENSATION, CONTRACTING PARTIES, CONTRACT FORM, AND THE PROSPECTS OF CONTRACTS

The very grave problems of estimating compensation for change-affected
members of the ruling stratum in Soviet-type states should not be regarded
as constituting an insuperable obstacle. It should be borne in mind that the
amount of compensation to be paid need not be very precise for it to be
seriously considered by those affected by the system's change. First, 'owners of the system' cannot themselves precisely estimate their prospective
income, given the vagaries of shortage economies, the impact of long-term
systemic decline, deteriorating living conditions, and so forth. Second, the
nature of the buy out contract is such that the closeness of the approxima-
tion of the price offered to the (unknown) reality matters less than its
closeness to the expectations of the sellers. Consequently, the present
writer proposes a rough estimate of the income *per* average representative
of the ruling stratum and an estimate of average compensation relative to
the income of the average person employed in the national economy as the
starting point for such an endeavor.

Next to be considered are the parties to the buy out contract. Here we
may envisage two possibilities. In the Soviet-type states where more or
less numerous alternative political elites already exist, they could become
parties to such a contract, the other party being the ruling group (with the
tacit, even if reluctant, approval of the ruling stratum). The situation would
be more difficult in those states where nothing resembling alternative political elites has emerged. Under the latter condition, another solution is
conceivable. A ruling group, conscious of the scale, extent, and the dynamics of crisis phenomena, may itself undertake the initiative. Supported

by some segments of the ruling stratum, it may decide to effectuate withdrawal from the economy and, to lessen the resistance of those most interested in maintaining intact the existing property rights structure, may decide to compensate them for such withdrawal. It would be difficult to describe this transaction as a contract in the proper sense of that word; rather it would be a 'quasi-contract' forced by the ruling group upon the (quite possibly) resistant segments of the ruling stratum.

Is such a buy out scenario a possible solution for the crisis-ridden Soviet-type states? Or is it only a more or less elegant theoretical construct which has not the slightest chance of being applied in the real world?

At the very least, various developments in the Soviet system tend to increase the possibility of the proposed solution. These developments act on the consciousness of the ruling stratum in two ways: either they decrease the benefits drawn by those parasiting on the system, or they weaken self-legitimization. As regards the former, the developments manifest themselves as follows.

1. Although there are no systematic surveys on the matter, the present author is of the opinion that **awareness of decreasing possibilities of rent extraction is rising among the representatives of the ruling stratum**.

2. The ruling stratum's **awareness of the dangers of declining health standards** in societies afflicted by 'real socialism' **is probably growing even faster** than recognition of the declining trend in the supply of some goods; and such dangers cannot be alleviated by privileged distribution through nonmarket channels - it is not possible to breath different air in the most polluted areas of the Soviet-type states.

3. No less evident - and as a daily experience even more uncomfortable - are **the effects of decaying municipal infrastructure**. A low quality pipe when it breaks deprives whole districts of central heating, hot and cold water, sewage disposal, and so forth. Such situations, which tend to occur with increasing frequency in Eastern Europe, are in some countries accompanied by electricity shutoffs, due to an inadequate supply of fuel for heating and lighting.

The consciousness of the ruling stratum is affected also by its perception of its declining legitimization or, to be more precise, **its declining self-legitimization**, since politically conscious groups in Soviet-type states have generally rejected communist legitimization from the outset. **What is important in the framework of systemic decay is declining self-confidence of the 'owners of the system' themselves.** A creeping feeling of impotence is affecting them to an increasing extent, since neither political mobilization campaigns nor modifications of the defective system seem to be able to reverse or even halt the decline. Thus, if nothing is left except the enrichment (and even that may be decreasing), why not give up the 'red man's burden'? At some point, with the costs of governance for the ruling stratum increasing and the rent derived therefrom [decreasing], tired and disillusioned totalitarians will become ready for negotiated - and, if early enough, also compensated - withdrawal. The first most probable step is the withdrawal from the economy.

REFERENCES

Cheung, S. N. S., 1986, Will China Go "Capitalist"? Hobart Paper 94 (2d ed.), Institute of Economic Affairs, London

Cheung, S. N. S., 1974, A Theory of Price Control, *Journal of Law & Economics*, Vol.17.

Hillman, A., and Schnytzer A., 1986, Illegal Economic Activities and Purges in a Soviet-Type Economy: A Rent-Seeking Perspective, *International Review of Law and Economics*, Vol.6.

Simis, K., 1982, *USSR: Secrets of a Corrupt Society*, Dent, London

Winiecki, J., 1986, Distorted Macroeconomics of Central Planning, *Banca Nazionale del Lavoro Quarterly Review*, Vol. 157.

Winiecki, 1987, The Overgrown Industrial Sector in Soviet-Type Economies: Explanations, Evidence, Consequences, *Comparative Economic Studies,* Vol.28, No. 4.

Winiecki, J., 1989, On Markets and Pseudo-Markets, *Economic Affairs*, No.9.

PART II

DETERMINANTS OF COLLAPSE OF THE SYSTEM

CHAPTER 6

HOW IT ALL BEGAN: SOURCES OF THE RECENT BREAKDOWN OF THE SOVIET ECONOMIC SYSTEM·

INTRODUCTION

The 'Spring of Nations' that took much of East-Central Europe by storm last autumn was without doubt a political phenomenon. An apparent abandonment of the doctrine of military intervention in subordinated East-Central Europe by the Gorbachev regime had encouraged change for some time. The Hungarian decision to dismantle border fortifications at the border with Austria triggered a flood of East German refugees to the West that put pressure on the East German communist regime. Once Honecker fell, Czechoslovak neo-stalinists found themselves isolated and the pressure applied skillfully by the opposition resulted in the smoothest possible transfer of power. The fall of Ceausescu completed the domino effect.

But all these spectacular phenomena, coupled with the unfolding of *glasnost* and *perestroika* in the Soviet Union itself have been **outcomes of long processes rather than spasmodic events** as they often seemed to outsiders. And, the processes were mainly economic in nature. This author

· *This article has appeared originally under the title:* How It All Began: Sources of the Recent Breakdown of the Soviet Economic System, in: Towards a Market Economy in Central and Eastern Europe, *Herbert Giersch, (Ed.),* **Springer Verlag**, Berlin, *1991.*

warned years ago that Soviet-type economies were entering an era of long-term decline [Winiecki, 1984].

There have been other determinants of change: ecological, social, demographic, etc. They all combined into what this author called quite recently **'the irreversible multifaceted decline of the Soviet system'. It is irreversible decline and responses to it by societies living under the system that have been instrumental in bringing about changes in East-Central Europe and the Soviet Union itself.** Let us follow the varied economic phenomena that all contributed, simultaneously or successively, to the downfall of that wasteful monstrosity.

SOURCES OF ECONOMIC DECLINE ENDOGENOUS TO THE SOVIET SYSTEM

What is worth stressing at the start is the endogeneity of the sources of economic decline. When the first signs of increased disturbances and decline appeared in the 1970s, some analysts, especially those sympathetic to the system, were pointing at the disturbances in the world economy as the source of the problems encountered by Soviet-type economies. They were never able to explain, however, why signs of stress and decline were as strong (if not stronger) in the Soviet Union, the net winner of two so-called oil crises, than in the smaller East-Central European countries. More perceptive was the view that the disturbances in the world economy exacerbated the distortionary, if not self-destructive, features of the Soviet-type economies.

To begin with, the traditionally stressed **distorted motivation** in Soviet-type economies that results, *inter alia*, in abnormally high levels of resource use became increasingly painful since the first oil price jump and commodity boom of the early 1970s. Quite obviously, with consumption of energy or steel *per* one dollar of GDP being 2-2,5 times higher in Soviet-type economies than in market-type economies, the former began to feel the cost of their high resource intensity much more strongly than before. Moreover, while saddled with a high resource intensity, Soviet-type economies, except the Soviet Union, have been facing a relative fall in domestic resource availability. It meant that these countries had to import more and more of their energy and industrial mineral inputs.

Although smaller Soviet-type economies obtained a large part of their imported inputs from the USSR, costs of obtaining these resources in the latter also rose sharply. Consequently, rulers of Soviet-type economies faced a dilemma. With resource imports from the USSR leveling off and later declining and imports from the world market difficult to pay for, due to weak export performance, their economies had a choice of either declining or undergoing a far-reaching change that would reduce resource intensity. This dilemma is shown graphically in Figure 1.

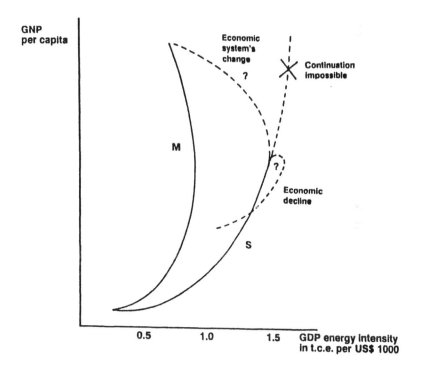

Figure 1: The Actual Pattern of Change of Energy Intensity in Market-Type Economies (M) and Alternative Future Paths of Energy Intensity in Soviet-Type (and post-Soviet-type) Economies

Summing up, an old weakness of the Soviet economic system became a matter of much greater urgency. High resource intensity emerged in the 1970s as a strong growth-inhibiting factor. Much less known, let alone estimated quantitatively, is what this author called **the twofold underspecialization** of Soviet-type economies It is the result of the Soviet style industrialization strategy and features specific to the Soviet economic system. The gist of the [communist] 'steep ascent' strategy was maximization of investment in the industrial sector in order to achieve the largest possible increase in its share of output in the shortest possible time span (all this conducted under near autarchic conditions). Investment within the industrial sector was in turn concentrated on heavy industry because it was assumed that without the capability to produce machinery and equipment, Soviet-type economies would not be able to overcome their backwardness (that they would become backward machinery producers was not the possibility envisaged at the time!).

This strategy, devised for the Soviet Union and later implanted in the smaller Soviet-type economies, was nonsensical from the start in the case of the latter. The foregone benefits of international specialization for small countries trying to produce as much as possible domestically resulted in an oversized industrial sector. This sector, however, has been decreasingly able to satisfy internal demand, since each new final good requires a range of new intermediate products for its manufacture at high cost due to the smallness of the internal market.

The issue of an import-substitution-based development strategy has been well researched with respect to developing countries. So it will only be noted that the degree of separation from the world market has been greater in Soviet-type economies than in LDCs, with correspondingly larger structural distortions.

But even more important were system-specific features of underspecialization. With central planning breeding excess demand, uncertainty and shortage, enterprises have been adjusting their behavior accordingly, trying to produce as much as possible of the intermediate inputs they need within the enterprise. In other words, enterprises in Soviet-type economies also pursue an 'import' substitution strategy, substituting their own high cost production for unreliable supplies ('imports') from other domestic enterprises.

However irrational in macroeconomic terms, such behavior makes sense for enterprises that need these inputs to fulfill their plan targets with respect to final output in order to obtain premiums and bonuses. For they are reasonably sure that cost overruns will be compensated one way or another by superior bodies in the bureaucratic hierarchy.

The effects of this microlevel 'import' substitution running counter to the fundamental economic logic and the established pattern of industrial specialization were especially severe. Since Adam Smith it has been recognized that growing wealth is achieved through increased specialization. Under central planning, however, real gains from the expanded division of labor - as more and more separable processes are carried out by firms specializing in them - have slowed down or were even reversed. The result was a hypertrophy of the industrial sector that in Soviet-type economies grew to much above the share in total output and employment typical for market-type economies at any level of economic development (see Figure 2).

This was one of the important reasons of **the growth-without-much-prosperity phenomenon** visible in Soviet-type economies almost from their beginnings. It again became costlier as Soviet-type economies shifted their attention to more sophisticated, technologically advanced goods in the 1970s. However, before this author turns to the intertwined problems of underspecialization, **inflexibility of Soviet-type hierarchical bureaucracies and slowness to innovate**, two important aspects of underspecialization should be stressed here.

First, Soviet-type economies not only forego a (large) part of the gains from the first industrial revolution, i.e., inter-enterprise specialization in production of goods within the quickly expanding market, but also the gains from the present industrial revolution. An important component of the latter is a rapidly growing specialization in the production of business services previously performed mostly within the industrial enterprises.

Also, the long neglect of a service sector, traditional and modern alike, has begun to affect more strongly the performance of Soviet-type economies. Undersized and long starved of resources, the service sector turned into an ever-stronger drag on economic growth. Especially since the mid-1970s, when ruling groups devoted more and more resources to propping up the declining performance of industry, the infrastructure of these economies began to decay at an accelerated rate.

Low quality inputs require extensive replacement and maintenance activities also in the service sector. **Without quantitatively large supplies, the reliability of services fell dramatically**. To give but one example, the breakdown rate of main water pipes in the USSR in 1976-1980 period was equal to 40 accidents per 100 km annually. This absurdly high rate increased to 100 accidents per 100 km annually in the next five-year period!

The disadvantages of the hierarchical economic bureaucracy in the Soviet economic system have been long recognized as a disadvantage. But again, it is the turn of the 1960s and 1970s that changed the old weakness into a fatal flaw. In this author's opinion, the shift in the role of the engine of economic growth from economy-of-scale-based to flexible, entrepreneurial and innovation-based industries has been at the source of the marked change for the worse.

If there ever existed an advantage of the Soviet-type economy over the market-type economy, it would be the former's capability to quickly (and often ruthlessly) collect resources and allocate them for the implementation of a few large projects. This capability gave Soviet-type economies an appearance of efficiency, as they were able to build large-scale plants: steel mills, cement plants, fertilizer plants, etc. The speed of allocation and collection in spite of the attendant waste allowed Soviet-type economies to catch up in some respects with Western market-type economies.

All this changed with the shift of the growth engine role to industries based on flexibility and other features antithetical to central planning. When Soviet-type economies began to expand less material-using, more value-added industries, so that a multitude of new products and more sophisticated versions of the old ones began to be manufactured, the sharply raised requirements of smooth management of complex coordination processes became too great a burden for the slow-moving bureaucracy. Signs of strain multiplied.

It is worth noting that technology imports, which were supposed to circumvent the barrier of hierarchical bureaucratic management, itself adverse to innovation, did not help much. On the contrary, the new and higher quality standards of products manufactured under Western licenses put an additional burden on domestic suppliers of inputs to these products. They required additional imports, upsetting foreign trade balances, and causing quickly increasing indebtedness. The only exception was the Soviet Union enjoying windfall gains from two very large oil price increases (but even that country could have used its gains in a different way, were it not for the extra import demand for Western intermediate inputs). It turned out that **bad innovators are also bad imitators**. Soviet-type economies found themselves under yet another pressure: increasing demand for imports in the face of the weak ability to export.

This ability to export to the world market, particularly to export manufactures, has been not only weak but declining over time. The case of Czechoslovakia is the most telling one. At the turn of the century, the Czech lands of the Austro-Hungarian empire were one of the strongest world centers of heavy industry (steel making, engineering). In 1948, Czechoslovak engineering goods still fetched the same unit price as West German goods. By the mid-1960s they were already receiving only half of the average unit price obtained by others on the EEC market. By the mid-1980s, they were receiving a dismal one-fourth. Other Soviet-type economies experienced similar declines as shown in Table 1.

In other product groups, the situation was not as bad as in highly sophisticated engineering, but on the average more and more goods had to be exported to earn one unit of convertible currencies. These developments contributed significantly to the fall in real wages, quite apart from the consequences of indebtedness that emerged as another constraint.

Table 1. Unit (Kilogram) Prices of Engineering Goods Obtained by East European Members of COMECON on the EEC Market Relative to Average
Prices Obtained by Exporters in 1965-1985 (in percentages: average
price equals 100 percent)

Country	1965	1970	1975	1977	1980	1985
COMECON (weighted average)	50	45	37	38	35	28
Bulgaria	32	39	36	34	30	25
Czechoslovakia	47	45	38	36	32	25
GDR*a*	58	47	48	44	37	33
Hungary	77	72	52	53	47	35
Poland	36	36	36	44	34	23
Romania	37	39	38	45	38	29
USSR	46	43	30	30	29	23

a without *intra*-German trade.

Source: E.D. Winiecki and J. Winiecki [1988]

AGGREGATE EFFECTS OF DECLINE: MUCH WORSE THAN SHOWN BY OFFICIAL STATISTICS

If official statistics in Soviet-type economies are taken seriously, then the
adverse effects of the range of interrelated economic determinants of
change should be regarded as surprisingly small. There was a slowdown in
economic growth rates of Soviet-type economies since the late 1970s, but
credulous analysts could still write, for example, that the growth record of
Soviet-type economies used to be outstanding but now is merely good [as
did Weitzman, 1987]. Those who knew better stressed for years, if not
decades, that official figures grossly overestimated the real growth, sometimes by more than 50 percent. American (C.I.A.) estimates, for example,
pointed out that Soviet economic growth was nearer to two thirds of the

officially published rates in the postwar (1950-80) period. U. N. estimates pointed to similar overstatements.

It is due to *perestroika* that these downward revisions of official figures were revised downward even further by Soviet economists themselves. According to Khanin, Soviet economic growth was barely above 50 percent of the official figures in the 1961-1975 period, whereas in the next decade the economy stagnated (growth of less than 1 percent annually), while official figures showed a relatively good growth performance of 3.5-4 percent annually.

Table 2.   Official Soviet Statistics and Varying Unofficial Estimates of Annual Economic Growth rates in the USSR, 1951-1985

Period	Soviet Official	ECE U.N.	C.I.A.	Russian Unofficial
1951-55	...	5.1	7.6	...
1956-60	...	5.2	7.1	...
1961-65	10.2	...	...	7.2
1966-70	6.5	5.4	5.1	4.4
1971-75	5.7	3.9*a*	3.7	3.2
1976-80	4.2	...	2.6*b*	1.0
1981-85	3.5	...	...*b*	0.6

a 1971-73 only.

b Alternative C.I.A. estimates are 2.3% *per annum* in 1976-80 and 1.9% in 1981-85

Sources: Soviet official statistics, European Commission of Europe Bulletin, 1980, U.S. Congress materials supplied by C.I.A. and Khanin [1988]

A smaller effort was made to estimate the economic growth of Soviet East-Central European dependencies. But those that were made showed a range of figures lower than the officially published statistics, at times more than 50 percent lower. The worst offenders in terms of the biggest discrepancies were East Germany, Romania and Bulgaria. These countries stagnated at best, if not went into decline. In fact, Polish statistics in the post-

Solidarity period also raised a lot of doubt. Instead of impressive 4-5 percent annual growth rate some estimates put it at 1-2 percent range at best.

If economic growth was lower than officially registered, especially toward the end of the period, inflation was higher - often much higher than published by the respective statistical authorities. This stemmed from the well-known phenomenon of hidden inflation in Soviet-type economies. Various estimates pointed to a substantial - and rising - hidden inflation. Accordingly, since hidden inflation estimates were markedly higher than official figures of real wage growth rates, Western studies confirmed Soviet-type economy consumers' perception of declining real wages and consumption. Both began to fall in the mid-1970s. The decline was the steepest, of course, in Romania and Poland but wages and consumption declined in every country.

Stagnating economies and falling real wages were coupled with increasing domestic imbalances. Except for Romania, communist rulers were afraid of the social consequences of reverting to Stalinist confiscatory measures with respect to excess liquidity in the hands of the population. Consequently, forced savings began to grow faster than in the past.

Repressed inflation (shortages) became more visible as a result. Thus, not only private consumption fell, often quite strongly, as in Poland or Romania, but also living standards declined due to longer queues. These developments, once they turned out to be a permanent feature of Soviet-type economies, became a determinant of decline in their own right. Noneconomic factors began to contribute to the accelerated decay of the Soviet economic system.

NONECONOMIC DETERMINANTS OF DECAY

For societies living under the Soviet economic system, the most important direct effect was **the fall in living standards**. This entailed the fall in real wages and consumption (see the preceding section and Table 3), as well as the still less easily estimated fall in living conditions (deterioration of housing, municipal infrastructure, transportation and telecommunications, and - last but not least - of environmental conditions). The continuing fall in living standards may well have convinced people living under communist rule that even the modest increases they had enjoyed since around the mid-1950s were over.

Table 3.   Monthly Average Real Wages In 5 Soviet-Type Economies, 1965-1982 (at 1975 constant prices; 1975=100)

Country/Year	1965	1975	1980	1982
Czechoslovakia	92.6	100	98.6	96.1
GDR	103.2	100	95.0	90.9
Hungary	90.4	100	98.6	96.1
Poland	88.0	100	91.0	67.3
USSR	82.7	100	99.8	95.7

Source: Askanas [1985]

Having formed such expectations, **societies at large**, not only individuals, **have assumed that the system is hopelessly inefficient**. As Wiles [1982] rightly stressed, years of broken promises brought about a widespread feeling in the Eastern part of Europe that 'not just the economy but the whole theocratic system is not good'. The earliest sign of the extent of such feelings were heated public debates on the 'reformability' of the Soviet economic system in Poland in 1980-81.

Such expectations transformed into attitudes and hence into deteriorating work effort, once they set in, became a separate, even if derived, determinant of decline affecting independently economic performance. Hopelessness begets cynicism and cynicism begets corruption, contributing to further deterioration.

There were some differences between Soviet-type economies in this respect. The dividing line was industrial tradition. In those Soviet-type economies that industrialized before communist rule, workers and bureaucrats simply would not perform below a certain (modest) level because they would not think it possible. On the other hand, in recently transformed, mainly peasant, societies, already low levels of performance would fall sharply to a much greater extent. Therefrom stem the differences in the extent of deterioration in work attitudes between Czechoslovakia, East Germany and, in part, Hungary, where these processes were less dramatic, and the remaining Soviet-type economies.

But socio-psychological consequences of falling living standards were only one aspect of the irreversible multifaceted decline that set in all over East-Central Europe and the USSR. Fast decline of urban infrastructure that made life in the cities decreasingly bearable has been affecting urban population in these countries in much the same way as the fall in consumption.

Less easily perceived but no less damaging in the long run was environmental pollution. **It turned out that the centralized system is even less able to take remedial action in the cases of diverging social and individual returns.** Unsubstantiated praises for authoritarian solutions to the contrary [see, e.g., nonsensical utterances by Kimball, 1973], pollution in Soviet-type economies has been very much worse than elsewhere in the world.

For example, East-Central Europe, excluding the Soviet Union, emitted in 1982 some 40.7 million tons of sulphur dioxide as compared to 18.6 million tons for the EEC countries. The above figures are more poignant if one takes into account that the former countries have slightly smaller territory and one fourth to one half of the living standards of the latter. On a *per capita* basis, emissions in East Germany have been more than four times larger than those in West Germany, and so were those in Czechoslovakia relative to those in Austria.

Other sources of pollution, as well as damage caused by mining, hydroelectric dams and other projects, contributed also to a much greater extent than in other countries. The worst situation with respect to land, water and forest damages is probably in the Soviet Union. To give but one example, between one-fourth and one-half of the black soil in the Soviet Union has been destroyed since collectivization [see Antonov, 1987]. But again, elsewhere in Soviet-type economies, things were not much better. A recent report of Czech economists points out that 54 percent of agricultural land is threatened by erosion, while 80 percent by souring [Zieleniec, Ed., 1989].

It is not surprising under the circumstances that life expectancy has been on the decrease in the Eastern part of Europe for years if not decades. Again, the worst case is the Soviet Union itself. A Soviet male was expected at birth to live less than 60 years according to unpublished 1979 census data leaked to the West in the early 1980s. [Feshbach, 1985]. Adult males live shorter and shorter in other Soviet-type economies as well. Hungary, Czechoslovakia and Poland registered the largest increases in mortality since the 1960s. The trend again accelerated in the 1980s. Figure 3 compares life expectancy in these countries with some Western countries. The dramatically diverging patterns of both groups of countries are there for all to see. Let me add that in other male age groups the situation is not any better.

The combination of economic and noneconomic decline made the societies not only more vulnerable, as shown by falling life expectancy, but also ever more ready to criticize and challenge the ruling elites. This in turn put more stress on the ruling stratum in the Soviet system, for a sullen and rebellious population requires both more extensive and intensive control as tired Polish apparatchiks, security policemen and *nomenklatura* bureaucracies learned in the 1980s.

Thus, **the costs of governance began to increase in the communist-ruled Eastern part of Europe.** At the same time benefits from parasiting upon the Soviet economic system have declined. The ruling stratum has been able to continue to appropriate the rent from ruling through allocation of goods in short supply for themselves but even this has become more difficult. For example, in Poland cars allocated to the ruling stratum at below market prices were distributed less often in the 1980s than a decade earlier. And this took place in spite of the fact that Polish rulers almost doubled the share of cars distributed in that way from some 20 percent in the 1970s to almost 40 percent in the 1980s. The reason for the decline: falling production coupled with increased exports.

But the allocation of goods for the parasitic ruling stratum was the least affected part of the good life of the communist *'privilegentsia'* (to use the brilliant term coined by the *Economist*). The degradation of the urban infrastructure affected them much more strongly. Since heating systems are centralized in the East, both old-age pensioners and arrogant *nomenklatura* representatives have shivered from cold and/or had to forego shaving for weeks in row. **It turned out to be much easier to allocate cottages, cars, color TV-sets, etc., to themselves than to avoid breakdowns of water, heating and sewage systems.** The best known case, which amounted to no less than the poetic justice, was the gas pipe breakdown that ruined - of all places - a part of the planning commission's building in Prague.

The consequences of the extraordinarily high levels of pollution could not have been avoided by the ruling stratum, either. A party secretary in a highly polluted Russian, Polish, Czech, or East German city has to breath the same air containing a lot of sulphur, nitrogen, lead, cadmium (you name it) - as everybody else. The consequences of systematic decay became increasingly a part of everyday life, not only for the ruled but also for the rulers. The Brezhnevs, Ceausescus, and Honeckers of the world did not notice it, of course. But policemen lower echelon apparatchiks and bureaucrats, and military officers - in other words the pillars of the system - might have repeatedly asked themselves **whether they still benefited from their relative position under the conditions of steep absolute decline.** Moreover, as this author has stressed elsewhere, not all segments of the ruling communist stratum have been equally strongly interested in maintaining the Soviet economic system. The police, but especially the military, have not been benefiting to the same extent from the system as did apparatchiks and bureaucrats [*see texts nos. 1 & 3*]. And when it became clearly visible that the system is not delivering what the military expects, i.e. modern weaponry in sufficient quantity and quality, members of the military were prepared to discard it more than others (if anywhere within the ruling stratum, it is among the professional military that Gorbachevites enjoy the strongest support). Soviet satellites did not have imperial ambitions but their professionals in the military also became more sensitive to the need for change. The performance of the Romanian military is particularly telling in this respect.

THE INEVITABLE BREAKDOWN

As a result, not only the costs of governance have been on the increase for quite some time in Soviet-type economies but also the benefits from running the economy and the country were on the decline. Such a situation made the radical change increasingly probable. As this author wrote in the Spring of 1989, 'at a certain point understood graphically as an intersection of falling benefits from parasiting upon the inefficient economic system and raising costs of containing the increasingly hostile society, the ruling stratum will become ready to accept the 'critical mass' of changes - including necessary political changes'[Winiecki, 1989]. **Once popular pressures grew, the whole edifice began to crack.** The MANES, THEKEL, FARES, already visible for quite some time on the wall for those able and willing to see, suddenly caught the attention of leading writers, scholars and politicians everywhere in the Western world. But this new awareness was simultaneous with the breakdown itself.

REFERENCES

Antonov, M., 1987, Polish Translation from Russian in: *Przeglad Techniczny*, No. 45.

Askanas, B., 1985, Niveau und Entwicklung der Reallohne in den RGW-Ländern im Vergleich mit Osterreich. WIIW, Wiener Forschungsberichte, No. 103.

Balassa, B.A. and associates, 1971, *The Structure of Protection in Developing Countries*. Baltimore 1971.

Congress of the U.S., 1982, *USSR: Measures of Economic Growth and Development, 1950-80*. Studies prepared for the use of the Joint Economic Committee, Washington, D.C., 1982.

-, 1985, *East European Economies: Slow Growth in the 1980s*. Papers submitted to the Joint Economic Committee, Vol. l, Washington, D.C.

-, 1987, *Gorbachev's Economic Plans*. Study Papers submitted to the Joint Economic Committee, Vol.1, Washington, D.C.

Feshbach M., 1985, The Age Structure of the Soviet Population: Preliminary Analysis of Unpublished Data. In: *Soviet Economy*, Vol.1, pp.177-193.

Holzman, F.D., 1979, Some Systematic Factors Contributing to the Convertible Currency Shortages of Centrally Planned Economies In: *American Economic Review*, Vol.69, No.2, pp.76-80.

Khanin, G., 1988, Economic Growth: An Alternative Estimate, *Communist*, No. 17, 1988, pp.83-90 (in Russian).

Kimball, T., I Felt the Winds of Change. *National Wildlife*, February-March 1973.

Mantorska, T., Demographic Situation in Areas under Ecological Threat. Institute of Economics of the Polish Academy of Sciences, Research Monograph (in Polish).

Little I.M.D., T. Scitovsky and M. Scott, 1970, Industry and Trade in Some Developing Countries, London.

U.N. Economic Commission for Europe (ECE), 1980, *Economic Bulletin for Europe*, Vol.31, No.2,

Weitzman, M.L., 1987, 'Foreword', In: P.Desai, *The Soviet Economy: Problems and Prospects. Oxford*, pp. vii-viii.

Wiles, P., 1982, Introduction: Zero Growth and the International Nature of the Polish Disease. In: J. Drewnowski (Ed.), *Crisis in the East European Economy*, London, pp. 7-17.

Winiecki, E.D., and J. Winiecki, 1988, Intra-Branch Structural Change in Poland and Other COMECON Countries and Specialisation for the World Market, Main School for Planning and Statistics, Warsaw, November, manuscript (in Polish)

Winiecki, J., 1984, Soviet-type Economies: Entering an Era of Long-Term Decline. Warsaw, mimeo

-, 1987a, *Economic Prospects: East and West*, Centre for Research into Communist Economies, London.

-, 1987b, The Overgrown Industrial Sector in Soviet-Type Economies: Explanations, Evidence, Consequences, *Comparative Economic Studies*, Vol.28, No. 4, pp. 13-36.

-, 1989, Der Preis der Privilegien und der Machterhaltung: Verfall auf der ganzen Linie ist der bestimmende Faktor fur Wandel im Sowjetsystem, *Frankfurter Allgemeine Zeitung*, April 28.

-, 1990, Why Economic Reforms Fail in the Soviet System: A Property Rights Approach, *Economic Inquiry*, Vol.28, No.2, pp.195-221.

Zieleniec, J., Ed., 1989, *Czechoslovakia on the Crossroad.* A Report by a Collective of Authors, Institute of Economics, Prague, mimeo (in Czech)

CHAPTER 7

HOW IT ALL BEGAN: THE IMPACT OF GORBACHEV'S *PERESTROIKA*[*]

What is really going on in the East, above all and most important in the Soviet Union? **Is it a momentous change or another thaw in a seemingly endless cycle of relaxation and repression under totalitarianism?** And if it is a momentous change, what should be Western attitudes and policies? (...) Does the West possess any leverage with which to prod the Soviet Union in the desired direction? This article is an attempt to answer the questions.

To begin with, it is necessary to sketch the *contours* of the next stage in the development of the Soviet system. Its first stage, under Stalin, was that of wholesale terror affecting everybody, including the ruling stratum: party apparatchiks, bureaucrats, policemen and soldiers. As usual under dictatorships, power was the main road to privilege and privilege to the acquisition of wealth. In this context, purges could be seen as the main road to power and wealth.

However, stakes in the game, played exclusively within the ruling stratum, were too high under the old dictator: the winners took everything, including the life of the losers. With the demise of Stalin, a new rule governing political (in reality, mostly personal) change was established: the winners take power, privilege and the means of acquiring wealth but leave the losers their life and (usually) also the acquired wealth.

---

[*] The full text of this article, written jointly with Jacek Szymanderski, in 1987, was published as 'The Gorbachev Challenge - A view from the East, in **The World Today**, Vol.45, Nos.8-9, 1989.

It is worth bearing in mind that the rewriting of these rules was undertaken for the benefit of the members of the ruling stratum . It was they who were unable to enjoy for longer periods the fruits of the wealth acquired during their political life. (This historical reference is important for - in the view of the authors - the new stage of the development of the Soviet system is also shaped by the interests of the ruling stratum in the present age of [system's] decline.)

After Stalin came, thus the next stage. Terror was maintained at the retail - not wholesale - level. It was less and less directed at the ruling stratum or the general public, and more and more at those hinting at their dissatisfaction with the system. 'Authorised' corruption through privilege continued unabated; 'unauthorised' corruption may have even increased, with the less severe penalties for the losers. Periodic aggravations of economic problems in the still growing economies were partly remedied by lessening central controls and providing room for lower-level initiatives. But when problems looked less urgent, while critique of economic mismanagement threatened sometimes to spill over into politics, central controls were tightened. Relaxation was superseded by repression.

It is this alternation of relaxation and repression that gave the impression of endlessness of system-specific cycles. But these cycles were neither characteristic of the first stage of the development of the Soviet system nor are they fully applicable to what is emerging as its third stage. Although the signals are varied and inconsistent, not only across countries and over time but also simultaneously within countries, criticism of the system is both more widespread and intensive. Reforms in the economic area are officially talked about (so much so that Mr. Gorbachev and his aides may even be convincing themselves that they were already introduced). Meanwhile, criticism is spilling over into other [walks of life], including politics itself, with only mild repression as a penalty.

Gorbachev in Moscow, Jaruzelski in Poland and the current collective leadership in Hungary seem to be making encouraging gestures to independent critics and reaching beyond the ruling stratum in their attempts at rejuvenating the old system or moving cautiously towards the new and less repressive and wasteful one.

It is an intriguing question whether the real goals of the Soviet, Polish, Hungarian or any other communist leadership are the same as the professed ones. Actually, the answer may not be all that important for future developments in the Soviet system. **Something else is much more important.**

It is that, according to signals coming out of the Soviet system, some ruling groups - or, to be more precise, majorities in the ruling groups - are beginning to understand that under the present circumstances of secular decline it is less and less possible to realise their own goals in complete disregard of elementary rights and basic interests of the societies they rule.(...)

However reluctantly, Gorbachev and the other leaders seem to be ready for a bit of 'give' in return for a hefty - but not total - 'take'. These signals are conflicting, since large segments of the ruling stratum, parasiting quite comfortably upon the system, are as yet unprepared for even a symbolic 'give'.

Every ruling group in the Soviet system is an emanation of the ruling stratum (...). Thus, for Gorbachev - or any other communist leader for that matter - there is no 'good tsar, bad officials' contrast because both the tsar and his circle, the ruling group, are the representatives of the stratum as a whole.

There remains, however, one important difference. The ruling group is the only one within the ruling stratum that is concerned with the real performance of the system, not just the distorted reports of that performance. The buck stops there. **They are between the Scilla of transaction cost constraint and the Charybdis of competitive constraint: the inefficient property rights structure does not generate increased wealth,** which threatens the superpower status of the Soviet Union **and increases the dissatisfaction of the population everywhere,** but a change in the property rights structure would threaten the rent extraction by the ruling stratum, which, dissatisfied, may turn to a rival ruling group from within its own ranks.

Given this relationship between the ruling group and the ruling stratum, it is very difficult for a ruling group to push for changes that would go much further than the consensus of the moment.(...)

At this point **it is necessary to stress certain long-term trends in the Soviet Union** that have been affecting both the behaviour of the ruling group and that of the ruling stratum. They are all related to the visible signs of stagnation and decline in the Soviet economy, society, environment and so on. The economic slowdown since the mid-1970s and the perceptible increase in the technological gap between the Soviet Union and the West (also in the military area) put the Soviet Union's capability as a superpower under strain, in three ways:

- First, in spite of the steady inflow of resources to the military research and development sector, its cost efficiency just like that of any other sector - has been in secular decline. Obviously, America's acceleration of military expenditure under President Reagan after years of neglect contributed to the widening of the gap. In this sense, we may talk about an American challenge to Soviet rulers rather than the other way round.

- Second, a stagnating economy is putting pressure on the Soviet industry's capability to re-equip the huge Soviet army with the succeeding generations of weapons.

- Third, the same stagnating economy is less and less able to shore up distant communist regimes established with Soviet military support.

The very existence of these constraints is a strong card in Gorbachev's hand in his disputes with the protagonists of the old style. Unpalatable changes are presented as a necessity since the traditional model of governance and management puts the Soviet Union increasingly at a disadvantage. But neither Gorbachev nor his domestic communist opponents understand that these adverse trends are going to continue whoever gets the upper hand, since economic reforms are a non-starter. They will not have a serious effect upon the economy - except to a limited extent upon agriculture. They are mostly institutional rearrangements, a long way off even from the modest Hungarian reforms adopted since 1968 which, except in agriculture, themselves yielded only limited and temporary results.

Nonetheless, such pseudo-reforms oblige the party apparatchiks and economic bureaucracy to step up their effort to control the economy, but without the commensurate increase in the rent appropriated by them from it, because the economic situation would continue to deteriorate. It would be possible, of course, to increase the share appropriated by the ruling stratum from the declining wealth. This happened in Poland in the early 1980s, but it is a temporary expedient only. Thus in, say, five years from now economic conditions will be worse. This deterioration may remain hidden if the present political course continues and Gorbachev really implements the shift of some resources from the military to the consumer goods-producing sector. Such a move, however, could pit him against the armed forces.

Under the circumstances of continued cautious flirtation by the ruling group with the both the intelligentsia and the masses, **the economic deterioration may prod Gorbachev and his group much further along the lines of economic and political change, regardless of the existence of differences between professed and real goals**. Whether they like it or not, they may be forced to move closer to the political and economic models of the West (with visible economic effects expected at best in 3-5 years from the moment of serious changes). In contrast, benefits of political change would become visible gradually, with some feedback effects upon economic performance (once serious changes are introduced).

However, both types of changes would reduce the possibility of the parasitic ruling stratum to appropriate wealth in the officially authorised way (through the *nomenklatura*, formalised privileges and so on) and the officially unauthorised way (through the flow of unpaid or underpriced goods and services in short supply to the ruling stratum, through outright bribery, and so on).

Sensible economic changes would have to introduce, *inter alia*, performance criteria for managers in enterprises based on efficiency rather than personal or political loyalty, thus depriving apparatchiks and bureaucrats of at least a part of their spoils at present allocated to them through the *nomenklatura*. The establishment of at least a modicum of independent opinion would allow the voicing of criticism of the system of officially approved corruption - formalised privileges for the ruling stratum, including special shops. Also, it would help to alert the general public to the most flagrant cases of the officially disapproved corruption.

But it is not only wealth appropriated through power and privilege but also power itself of the ruling stratum that would be gradually eroded by the increased number of participants in the game and the introduction of some efficiency-based criteria. And there is another factor: the imprint of the totalitarian system on the minds of the representatives of the ruling stratum. A more open political atmosphere leading to a more critical climate frightens them. They perceive themselves as engaged in a zero-sum game; it is either 'we control them' or 'they control us'. They fear they will lose everything. Finding room for compromise with the oppressed, even in their own long-term interest, does not come easily to people with a totalitarian frame of mind.

Thus, sooner or later such curtailment of power, privilege and wealth would generate a reaction from those most affected by these changes, i.e., [communist] party apparatchiks and bureaucrats (including party apparatchiks in army uniforms: political commissars in the armed forces). Let us assume the worst, i.e., that they succeed in ousting Gorbachev and suppressing public discontent. Or, even better, that they succeed in 'Brezhnevising' Gorbachev himself. What would be the effects of such a *coup*?

First of all, the economy would deteriorate faster (as shown by the examples of Romania and Poland, each in a somewhat different way). The gap with America and its allies would increase further, even with the reallocation of resources towards the military sector rather than the other way round, since increasing complexity penalises the rigid system disproportionately strongly. A post-Gorbachev ruling group would face not only the fast-declining Soviet capability to influence the world outside its borders - including the adjacent East European dependencies - but also the declining quantity and quality of goods and services inside its borders, both as a result of declining supplies of natural resources and as a reaction of the frustrated expectations of Soviet producers/consumers.

All the other adverse effects of the traditional system would intensify, too. For **the Soviet state is not only affected by economic decline but also by the decline in almost all other walks of life**: the environment, public health and so on. It is probably this overall deterioration which may convince many defenders of the traditional system that without change they may not be able to shield their privileged position, and even themselves personally, from the consequences of the decline.

To illustrate the above, here are some cases. The socialist industrialization succeeded in severely polluting half of Lake Baikal, the biggest lake in the world containing about 20 percent of world reserves of drinkable water. The local party secretary and his apparatus may still be able to have the water brought for them from the other unpolluted, or less polluted, half of the lake. However, both the party secretary and his family and the workers with their families will have to breathe the polluted air in areas of heavy sulphur dioxide emissions - 2-2.5 times higher on a per capita basis in the Soviet Union than in the West; still higher (4-4.5 times) in Czechoslovakia and East Germany. There is no way of avoiding that.

The same may be said about the effects of the decaying infrastructure - the result of long neglect and the more recent decline in investments. A member of the ruling stratum may still have a chauffeured car (there are about 600,000 of them in the Soviet Union) but on reaching home he will be shivering from the cold, together with thousands of other inhabitants of the district because a pipe has burst somewhere in the neighbourhood. Or he may suffer with everybody else from heating and power cuts caused by fuel shortages.

Lower-level representatives of the ruling stratum who will be the first to feel the pinch of this comprehensive decline are not going to turn democrats overnight as a result. They may even be angry with the present ruling group and warmly applaud the coup that promises to restore the 'good old days' of uninhibited tyranny and corruption. But **if things get continually much worse for a couple of years, then they may have no choice but to go along with the next change, however distasteful it might have seemed to them before.**

Already life is putting so many pressures on the Soviet male that he is expected (at birth) to live less than 60 years, according to unpublished data from the latest Soviet census. How much further to the level of Burma or Zimbabwe must Soviet health deteriorate before its implications become clear for those in power? All the symptoms point to a growing (communist) *fin-de-siécle* mood. Some segments of the ruling stratum that benefit less from the traditional economic system, e.g., the professional soldiers may take cognizance of the fact at some point in the future. And it is the post-post-Gorbachev ruling group emanating from among them that may push through long overdue changes which many in the East and the West expect from Gorbachev and his group.

These are, in the authors' view, the most important elements of the situation in the Soviet Union and the other East European states. They are **only remotely related to the ruling group's goodwill, goals or intentions. They are determined, above all, by the self-destructive nature of the system** which, after reaching a certain level of complexity, begins to bring zero or even diminishing returns - and not only in the economic sphere at that.

Do these developments - both current and prospective - pose a challenge to the West? Do they put the West on the spot? They do not threaten the West politically or economically. However, a post-Gorbachev 'counter-reformer' may find it tempting to try to 'solve' the system's decline by the military conquest of Western Europe whose resources could prolong the existence of the system for a couple of decades. In fact, the same temptation may be felt by Gorbachev himself in a few years from now when his present pseudo-reforms turn out to be a visible flop. The latter seems to be psychologically less probable, though. However, the West has taken note of and lived with this threat for decades; it should be prepared to live with it a couple of decades longer.

If there is any 'challenge' at all, it is one of Western policy response to the developments in the Soviet system. Here, however - contrary to widespread expectations - the West's capacity to influence these developments is very limited. Moreover, as will be shown below, most Western actions under consideration now may make the desired outcome less, not more, probable.

It is, of course, true that the present trends in the Soviet system are advantageous to the West in the East-West context. Decreasing capability of an aggressive competitor is an advantage in itself, quite apart from *glasnost* and *perestroika*. But it would be even better to have a competitor who radically decreases his aggressiveness and increasingly devotes his energy to internal rather than external expansion (as post-1945 Germany and Japan did). It is the - still distant - promise of such a change held by the present developments that should make the West view Gorbachev's attempts sympathetically.

The West's attitude should be that of a careful but sympathetic observer, conscious of his own limitations. It should not behave as a tough bargainer trading capital and technology for some highly visible political concessions (usually unimportant in the long run), a position sometimes adopted by conservative 'realists'. Nor should it rush in with government loans and technology licenses, a position adopted even more often by left-leaning 'do-gooders'.

New large-scale credits would reduce the pressure on the ruling group to change the system further. The inflow of capital would loosen for the time being the resource scarcity constraint put upon the Soviet economy by its declining performance. It is widely accepted by now that large-scale Western credits in the 1970s postponed for about a decade the much-needed beginnings of a reform movement towards a market-type economy. Capital inflow would also help to halt the decline in the system's capacity to supply the Soviet army with the next generation of weapons because at least a part of the obtained credits could be diverted to military purposes. At the very least, such credits would eliminate the possibility of a temporary reverse flow of resources - from the military to the civilian consumer sector - in order to (artificially) show quick results of *perestroika*.

The same applies to the lifting of restrictions on the transfer of militarily sensitive technology - as promised, for example by Mr. Johannes Rau, the former leader of the German Social Democrats, and later by the West German Foreign Minister, Hans-Dietrich Genscher. The increasing technological lag, just like the decreasing economic capability to rearm, is one of Gorbachev's trump cards in his struggle against the protagonists of the old style of political governance and economic management. To permit the unrestricted flow of technology would allow the reduction of the gap without far-reaching economic change. A similar effect would be produced by large-scale and lasting cutbacks in the American R & D effort, since the gap would again decline after some time without the change in the Soviet system.

To increase the chances of the movement in the Soviet Union towards what is commonly regarded in the West as civilised political and economic standards, the West should take a long-term view. Such a long-term view fits in well with long-term Western interests: the reintegration of Europe within the framework of the Western civilisation. It is within this framework that the flirtation of the ruling groups with the politically dispossessed societies of the Soviet Union and smaller East European countries should be applauded, and rewarded in a symbolic way. The same applies to moves toward economic sanity.

A new strategy, similar to Zbigniev Brzezinski's 'bridge-building' in the 1960s, needs to be formulated. But instead of choosing, as then, between countries, the West should now try to choose between levels of linkages. It should be patiently explained to Soviet and other communist authorities that lasting confidence comes only from multiple interactions at a subnational level. This applies to contacts between various independent political, professional and cultural groupings, associations and parties as well as to contacts between business firms. In the longer run, they are much more important than exchanges of observers at military manoeuvres or long-term agreements on economic cooperation.

The West can do little to speed up the process of change forced upon the Soviet Union and its dependencies by the self-destructive character of the system. This is an internal process; its dynamics cannot be much influenced from outside. But there is a strong probability that, in the longer run, it is going to be carried much further than both its proponents and opponents in the East perceive at the moment. It is obviously better if this happens without traumatic reversals of the post-Gorbachev variety described above, but the process of decline and attempts to stave it off also have their own dynamics and are going to continue regardless.

The West can slow down the process by rushing in, bearing gifts. It cannot, however, speed it up. But, if the West does not - in an act of folly - disarm itself, thus inviting aggression as a (temporary) solution to the decline of the Soviet system, the change in that system is going to come sooner or later.

A chase after the surrealistic chimera of central planning that started with a loud bang is ending with a whimper. **Political control to impose** the coercive utopia upon the population is increasingly becoming a burden for the ruling stratum itself. This (so much uglier) *fin-de-siécle* is going to dictate the need to offer successive concessions to dispossessed societies. They will come neither from the benevolence of the Soviet rulers, nor from Western acts of commission or omission. The process goes by fits and starts but is, in the view of the authors, inevitable.

CHAPTER 8

HOW IT ALL BEGAN: REAGAN AND THE SOVIET COLLAPSE·

Many commentaries ascribed what was happening behind the late Iron Curtain to the pressure on the Soviet Union applied by President Reagan's administration. However, 'reversing the tide of history' cannot be created *ex nihilo* by political will alone, or even by political will coupled with accelerated military expenditures. MANES, THEKEL, FARES has already been on the Kremlin wall for some time and the pressure, applied to a creaking Soviet economic machinery, put it virtually to a halt. Incidentally, had the accelerated military expenditures been the sufficient measure in this respect, the reversal would have taken place during President Harry Truman administration. But the resolve of that [other] great American president could only stop the advances of communism in Europe, not to reverse them.

INABILITY TO COPE WITH ECONOMIC CHANGE

How it all began, then? The seeds of self-destruction were all embedded in the system and they were largely economic. For those who would object that such a barbarian political system could not last long the answer is simple. The Assyrian empire lasted thousand years (with an interruption)

· This is a manuscript of an article submitted by the author in 1991 to **The Spectator** but not accepted by the journal (most probably under the impression of the communist putsch). The present writer regards it, however, as an important complement to a piece about Gorbachev's reforms (see the preceding text).

because economic change was so slow as to be imperceptible. Therefore rulers knew how much to take away from the peasants, so that most of the latter survived until the next harvest. They were hardly bothered by other economic questions.

The Soviet empire collapsed primarily because the system could not cope with economic change. External events and leaders' own policy decisions amplified self-destructive features of the system. By coincidence, most important developments took place at about the same time, that is [in] early 1970s. America seemed to be exhausted, morally and economically, at the time, while the Soviet empire looked stronger than ever (Toynbee was right is stressing that empires appear strongest just before the fall!).

Thus, almost without being noticed as a problem for the Soviet world, shock waves were generated by the first oil crisis. It exacerbated the long standing weakness of Soviet-type economies, namely the fact that they used 2-3 times more of basic resources (energy, steel, cement) than normal economies to produce the same output. With the oil price jump this feature became increasingly painful, first for smaller East European importers of energy and later for the Soviet Union itself.

It became obvious that the traditional wasteful pattern of economic growth cannot last for long. But to change it, economic system's change was needed. Since this was not forthcoming, growth had to decline. And it did although doctored official figures did not reveal the depth of the fall.

Yet another feature of the Soviet system became increasingly costly at about the same time. Since late 1960s or early 1970s at the latest a shift in the economic 'growth engine' role occurred in the world economy. Industries based on the economy of scale yielded their dominant positions to those based on flexibility, entrepreneurship and innovation. This pulled the rug from under central planning. (...)

As the Soviet Union and its satellites tried to produce a multitude of new products and more sophisticated versions of old ones, sharply raised requirements of smooth management of complex coordination processes became too great a burden for the slow-moving hierarchical bureaucracy. Signs of strain multiplied.

Of course, little would have happened if the Soviet empire decided to continue producing, symbolically speaking, rails and nails. But they in all their ignorant arrogance (God bless it!) wanted to 'catch up with and surpass' the West.

The shift to industries based on features antithetical to the Soviet system exacerbated yet another weakness, namely international competitiveness. For years they were selling more and more and getting less and less, as their industries were inexorably falling behind those of outward looking economies. But the ambition to produce more sophisticated manufactures generated extra demand for imports because domestic industries turned out to be unwilling or unable to produce higher quality inputs to new products. With limited ability to increase exports, indebtedness began to rise rapidly in the second part of the 1970s.

On top of that [Soviet-type] economies slowly but surely became more and more distorted, as industry (Marxist pet sector) sucked in resources from the whole economy and became ever larger. By late 1970s industry had a share in national product higher by 1/3 and that in employment by 1/4 than in other countries at a similar level of development. But this was only an illusion of the industrial might. As enterprises tried to produce everything within their own factories (to avoid unreliable suppliers), what they made cost up to ten times more than comparable products from specialised firms even in their own inefficient economies.

With the amplified effects of various economic woes something [had] to give. The first were living standards that began to decline everywhere from mid-1970s. Then, economic growth fell in some countries to or below zero at about the same time. Military expenditures continued to get their enormous share. But just because it was already enormous in the USSR (20-25% of national product) it could not be increased any more, while requirements of rapidly changing technology put increasing demands on decreasingly efficient Soviet economy.

THE ROT SPREAD BEYOND THE ECONOMY

Economic stagnation or even decline that became ever more obvious since the mid-1970s (in spite of official statistics to the contrary), were accompanied by other, non-economic but largely [Soviet] economic system-generated phenomena. First, as industrial sector, and especially armaments industry, sucked in ever more resources, urban infrastructure began to decline faster. One example is worth quoting here: in 1976-1980 *pyatiletka* trunk water pipes in the Soviet Union registered 40 breakdowns a year per 100 km of pipes but this horrible rate increased to 100 breakdowns per 100 km in the next *pyatiletka*. And, since at the oil and gas pipelines pipes had to be changed every 2-3 years, there were few pipes left for other purposes!

Decaying urban infrastructure and increasing pollution (worst in the world) were extremely important determinants of the systemic collapse because they affected not only the ruled population but also the ruling stratums in these countries. The Brezhnevs, Ceausescus, and Honeckers of the Soviet world did not notice it but they had demoralising effects on policemen, lower echelon apparatchiks, bureaucrats and military officers. **Many asked themselves (and, after a bottle of *vodka*, even their colleagues) whether they still benefited from their relative position under the conditions of steep absolute decline.**

It is in such conditions that the Soviet empire greeted its *Nemesis*: Ronald Reagan. Most probably, President Reagan was convinced by the analysis of his advisors who (fortunately for us all), did not belong to the usually dominant bunch of left leaning wishful thinkers and stressed the rapidly deteriorating economic and other conditions in the Soviet Union. **The policy suggested itself: accelerated technological race will reveal all the weaknesses of the Soviet economic machinery** that needed more and more to produce less and less of sophisticated products (military, as well as non-military).

It is in my opinion President Reagan whom we owe '*Gensek*', and later President, Gorbachev. As Soviet economy, trying to respond to the Reagan's challenge, was brought to a halt (economic growth in 1981-1985 fell down to zero), the octogenarians on the *Politbureau* realised that they need somebody who will be able to radically modernise the Soviet system to improve significantly its performance - even at a cost.

But what they did not realise, was that **a car on its last stretch cannot run faster. If the driver puts his foot on an accelerator, the creaking**

machine will fall to pieces, like inspector Clouzot's car in the final scene of the 'Pink Panther'. Gorbachev's program of *'uskorenyie'* (acceleration) had exactly that effect. The Soviet economic machine began to unravel, additionally disturbed by half-hearted (and often half-baked) *'perestroika'*, that is [typical socialist] reformers' tinkering. **Without Gorbachev, that is without Reagan, the Soviet Union could have rotted at a slower rate, unraveling in mid- or late 1990s rather than a decade earlier.**

It is that decade of freedom that we all owe to the resolve of President Ronald Reagan. But 'the tide of history' was already on our side for some time.

PART III

POLITICAL ECONOMY OF SYSTEMIC CHANGE: FEASIBILITY OF THE PROCESS

CHAPTER 9

SHAPING THE INSTITUTIONAL INFRASTRUCTURE*

In Eastern Europe (...) general rules and market institutions are often non-existent, and a major problem is to create market economies while simultaneously building the supporting institutions. We describe the type of institutions inherited from Soviet-style economies and show institutional reforms and macroeconomic policies may have limited effects due to the interdependence and lack of complementary market institutions. Without a 'critical mass' of market institutions, the benefits of market are slow in realization. The advantages of reforming existing but distorted institutions over building new ones is stressed.

THE INSTITUTIONAL LEGACY OF THE SOVIET ECONOMIC SYSTEM

Throughout its history the Soviet economic system displayed major deficiencies that led to its decline and eventually to its demise. These deficiencies stemmed from problems that were inherent and thus unsolvable within the institutional setting of the Soviet-type economy. Its institutions made the Soviet or any other classic socialist system a sure loser in the long run in a competition with market economies. This insight, first

---

* This is a slightly abbreviated version of an article 'Shaping the Institutional Infrastructure', that appeared in **Economic Inquiry**, Vol.32, January 1994. It was first presented by the author at a Kiel Week Conference in June 1991.

enunciated by Ludwig von Mises back in 1920, has been for quite a few decades lost to modern minds.

Centralization of economic decision making generated unwieldy, mammoth bureaucracies which attempted to cope, unsuccessfully, with **the 'knowledge problem'** - in the Michael Polanyi/Friedrich von Hayek sense [Lavoie, 1985]. The presence of the communist party apparatus added to the confusion. The central planners' inevitable ignorance and their crude plan corrections were made worse by political campaigns and *ad hoc* interventions.

The most serious consequence was **the loss of economic agents' initiative, entrepreneurship and innovativeness.** Whatever initiative was left was used outside the framework of aggregate wealth creation, which is what economic activity is mostly about. Avoidance of contradictory rules, innovative padding of firms' and other organizations' reports, obtaining those plan indicators that were easiest to implement, and collecting resources to ensure the implementation of plans regardless of costs became the major areas of economic agents' initiative.

The foregoing points to another, ultimately unsolvable problem of the old institutional setting, namely **the 'incentive problem'.** Central planners and their political masters made extremely costly mistakes. These happened because of their inevitable ignorance, due partly to the impossibility of obtaining the incommunicable, tacit knowledge residing in hundreds of thousands of economic agents and partly to the fact that by centralized price setting they destroyed the informational content of market prices (for economic agents reveal their partly tacit knowledge through actions that in turn affect prices). But their mistakes were compounded by the fact that even communicable knowledge reached them in a highly distorted shape due to a structure of incentives that severed the link between efficient performance and reward. For it turns out that there is a sea of difference between being paid for what one sells on the market and for what one reports to one's superiors in a multilevel hierarchy. Agency costs (in the sense of Jensen and Meckling [1976]) turned out to be exorbitant in state-owned enterprises, especially under the conditions of measurement without markets [Szymanderski and Winiecki, 1989; Winiecki, 1991a].

This in turn leads us to the third unsolvable problem, i.e., the problem of **'property rights'**. The degree of control over management in the Soviet system, in spite of the ability of the central planners and their political overseers to impose the heaviest possible penalties, including imprisonment, was only formally absolute. In terms of their ability to generate expected behavior it was a fiasco.

Neither control over the flow of real resources into and out of enterprises by the multilevel planning hierarchy nor over the flow of financial resources by the state's monobank helped very much in the face of strong informational asymmetries between higher-level bureaucrats and enterprise managers in favor of the latter. Since the flow of financial resources was always subordinated to the planned flow of goods and production factors, the monobank, that had been designed as a control body, ended up as a mere cashier paying for whatever real resource flows took place in the economy. This situation was exacerbated by the *ad hoc* interventions of planners and apparatchiks protecting their rents in various enterprises, which, added to their traditional concerns with quantitative output targets, made them validate most unplanned cost increases [Winiecki, 1989a and 1991a]. From this combination of distorted incentives and property rights stemmed the well-known 'soft' budget constraint of state-owned enterprises under Soviet socialism [Kornai, 1979 and 1986].

Thus the substitution of centralized decision making for market incentives and state ownership for private ownership with transferable property rights in the end made effective control over the economy impossible. Decisions were invariably costly and resulted in persistent excess demand, shortages and uncertainty. Centralization of decisions and wrongly structured incentives ensured that quantities produced with much fanfare (and largely overstated figures) were of low quality and technologically obsolete. By the 1950s planners were already tinkering with the system, trying to alleviate institutional deficiencies that were visible by then. The failure or, at best, marginal improvements occasioned by these attempts suggested the unsolvability of the problems in question, but at the time the system's failures were interpreted as evidence of growth problems. However, as an old Eastern European joke had it, problems of growth were followed by the growth of problems. The story of how the Soviet economic system began to unravel is not of primary importance here, though[*see text no.6 above*]

What matters is that these reformers tinkering with the system tried to inject some bits and pieces of the market, at times - as in Hungary after 1968 - with the effect of creating a parallel system of indirect economic inducements alongside one of direct planners' commands. However, until the very end the market was subordinated to the planners. Whenever problems cropped up, market measures were held in abeyance, while commands (direct or in the guise of 'recommendations') got the upper hand. This situation led Janusz Beksiak [1988] to call nominally autonomous, reformed socialist enterprises 'enterprises until further orders'.

INDISPENSABLE MARKET INSTITUTIONS AND THE REQUIREMENTS OF MACROECONOMIC POLICY

Governments in all the post-Soviet-type economies face the same problem of creating the institutions (general rules, organizations, and policy instruments) indispensable to the normal functioning of the market system. It is obvious that these institutions cannot be created overnight especially in countries where the political system is also in a state of transition and may be limited in its ability to tackle some of the more complicated issues of establishing - or in some cases re-establishing - market institutions. (...)

Almost all aspects of economic activity require immediate attention, almost all require new laws, institutions and policy measures. But only a few issues at a time may command the attention of governments coping with the obstacles posed by inherited institutions. For it is the government, the main source of institution-building initiatives at the early stage, that is most likely to discover these obstacles in the course of its attempts to facilitate the transition to a market economy.

Those who question the propriety of such a road to the market should consider the 1979 quote from James Buchanan on economics as a game within rules (...). Friedrich von Hayek [1973] also expected 'general rules' to be set by the state. And in most aspects, post-Soviet-type economies lack even these basic general rules.

The supply of institution-building by the government is determined not only by the government's capacity to act, but also by the government's own needs. Leaving aside the government's theoretical and ideological preferences, [measures] are dictated to a large extent by the pressing need to cope with the severe macroeconomic imbalances these countries have inherited. This was the case in Poland, which approached hyperinflation in the autumn of 1989, of Hungary, with its ballooning foreign debt and an unbalanced economy facing an annual inflation rate of 20-30 percent, and of Czechoslovakia, although the economic situation there was not so bad as in Hungary (to say nothing of Poland). Nowhere else does the term 'coping state' [Hirschman, 1981] find better reflection than in the activities of both the executive and legislature in the post-Soviet-type economies as they try to build the rudiments of a market economy from scratch.

The pressing need to equilibrate economies still in transition to the market requires room for exercising macroeconomic policy, and it has turned out it is in this area that governments have concentrated their attention with respect to institution-building. Thus, monetary policy requires as a first step the liquidation of the state's monobank and the creation of a two-tier banking system. This does not give the government the room to maneuver (for good or bad) it has in mature market economies, but at least in the central bank it has an instrument with which to institute stringent monetary policy For a policy tool the central bank has to rely almost exclusively on its real positive main lending rate, given the current nonexistence of open markets for short-term government securities in these countries (an institution to be developed in some unspecified future). (...)

Poland and Hungary were fortunate in that communist reformers in both countries had split the state monobank into a central bank and commercial banks in their last years of rule. Since 'soft' budget constraint ruled supreme, the central banks' policies and credit expansion by commercial banks were severely distorted, but at least organizational reforms were made and some knowledge as to the proper behavior of banking officials was acquired by the personnel (even if not necessarily put into practice). Czechoslovakia was not so fortunate and had to create its two-tiered banking system after its change of government. This, however, was offset by the less serious macroeconomic imbalances in the Czechoslovakian economy, which allowed the government to devote more attention to institutional measures.

Incidentally, the Polish *cum* Hungarian case, as opposed to the Czechoslovakian, displays ambiguous effects from earlier tinkering with the Soviet-style economic system. On the one hand, Vaclav Klaus [1990] has argued that the decentralization of economic decision making without simultaneously linking decision making to capital risk (that is, without changes in the system of property rights) generated stronger inflationary pressures. On the other hand, the very existence of previously misused institutions (phony commercial banks, phony bonds or no less phony stocks) in the radically changed conditions of a real transition to a market economy cut the time needed to establish these institutions and make them operate with some semblance of efficiency Therefore, although these earlier attempts at reform have resulted in some extra costs, they have also brought some benefits, the latter realized largely after the demise of the Soviet system.

A modicum of efficiency is probably as much as one can expect from these newly established or adapted institutions at this time. Although with the establishment of a two-tier banking system the discount rate becomes the main policy instrument of the central bank, policy instruments from the old institutional setting are still in use (such as refinancing credit as the only source of credit expansion for most commercial banks, credit rationing, etc.). Furthermore, the very fact that commercial banks are still state-owned organizations makes them behave more like bureaucracies than businesses. Therein stems the high tolerance of mutual indebtedness among state-owned enterprises in both Poland and Hungary (and now, increasingly, in Czechoslovakia).

This occurs in spite of the fact that in many cases delayed payments are so much higher than delayed receipts that they cannot conceivably be covered by future cash flows. But banks tolerate that, and their willingness to act decisively, i.e., to refuse further credits to such firms probably will not increase very much until they are privatized (yet another urgently needed institution-building measure!).

Similar concerns exist with regard to fiscal policy. Here, too, certain institutional measures have to be undertaken for fiscal policy to play a role in equilibrating the economy Implementing these institutional changes has occupied much of these governments attention from the very beginning of the transition process.

Balancing the budget has been a problem for all three governments, but most urgent for Poland. Increasing revenues has required, first of all, improved tax collection, as well as curtailment of the plethora of tax exemptions. Although this task could be viewed as an attempt to make the 'soft' budget constraint of enterprises harder (a policy measure), it should be noted that the shift to market-type policies also required measures that would equalize conditions for enterprises, among them simplification and equalization of tax regimes across enterprises (an institutional measure). Thus quite apart from the universal long-term aim of introducing VAT, interim tax measures have aimed at creating more equal conditions for competing enterprises.

On the expenditure side, substantial reductions of subsidies, greater tax discipline and significantly tighter monetary policy - all taken together - have put to the fore the question of unemployment and, consequently, whether existing institutions will be able to deal with the emerging problems. Employment offices, the heritage of the old system, were originally designed to control the flow of labor, just as the monobank was designed to control the flow of money, and both failed for the same reason. Here again the government's scarce time has had to be occupied with institutional measures: devising general rules for unemployment benefits, extending the area of responsibility of employment offices, devising crash programs to train personnel for these offices, etc.(...)

Obviously, the effective use of economic policy, i.e., policies that influence the actions of economic agents through the pressure of market incentives in contrast to planning directives, required as a prerequisite domestic price liberalization. The lifting of price controls drawn intense attention due to the role of prices in the devised 'shock therapy'. Although in many cases freeing prices did not require changing already established rules, in some cases it did, for example in the case of housing maintenance pricing. Pricing decisions in such areas were, however usually postponed in the early transition period.

Foreign economic policy has required even more institutional changes. The choice of the foreign exchange regime (most post-Soviet-type economies have adjustably pegged exchange rates), the extent of currency convertibility, whether economic agents should be allowed to maintain accounts in both domestic and foreign currencies, as well as trade policy-related measures (customs duties and their structure, tariff exemptions, export restrictions and import quotas, tax refunds), all required the establishment of new sets of rules.

Altogether, **the transition to a market system has required not only policy decisions, i.e., choices within rules, but also institution-building, i.e., choices among rules.** The pressing need for economic stabilization, coupled with clearly stated preferences for liberalization and - within that large area - the governments' perceived needs for effective policy instruments for short-term adjustments, dictated to a large extent the actual content of the supply of institutional measures. Demand in other areas (e.g., privatization, demonopolization) has been left unsatisfied - or at least much less has been done there.

However, **the choice of what problems to address first was affected as much by the scarcity of time as by anything else.** Some institutional reforms required further institution-building to reap fully (and sometimes to reap at all!) the efficiency benefits of the market system. It is for this reason that the benefits of a shift to the market system grow incrementally rather than once-and-for-all - and this in spite of the 'shock therapy' which introduced a very short time span.

Badly needed is a recognition of the fact that although a package of wide ranging - and often painful - reforms was implemented right at the start of the transition, this in no way means that efficiency and, accordingly efficiency-based benefits will also be forthcoming in a large chunk shortly thereafter. For the critical mass of measures is a minimum necessary to get the ball rolling, while benefits accumulate only over time, as the buildup of market institutions moves up along the supply curve narrowing the gap between the demand for and supply of these institutions.

Thus **the demand for market institutions is very great from the start, while the supply - in spite of strenuous efforts - is of necessity lagging behind. Only time may narrow the gap** (as shown in Figure 1).

Major issues may have to be left unattended for now, and - what is worse - steps already taken may not bring about the expected results because other, related steps have not yet been accomplished due to lack of time, underappreciation of the importance of some measures or simple neglect.

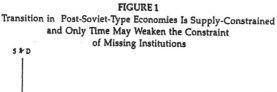

FIGURE 1
Transition in Post-Soviet-Type Economies Is Supply-Constrained
and Only Time May Weaken the Constraint
of Missing Institutions

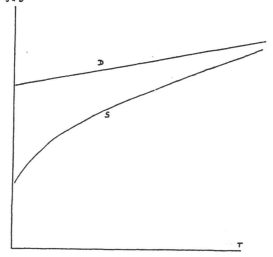

S and D — supply and demand for institutions axis
T — time axis

Unfortunately, governments in post-Soviet-type economies have been guilty to a lesser or greater extent of failing to appreciate the importance of the foregoing difficulties. This is partly a consequence of the general lack of experience with the transition from planned to market economies and the resultant ignorance of some of the related difficulties (such as an one-time fall in output early in the transition; see [Winiecki, 1990 and 1991b], partly from the lack of appreciation of the time factor mentioned above, and partly from the temptation to 'sell' the stabilization and systemic change programs to the general public by promising rapid improvements in living standards. **The impression given was that results would be apparent in months, rather than years.** The political costs of succumbing to such temptation have been very serious.

TIME AS A FACTOR IN INSTITUTION-BUILDING

Leaving aside the contributions of ignorance and policy mistakes, **a scarcity of time has emerged as the most serious problem in building institutions** aimed at achieving the higher economic efficiency associated with the shift to a market system. Two case studies illustrate the point. They show how the benefits of choosing the right set of rules can remain unrealized due to the linkages between the newly established general rules and other, conflicting, associated, or as yet nonexistent but necessary rules, as well as nonexistent but necessary organizations. (...)

The first deals with privatization proper, that is, the transfer of state assets into private hands (regardless of the chosen method of privatization). The privatization laws already enacted in each country required a lot of work but represent only the tip of the iceberg in institution-building associated with privatization.

One of the issues that emerged while working on the privatization legislation in Czechoslovakia, Poland and Hungary has been reprivatization - the return of assets to their former owners. This issue has been extremely complex due to the different legal status of earlier nationalizations (which sometimes have no legal status whatsoever!), as well as to the different states of 'recognizability' of nationalized assets. (There is a big difference between assets that can be returned - for example, a pharmacy taken away from its owner in a house that still exists - and those that have to be valuated somehow - for example, a factory which has become many times larger in the meantime).

Two different problems emerged. The first was the elaboration of general rules of reprivatization/compensation (the latter in case where reprivatization was thought desirable but impracticable). The second was not of an institutional but a psychological nature, but one that yields to institutional solutions. Since uncertainty generated by the claims of former owners casts a shadow over the legal status of some enterprises, their privatization would have to be delayed. So far these problems have been best solved in the Czech privatization bill which gives former owners of industrial assets compensation in the form of extra investment coupons with which to bid for shares in privatized state enterprises. (...)

The interdependence of rules is more visible in the case of the separation of state property from that of municipal and other local authorities. For example, in Poland the privatization of shops, restaurants, etc., had to wait until the passage of the law on municipal authorities (that came into being after forty years of communist centralization) legally able to sell or lease municipal property. However, before actual sales could occur, the local authorities had to establish clear property rights to each individual piece of real estate. (...)

The foregoing considerations are concerned with what is sometimes called privatization 'from above', which stresses the role of the state in setting the institutional framework for the transfer of its assets. An alternative is privatization 'from below', i.e., the legal formation and expansion of new private firms. These two routes complement one another in altering the proportions of economic activity controlled by the private and state sectors. A natural reaction to the failed centralization of the Soviet economic system and simultaneously a recipe for freeing people's initiative would be the passage of a 'charter of economic freedom' allowing anyone to open any business subject to well-defined limitations. The elaboration and passage of such a law would not be very difficult under current political conditions: in fact, such a law was passed in Poland toward the end of the last communist government's rule.

Welcome as this embodiment of economic freedom has been, it represents only the beginning of the institutional story. It did stimulate entrepreneurial activity in Poland where after the passage of this law the rate of formation of new, almost entirely private, firms shot up. The same happened in Czechoslovakia, where during the first nine months of 1990 a quarter of a million small business were established (despite the lack of familiarity with business practices due to the forty-year prohibition of private business activity in that country).

Yet Polish and Hungarian private businessmen complain about various sectoral and occupational regulations from the bygone era that are still in force and hamper their activity. Again, administrative measures often uncover such obstacles, and quite often legislative measures are necessary to remove them.

But the foregoing will still give people only the right to exercise initiative. However important this is after years of limitations and outright prohibitions of private economic activity, it does not in any way increase the probability of success. To illustrate the point, let us look at the example of Poland, where in the 1976-86 period the average size of the private industrial firm in terms of employment increased from 1.6 to 2.6 persons per firm (and the statistics included the owners as well !).

Obviously under communist regimes the private sector, if permitted at all, was allowed to exist but not to expand. Besides legal restrictions, there was also lacking financial institutions geared to the needs of small private businesses; private firms had the lowest priority for credit from the state monobank. Now the legal restrictions are gone, but a network of institutions supporting the expansion of the small business sector does not yet exist. What is needed is small-business development banks, insurance companies oriented toward naturally riskier small businesses, venture capital institutions, and innovation centers to encourage risk-taking by sharing the cost of developing new products and processes. **Without such institutional support, firms in post-Soviet-type economies will consist of a large number of very large enterprises (privatized or not) and a sea of minuscule firms, too small to ever be able to become reliable suppliers of products and services to larger firms.**

Thus, there is a pressing need for Western expertise in finance markets and other areas as well. However, more than expertise may be needed to establish the fundamentally important institutional conditions for the growth of the private sector. I am generally skeptical about the effects of public financial assistance. I think the experience of bilateral and multilateral assistance to developing countries by and large supports this skepticism. Nonetheless, judiciously injected 'seed' money may in well-considered cases do a lot of good. Building the network of institutions supporting the growth of the private sector belongs in this category. Instead of supporting large industrial projects, Western bilateral and multilateral donors would do much better by using a fraction of their money to endow newly established financial institutions with badly needed initial capital and Western expertise. (For example, retired managers could run these institutions for three to five years while simultaneously training their local successors.)

Of course, even without this network of supporting organizations some private firms would grow fast (and some did grow fast in Hungary and Poland in the last two years). But in order to make this phenomenon economically significant, that is, to obtain the strong spillover effects of increasing vitality, size and efficiency of the private sector, these supporting institutions are absolutely necessary. Otherwise, the benefits of shifting to a market system will remain limited for years to come. And it is these limited benefits - in stark contrast with the heavily front-loaded costs - that are the main source of public discontent.

RECONSIDERATIONS AND CONCLUSIONS

The previous two sections of this paper considered a series of interrelated themes. The first of these stressed that **the governments in post-Soviet-type economies have of necessity concentrated on certain priority areas in shaping the institutional infrastructure of their evolving economies.** Attention has centered on establishing the rudimentary institutional framework needed to make post-Soviet-type economies responsive to macroeconomic policy measures, as well as on creating the basic institutions necessary for future integration with the world market (and for making the domestic economy responsive to stimuli coming from there).

It was the large and rapidly growing internal and external imbalances in the countries economies during the pre-transition stage that required the concentration of efforts on these areas. Since monetary and fiscal measures, coupled with liberalization of domestic prices and liberalization of foreign trade and payments, constitute the core of all these countries' stabilization *cum* liberalization programs, these priorities were generally regarded as acceptable. Other areas in need of institution-building got less attention, although it should be noted that in Czechoslovakia work on privatization has advanced almost simultaneously with institutional changes in the monetary, fiscal and foreign economic policy areas.

This is not surprising. Having inherited the least disequilibrated economy among the former socialist countries, the Czech government could

devote less attention - in relative terms - to restoring some measure of economic equilibrium and more to introducing institutional changes to other
areas in need of market institutions. I do not mean to say that macroeconomic stabilization was neglected. On the contrary, in the pre-transition
year of 1990 the money stock grew in nominal terms by only 1-2 percent,
while prices increased sharply (...). The budget deficit was also sharply
cut.

The second theme concerned **the interrelatedness of institutional
change both within and between various areas of the national economy**. The necessity of building market institutions from scratch has meant
that the lack of institutions in one area (e.g., the law separating state property from municipal and local authorities property) has constrained institution-building elsewhere (here, a change in the property rights structure,
that is, privatization).

Furthermore, certain general rules, such as those establishing fundamental economic freedom, require in order to release entrepreneurial activity an extensive review of many existing industry-specific and real
property-related laws with the aim of removing obstacles to entrepreneurship.(...) I have stressed that **for possibilities to become realities, institutional support in the form of a network of institutions geared to meet
the needs of the dynamically growing small business sector is needed**.
It is, however, my opinion that the governments of all the post-Soviet-type
economies not only did not give priority to this type of institution-building
(which is not surprising) but underestimated its importance. It is one thing
to keep an issue on the back burner for the time being, given the crowded
agenda [see Simon, 1987], and another to overlook the importance of the
issue).

The interelatedness of various institution-building measures has
strongly affected the performance of these economies during the early
transition phase to the market system. The demand for institutions needed
to establish a 'workable', that is, relatively efficiently functioning market
economy has not only been high, but also 'inelastic' in the sense of a certain critical mass of institutions necessary to get the ball rolling. But the
supply of institutions, policy mistakes aside, has been primarily constrained by the capacities of both governments and parliaments to elabo-

rate the necessary measures. Rephrasing Kornai's well-known term, post-Soviet-type economies have turned out to be supply-constrained as far as market institutions are concerned - at least in the short-to-medium run.

My third theme concerned **the efficiency and welfare effects of institutional changes lagging behind the needs of a 'workable' market economy**. Without the needed critical mass of market institutions, the benefits of a shift to the market system will be realized to a limited extent only. For there is a difference between the set of macroeconomic policy and liberalization measures that together form a stabilization cum liberalization program and the set of market institutions needed to create a 'workable' market economy. Only the latter, preceded, of course, by the former, brings large benefits from distinctly higher efficiency.

Unfortunately, understanding of the [issues] outlined here has been rather limited. From this failure arose a lot of confusion and disappointment. After the 'big bang' [or 'shock therapy' as transition program has alternatively been called], the radical change of economic regime, after large costs at the start of the transition, the benefits of the market system were for many surprisingly slow in coming. The disappointment has been aggravated by the fact that governments often announced unrealistically short time horizons for improvements in living standards. For example, the Polish government announced in its program that visible improvements would be seen by the second half of 1990. The more realistic expectations of the authors of a program of stabilization and systemic change, prepared about the same time at the request of the parliamentary club of *Solidarity*, were that an improvement in living standards would not occur until after the completion of the program [see Beksiak, Gruszecki, Jedraszczyk, and Winiecki, 1989] (...). The Hungarian government, distancing itself from the 'big bang' approach, also made unrealistic promises. Both governments paid for this behavior at the ballot box.

In conclusion, I would like to stress a point that may seem quite obvious now, but certainly was not (at least not to everyone) at the beginning of the transition programs in the post-Soviet-style economies. It is much easier to restore distorted but existing market institutions than to build them from scratch. Accordingly, the effects of stabilization and liberalization programs in countries with distorted markets are often visible much sooner and are initially markedly larger than in countries without markets where missing but interdependent institutions lower the effects of the measures undertaken.

Therefore, the easy optimism of some Western experts, based on the experience of Latin American and Asian countries, may seem unfounded. Differences of opinion center less on the choice of measures or their sequence than on the time horizon before these measures raise the level of efficiency in the economy.

My second conclusion concerns the prospects of the post-Soviet-style economies in East-Central Europe *vis-a-vis* that of Eastern Germany. The usual reason underlying the much more optimistic expectations with respect to the latter country is the financial might of Western Germany and the billions of *Deutschmarks* that now flow and will continue to flow eastward in years to come.

I regard this reasoning as a very narrowly focused one. Financial resource flows matter especially where they make it easier to bear the social consequences of a very rapid transition to the market. But what matters even more is the fact that Eastern Germany, instead of building hectically the rudiments of the market system from the ground up, and for some time without visible signs of improvement in efficiency as have Hungary Poland or Czechoslovakia, got at the start all the institutions of the market economy in an already well-developed form. In addition, it received law and order, a stable currency and - last but not least - the pooling of risk given the much larger size of Western Germany. It is these much less often mentioned institutional benefits that the former G.D.R. has received and that the East-Central European countries may capture only with great effort - and only in the longer run.

REFERENCES

Beksiak, J., 1988, 'On Authentic and Socialist Enterprises'. Paper presented at a seminar on Proposals for the Transformation of the Polish Economy. Warsaw, SGPIS, 17-18 November, (in Polish).

Beksiak, J. R. Gruszecki, A. Jedraszczyk, and J. Winiecki, 1989, 'Outline of a Programme for Stabilization and Systemic Change', in The Polish Transformation: Programme and Progress. Centre for Research into Communist Economies, London, July 1990.

Buchanan, J. M., 1979, What Should Economists Do? Liberty Press, Indianapolis, 1979.

Ellman, M., 1989, Socialist Planning, 2nd ed., Cambridge University Press, Cambridge.

Gruszecki, T., and J. Winiecki, 1991, 'Privatization in East-Central Europe: A Comparative Perspective', Aussenwirtschaft, No. 1.

Hayek, F. von, 1973, Law, Legislation and Liberty, vol. 1, Routledge and Kegan Paul, 1973.

Hirschman, A. O., 1981, Essays in Trespassing - Economics to Politics to Beyond. Cambridge University Press, Cambridge.

Jensen, M. C., and W. H. Meckling, 1976, 'Theory of the Firm: Managerial Behavior, Agency Costs and Ownership Structure', Journal of Financial Economics 2(4), 1976, 305-60.

Klaus, V., 1990, 'Political and Economic Reform in Eastern Europe: The Case of Czechoslovakia', MPS General Meeting: 'Europe in an Open World Order, Munich, 2-8 September.

Kornai, J., 1979, 'Resource-Constrained versus Demand-Constrained Systems', Econometrica 47(4), 801-19

-, 1986, 'The Soft Budget Constraint', Kyklos, 39(1), 3-30.

Lavoie, D., 1985, National Economic Planning. What Is Left? Ballinger, Cambridge, Mass..

Mises, L. von, (1920), 1935, 'Economic Calculation in the Socialist Commonwealth', in: Collectivist Economic Planning: Critical Studies on the Possibilities of Socialism, edited by F. von Hayek. Routledge and Sons, London.

Ohashi, T. M., 1980, 'Privatization in Practice: The Story of the British Columbia Resources Investment Corporation', in: Privatization in Theory and Practice, edited by T. M. Ohashi and T. P. Roth. The Fraser Institute, Vancouver.

Simon H. A., 1987, 'Politics as Information Processing', LSE Quarterly 1(4), 345-70.

Szymanderski, J., and J. Winiecki, 1989, 'Dissipation de la rente, managers et travailleurs dans le systeme sovietique: les implications pour un changement du systeme, Revue d'etudes comparatives Est-Ouest, 20(1)

Winiecki, J, 1987, 'Why Economic Reforms Fail in the Soviet System. A Property Rights-Based Approach', Institute for International Economic Studies Seminar Paper No. 374, Stockholm, January.

-, 1989a, 'Large Industrial Enterprises in Soviet-Type Economies: The Ruling Stratum's Main Rent-Seeking Area', Communist Economies 1(4), 363-83.

-, 1989b, "How To Get the Ball Rolling." Financial Times, 13 January.

-, 1989c, 'Privatization en las economias de tipo sovietico', Estudios Economicos, no. 4, 1989c, 145-63.

-, 1990, 'Heilsamer Druck. Ostreformen: Realistische Zahlen' Wirtschaftswoche, no. 44, 1990, l04-06.

-, 1991a, Resistance to Change in the Soviet Economic System. Routledge.

-, 1991b, 'On Inevitability of Output Fall in Early Transition to the Market: Theoretical Underpinnings', Soviet Studies, no. 4.

The author would like to thank Ms. Pamela Martin, Economic Inquiry copyeditor, for her valuable assistance in the writing and editing of this manuscript.

CHAPTER 10

POLITICAL ECONOMY
OF 'BIG BANG'

INTRODUCTION

The most vocal debate on the transition of Eastern Europe to democracy and capitalism has been, of course, one between those who believed in the aim of establishing a capitalist market economy (whether or not unencumbered with a dose of state intervention) and those who would rather see post-communist countries moving along some more or less unspecified 'third road'. This put both free marketeers and new Keynesians, whose macroeconomic views dominate the thinking of international financial institutions, in one camp. Both criticised the so-called gradualists who, directly or indirectly, usually showed their sympathy for the search for alternatives. (...)

'BIG BANG' VS. GRADUALISM REVISITED

Architects of the 'heterodox' stabilization *cum* liberalization, i.e. new Keynesians, and free marketeers have been much closer on other than macroeconomic management issues and could therefore agree on a range of arguments in the area of general economic theory and institution-building, including privatization. These arguments largely supported the 'big bang' concept and its political economy implications.

To begin with, both groups of analysts agreed with the argument of interrelatedness that spoke in favour of a 'big bang'. The economy is an interrelated whole, not an unrelated collection of bits and pieces, as stressed by a free market-oriented practitioner, former minister of finance and architect of New Zealand's far-reaching liberalization [Douglas, 1989 and 1990]: The same views were expressed by economists belonging to both persuasions [see, e.g., Dornbusch, 1990, and Blanchard *et al.*, 1991 on the one hand; and, e.g., Siebert, 1991, as well as Winiecki, 1989a and 1992a, on the other). Most of them could agree on general equilibrium grounds, except for Hayekians and Schumpeterians, who questioned the usefulness of the general equilibrium approach, but agreed on interrelatedness on other grounds.

An economic argument about the interrelatedness of an economic system **leads to a political economy argument based on the difference between the time of sowing, i.e. creating market institutions, and time of harvesting, i.e. reaping benefits of better performance of the economy** [Winiecki, 1992a]. As there is a time lag between these two periods, it makes good politics to start with a c r i t i c a l   m a s s of measures, or as large a package as possible, to cut short the time span between the beginning of each period. It is also a strong argument in favour of 'big bang' and against gradualism. This is best explained in Figure 1.

As stressed elsewhere by this author [*see the preceding text*], demand for capitalist-economy institutions is very great from the start, while supply - in spite of strenuous efforts - grows only with the passage of time. Improved performance, however, is a result of a substantial narrowing of the gap between demand for and supply of these institutions, illustrated in a stylized manner in Figure 1 as a decrease in the distance between S1 and D.

The start, with a large package of measures, influences the pattern of narrowing this gap. In contrast, spreading the range of measures over a longer period, as suggested by 'gradualists', has adverse implications for performance. It means less coherence between the - necessarily interrelated - rules of the game and less efficient performance of the emerging capitalist market economy over a longer time span. This is illustrated in a stylized manner in Figure 1 by narrowing the gap between S2 (supply of institutions under a gradualist alternative) and D.

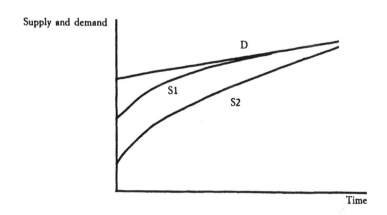

Figure 1. Demand and Supply of Market Economy Institutions

The foregoing means, **in political economy terms,** that **the costs of transition are borne by the society over a longer period, while the benefits of improved performance come later.** Since the political capital of new governments is strongest at the beginning of transition, when there is a lot of enthusiasm about newly-regained freedom and the memory of past failures of the Soviet-type economy (STE) is still strong, **lengthening the time span between the start of transition and the time when the new economic system begins to perform satisfactorily strains the patience of the population.** As such, 'go slow' approach of gradualism endangers the success of transition.

The rapid transition has other political economy benefits as well, also stressed by theorists of both persuasions. It is, thus, emphasised in institutional terms that **the fast speed of transition, characteristic of 'big bang', gives little time to organized interest groups to mount the effective counter-offensive.** This argument is also mentioned by practitioners [see Douglas, 1989 and 1990], as well as political scientists [see, e.g., Haggard and Webb, 1993] but it is doubtful whether this argument retains its strong validity in the post-communist era of transition to democracy and the capitalist market economy.

It should be kept in mind that in these countries there has not only been a deficit of market institutions, but also of political and other institutions mediating between economic agents and those between economic agents and the state. Strenuous efforts have been made to create the former; at the same time, the process of self-organization of society has been taking place. Thus, in the early transition period, when the political capital of new governments has been very high, they faced a largely unorganized society. Old institutions were discredited and, as such, not an effective conduit for demands of group interests, while new ones were in the making (only the Polish 'Solidarity' trade union has been an exception but even that was not very vocal in the early period of high political capital of 'Solidarity'-emanated government).

Yet another argument acceptable to both persuasions was **the credibility-enhancing role of the 'big bang'** [see Douglas, 1989 and 1990, as well as Polish deputy prime minister in 1989-1991 period Balcerowicz, 1992, and Czechoslovak minister of finance and currently Czech prime minister Klaus, 1990]. Interestingly, political scientists see in a large package the opportunity to offer some 'sweeteners' to reduce the resistance of some important interest groups (see, e.g., Waterbury, 1989, and Haggard and Webb, 1993), while no practitioner quoted so far dwelled on this aspect of the 'big bang'. On the contrary, **the 'big bang' was seen as a strong signal to the population that the government was serious about transition,** and the breadth of measures included in the particular package excludes the probable rollback, as often happened with various piecemeal reforms in the communist past.

Representatives of both theoretical persuasions, as well as practitioners, saw **the need to proceed with privatization as fast as possible,** even if not all practitioners agreed on what was the speediest way possible [see Gruszecki and Winiecki, 1991 and Winiecki, 1992d]. Theorists of both persuasions agree that speed is essential. As Dornbusch [1990] rightly stressed, in the case of privatization it was more important to do it fast than to do it right. Therefore various shortcuts should be tried. Usually the Czechoslovak style 'citizens' privatization' was preferred, but political economy considerations added important concessions to employees as a necessary part of any shortcut privatization [see, e.g., Lipton and Sachs,

1990, on the one hand and Beksiak et al., 1989, and Giersch, 1991, on the other]. There were, however, it should be noted, staunch critics of any shortcuts also among free market-oriented economists [see Kornai, 1990].

Yet another aspect of privatization could be used as a political economy argument in favour of a 'big bang', including as fast privatization as possible in the package. As is argued convincingly, the allocation of resources by non-owners is not only less efficient because of wrongly structured wealth incentives and the skewed distribution of risk, but also due to the great opportunity for corruption resulting from the situation where old controls by the state apparatus are even less strong than in the communist past, while opportunities for corrupt deals, profiting managers at the expense of the owner (ultimately, society) increase sharply. Since cases of unjustified enrichment by the *nomenklatura*-appointed managers provoked much of hostility [see, e.g., Winiecki, 1989b], the reduction of that opportunity through rapid privatization seemed preferable [see Schrettl, 1991]. Nonetheless, at the same time there was the understanding that doing things fast meant that not all would be done well - and that governments should be prepared to take the flak on the various occasions where (unavoidable) errors were made [see DeMuth, 1990]. It is interesting, however, that although arguments in favour of a 'big bang' were compelling both in terms of economics and political economy, they did not help to establish (or coalesce around) some rudiments of transition theory. The next section tries to put the foregoing into some systematizing format, using both neo-institutional classical writings and recent publications.

POLITICAL ECONOMY-SENSITIVE TRANSITION STRATEGY: A SYSTEMATIC APPROACH

Some most recent writings by Balcerowicz [1993] and Levy [1993] seemingly try to correct this deficiency. To begin with the former, Balcerowicz points to **the existence of what he calls periods of 'extraordinary politics' following major discontinuities in countries' history**. During these periods the level of readiness of a society to accept far reaching economic changes increases sharply. Over time, however, the 'extraordinary politics' gives way to the ordinary politics as described by public choice theorists, and readiness to accept radical changes (with their inevitable economic and non-economic costs) declines also to a level normal for a given society [Bruno, 1992, calls it the effect of 'reform fatigue']. **The strategy of a politician who tries to accomplish such radical changes is to try to implement as large a package of measures as possible during the period of 'extraordinary politics'**, thus tapping the political capital of the period following a discontinuity.

Unfortunately, the implementation of various components of a 'big bang' package takes more time in some than in others, [with] institutional change (and especially privatization) requiring much more time than stabilization and liberalization. Therefore, an important part of the transition has to take place under much less propitious circumstances, i.e. after the political capital of the period of 'extraordinary politics' has been exhausted. However, Balcerowicz does not offer a clue as to how to pursue transition strategy afterwards.

Although Balcerowicz presented his scheme within the framework of transition of post-STEs, it certainly has a more general validity. So has another scheme presented by Levy within the framework of his study of political and organizational capabilities as determinants of trade and investment reform programs in LDCs, using a two-variable scheme that is reproduced in Figure 2.

Levy defines political obstacles as those related to costs imposed on interest groups in the society that are important to government or even to the stability of the regime. Organizational obstacles stem from the fact that government bureaucracy is unable to implement successfully the reform-related tasks. The tabular form of Figure 2 with its dichotomous High/Low classification immediately separates uninteresting and interesting cases. Quadrants I and IV, where both capabilities are alternatively low or high, obviously belong to the former category. Levy rightly stresses that in the case of low political and organizational capabilities the probability of success is close to zero, while in the alternative case success seems assured.

Much more interesting are cases from Quadrants II and III. Levy's prescription for the case of high organizational capability and low political capability (Quadrant III) is to apply Hirschman's [1963] concept of

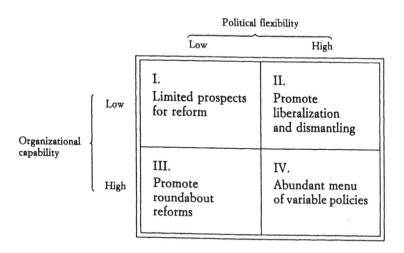

Figure 2. The Impact of Political and Organizational Capabilities
on the Design of Reform Programs

roundabout reforms. Rather than tackling head-on powerful interest groups benefiting most from inefficient policies, the government should try to strengthen the constituency for further reforms by providing opportunities for efficient economic agents. Cases from Quadrant II face the opposite problem, namely low organizational capability and high political capability. Levy's approach here is to concentrate on a few tasks essential for success of reforms which should be pursued with the support of specialists from abroad, while all other elements of the package should not be organizationally intensive (Levy calls them "stroke-of-the-pen reforms"). The scheme is interesting as it brings another variable (organizational capability) into the picture. However, its disadvantage is that it is static. There is no time frame. Countries belong either here or there. We learn nothing as to what happens, for example, if political capability declines over rime (although some answers are implicit in Levy's scheme).

Therefore, the present writer sees an advantage in amalgamating both approaches by drawing on Balcerowicz with respect to the time frame, that is, stages of transition, and on Levy with respect to the level of competence frame, that is, the organizational capability associated with preferences for certain types of measures.

Neither the scheme proposed by the present writer nor those of both authors referred to above are completely new. The situation Balcerowicz refers to is best understood within the framework of North's [1979] concept of 'social reformers'. The presence of such reformers signifies the departure from the situation, where the state acts in a predatory manner, thus enhancing attempts to reduce transaction costs in the economy. Also, following Olson in his 'Rise and Decline of Nations' (1982), the scheme in question stresses major discontinuity as a source of improved performance made possible by the weakening of interest groups resulting from the discontinuity in question.

Apart from the previously mentioned relationship to Hirschman, Levy's scheme also bears some similarity to another, albeit less well known Olson's concept. In Olson's [1987] view, it is only at a more developed stage, when organizational capability improves significantly, that the state can afford to become more interventionist, launching various sophisticated schemes which are impossible to implement properly and at a bearable cost at lower development levels. As seen from the last two paragraphs, the schemes in question have a distinguished neo-institutionalist pedigree. The present writer posits that we may gain some understanding of the political economy of transition by applying Olson's modified scheme, based on changes of political capital over time and changes in organizational capacity (also over time), to transition measures.

'Big Bang' and After

A look at the critical mass of measures called 'big bang' from this perspective brings a better understanding of various transition phenomena. First of all, it supports the 'big bang' approach as such *vis-à-vis* the 'gradualist' alternative. At the start, political support for radical change was undoubtedly very high (to be more precise, this author refers only to countries where political change had already been accomplished before the beginning of economic change [see Winiecki, 1990 and 1992e]). As proper for the period of extraordinary politics, such a situation called for a large package of measures whose composition, however, should be decided on the basis of another variable in our scheme, namely organizational capability.

By and large post-communist countries cannot be said to have high organizational capability in terms of modern public administration. It varies across countries, of course, as some of them (the Czech Republic and, to a smaller extent, Hungary) had the tradition of good public administration in pre-communist times, but even there half a century of corrosive communist influence did great damage. Therefore, Levy's prescription should apply here, namely that absolutely essential organizationally-intensive measures should be included in the package, while all other measures should emphasize the dismantling of existing barriers rather than modifying complex schemes.

In the view of the present writer, both stabilization *cum* liberalization and institutional change (including privatization) as parts of the 'big bang' fit reasonably well into the prescriptions generated by the scheme. Organizationally-intensive essentials of establishing foundations of macroeconomic management had to be pursued regardless of difficulties. At the same time, other measures were of the deregulation type, i.e. dismantling existing barriers. Price liberalization, foreign-exchange liberalization (introduction of limited convertibility), elimination of a large part of production subsidies, etc. are precisely the 'stroke-of-a-pen' reforms - in Levy's term - that are absolutely essential but, fortunately, do not require high organizational capability.

On the institutional - change side, almost all the measures require high organizational capability (changes in the taxation system, customs system, changes in or - indeed - the establishment of a rudimentary financial system, etc.). Therefore they had to proceed at a rather slow pace. An exception was the dismantling of barriers to expansion of the 'generic' private sector, that is, the one established from scratch (rather than being transformed into private from state or cooperative ownership). This process is sometimes called privatization 'from below' [see, e.g., Gruszecki and Winiecki, 1991].

A questionable departure from the organizational capability-based prescription has been **various schemes of wage control**, criticised by free marketeers. Let it be noted that these schemes **are questionable also from**

the political capital time-frame viewpoint. As stressed already at the start of transition [see, *inter alia*, Beksiak *et al.*, 1989, Beksiak and Winiecki, 1990], these schemes are also political capital-reducing ones, as they shift the conflict from the microeconomic to the macropolitical level. It is the government that becomes a party to every conflict resulting from wage claims in state-owned enterprises. As a result, **political capital tends to be dissipated at a faster rate than under the wage-liberalization alternative.**

In reality, the outcomes were far worse. The said departure - that is, unfortunately, at the same time a linchpin of a 'heterodox' programme - not only contributed to faster erosion of political capital but, in consequence, also shifted politically difficult decisions from the period of 'extraordinary' to that of 'ordinary' politics. Closing unprofitable firms, especially large SOEs is always difficult. It might have been easier, however, to do it when people were more ready to make sacrifices.

But the rejection of free marketeers' reasoning that the price of labour should be freed together with freeing other goods and factor prices (at least in the competitive sector), led to *de facto* **postponement of bankruptcies.** Wage controls of one sort or another made it more difficult for enterprises to price themselves out of the market *via* wage and, consequently, cost and price increases that were negatively verified by the market. With fewer (Hungary) or almost no (former Czechoslovakia and Poland) enterprises going bankrupt in the period of early transition euphoria, **the politically very sensitive task was shifted to a period when its implementation was known to be much more difficult.** Delays in structural adjustment and structural change resulting therefrom make the political economy of transition under the 'heterodox' programme much more difficult than under its free market alternative.

The application of the modified Balcerowicz/Levy scheme helps to explain the relative success of some measures *vis-à-vis* others included into the package. Price liberalization, as a 'stroke-of-a-pen' measure, is easier to implement than, say, tax-system changes, and although the latter belong to essentials they cannot be expected to succeed in the time span of 'extraordinary politics'. Continued in times of 'ordinary politics' they become an object of criticism from those who tend to lose from proposed changes (quite apart from criticism of more or less obvious conceptual and implementational errors!).

The scheme also helps to explain the relative success of privatization 'from below' (expansion of the generic private sector) versus privatization 'from above' (ownership transformation). The dismantling of existing barriers to entrepreneurship comes easier due to the nature of necessary measures that are not organizationally intensive, while privatization requires a very dense legal, administrative and financial framework of rules, as well as private and public sector suppliers of necessary privatization-related services. As an aside, it should be noted that even various privatization 'shortcuts' are markedly more organizationally intensive than the simple dismantling of barriers. For these reasons, the fast-growing share of the private sector in employment and GDP in post-STEs is to a much greater extent the outcome of privatization 'from below' than 'from above'.

The scheme also gives us political economy-based clues as to how to proceed when political capital changes over time, i.e. its level falls from the heights achieved during the period of 'extraordinary politics' to the level more normal for periods of 'ordinary' politics. However, before entering the field of policy recommendations, this author turns first to the political economy consequences of the legacy of the STE past for the transition process. For it is the opinion of the present writer that only after combining insights from the preceding considerations with those from system-specific knowledge of the past may a clearer set of recommendations emerge.

As stressed strongly by this author (most recently in Winiecki, 1993c) the use of knowledge about the STE past would strongly affect predictions of the outcome of early 'heterodox' stabilization programmes applied throughout East-Central Europe. Output would be expected to fall sharply (as it duly did) and inflation, after an initial sharp acceleration and deceleration, would continue at a relatively high rate for quite some time. Such expectations of the behavior of a real economy must of necessity alter political economy reasoning of governments and ruling coalitions in countries in transition.

A strategy based on catchy slogans such as: 'First, a short period of severe belt tightening and later a marked improvement' (a promise of the first

Polish post-communist government) was clearly not viable in the medium
run. Medium, not short run, because a period of macroeconomic difficulties would obviously - in terms of the scheme applied in this article -
stretch beyond the period of 'extraordinary politics' and the associated
greater willingness of the public to bear the costs of transition. Policy-
makers would have to face the fact that severe problems would still persist
under politically much more difficult conditions, when the population's
dissatisfaction increased significantly, while political opposition and
newly formed (or reformed) representations of interest groups began to
press their demands with greater force than before.

The use of STE knowledge, if applied in economic policy-making of
post-STEs, might result in some positive corrections of actual outcomes.
Somewhat less stringent monetary restraint at the start and later avoidance
of large swings in money supply [see, *inter alia*, Winiecki, 1992e and
1993c] would create a better environment for adjustment of state and private enterprises. Furthermore, the proposed limitation of access to credit
for the largest state-owned enterprises (SOEs) would improve that access
for relatively more efficient medium-sized state enterprises, reinforcing
their capacity to adjust. Also, better understanding of the pattern of SOEs'
profitability at the beginning of transition could result in some fine-tuning
of the process of reducing the level of subsidies.

However, the present writer is convinced that the effects of all these
corrections to macroeconomic policy would counterbalance only in part
the output, employment and wage level-reducing impact of unavoidable
fundamental adjustment of post-STEs in transition. This, in turn, means
that not only institution-building, including privatization, but also a difficult macroeconomic situation - even if somewhat less difficult than has
been the case - would be carried into a period of "ordinary politics".

RECOMMENDATIONS FOR THE UNAVOIDABLE
PERIOD OF 'ORDINARY POLITICS'

Some policy recommendations are - as signaled in the preceding section -
implicit in the modified Balcerowicz/Levy scheme applied here. Once the

early enthusiasm evaporates and resistance to change increases, the bunching of a large package of measures ('big bang') ceases to be a viable option. Even a continuation of the same package may meet too strong a resistance of absolute or relative losers, whether short-term or long-term ones. Evidently, at least some modifications of the strategy are called for.

The modified scheme calls for increasing the role of 'stroke-of-pen' measures, not requiring high organizational capacity, in the mix of transition measures. Also, following Hirschman's [1963] concept of 'round about reforms', **the second phase of transition should promote measurers that strengthen the position of efficient economic actors in the economy.** It is these actors that, by and large, make a constituency in favour of a transition to the capitalist market economy, and their increasing numbers and better performance improve the probability of success. Thus, the strategy for the second phase should avoid - to the extent possible, of course - head-on conflicts with interest groups hostile to change (first of all with the public enterprise sector, especially large SOEs that were traditionally the beneficiaries under the STE regime).

The foregoing means that **measures strengthening the private sector,** especially the non-agricultural private sector, **should weigh much more than in the earlier phase.** Only the fast expansion of the private sector may, over time, alter the balance of power in domestic politics to the advantage of those in favour of transition.

There are still some inherited idiocies from the communist past, the dismantling of which may facilitate the expansion of the private sector. However, over time, the weight of organizationally-intensive measures supporting the private sector will necessarily increase. Thus, first of all, the second stage of transition should include institution-building measures creating a financial sector more responsive to the needs of small and medium-sized firms. Also, support should be given to private entrepreneurs willing to buy SOEs. It is obvious that profits generated in their original, even fast expanding, private firms would be insufficient to take over SOEs with much higher asset value.

Here, however, conflicts are probable, since neither managers and trade unionists, nor workers in targeted state-owned enterprises are often willing to accept external owners. The former would usually lose their position or influence, while the latter would have to work harder. And, after decades of moral corrosion under communism, better pay and opportunities for advancement (without *nomenklatura!*) may not necessarily be seen as an acceptable *quid pro quo*. Wherever such resistance is encountered (strongest in Poland, Slovenia and in successor states to the former Soviet Union), a 'roundabout' approach should be used in privatization.

If no other option seems able to overcome the resistance of insiders (managers, trade unionists and workers), employee-share ownership (ESOP) should be offered to pacify the resistance [on this, see Winiecki, 1992d]. The present writer's expectations, reinforced by experience, are that, in the short-to-medium run, these enterprises would be threatened at worst with bankruptcy and at best would encounter an investment barrier to even simple reproduction, let alone expansion. In such circumstances external core investor would become much more welcome. And it is only then that financial opportunities for a private entrepreneur willing to undertake such buy-in would become available.

This author agrees with a possible criticism that some of those enterprises may turn out to be beyond rescue after their ESOP experience but this criticism goes only so far. In the second phase of transition, first-best solutions from the economics viewpoint are often unavailable and, accordingly, second-best ones should be implemented (in fact, some first-best solutions may not be available even in the first phase of 'extraordinary politics'). And second-best solutions are clearly more costly.

Next, promoting further economic openness and/or defending against encroachments upon it belong to the same category of measures crucially important for the performance of a much more flexible and outward-oriented private sector. Openness of the economy is very important for its further growth (...).

Some otherwise popular measures such as strengthened law enforcement also indirectly favour the private sector whose ability to pursue business opportunities is hampered by the rules' instability, non-uniform application of these rules, and, last but not least, corruption. Strengthening the judiciary, the establishment of a framework allowing for private arbitration, as well as improving enforcement - all belong to that category. Less popular will be measures promoting the shift of private economic activity from the unregistered ('grey') to the registered economy. This writer agrees with Kornai [1992] that modifications of fiscal rules should increase incentives to obey the law. Senseless persecutions will only push many of those operating in the 'grey' economy deeper into illegality, and deter many others even from trying to be entrepreneurial. Clearly, both carrot and stick should be used in the attempts to bring the 'grey' sector within the law. Even the proposal of partial tax abolition, however, meets with indignant howls of believers in 'absolute' justice in some countries (e.g. Poland).

It is worth noting that there are interlinkages between various private sector-strengthening measures recommended here. Turning again to Kornai [1992], private businessmen look at the possible shift to the registered economy in terms of a trade-off. They may consider giving up some income (that is, pay taxes) in return for legal protection, and an opportunity to benefit from facilities whose use is impossible while they remain in a 'grey' economy. For example, the already recommended improved access of entrepreneurs to the services of the financial sector (better access to credit and other financial services) may become a carrot, enticing private entrepreneurs to move out of the shadows of 'grey' economy.

The inverse of recommendations to strengthen the more efficient private sector through the use of 'roundabout' measures should be **recommendations to weaken (or reduce the extent of losses resulting from the activities of) politically strong but economically inefficient economic agents in the public enterprise sector**. These are located within that sector in large SOEs. The strongest political pressure against change comes from that quarter and, with reduced room for manoeuvre for the government, **the strategy of attrition** seems the most suitable.

It is obvious that giving in to all demands for the abolition of old debt and new credits and/or subsidies would push economies in transition back to where they started. Thus, **the strategy should be to give as little money as politically feasible** to state mastodons, **support people rather than inefficient production, and if inefficient production cannot be avoided for the foreseeable future, then money should be given on** *quid pro quo* **basis,** i.e. in return for the (enforceable) promise to slim down oversized enterprises. Redundancies should be instituted - to the extent possible - through a wide exit from employment in these enterprises (the departure of pensioners, voluntary departures, etc.) and tightly controlled entry. Attrition, quite apart from economic benefits (lower budgetary expenditure) would generate political benefits over time, since increasingly smaller unprivatized state enterprises would be ever less able to influence political resource allocation (i.e. through the state budget or state-determined credit allocation).

Finally, it should be realized that the resistance to privatization at any cost, including cannibalization of assets by enterprise management and workers, is not necessarily as bad as it is sometimes portrayed. For enterprises whose managers and workers resist privatization, through selling assets and leasing empty factory and office space to obtain money that will enable them to continue as before without privatization, do in fact little else but privatize! Assets that are sold or leased find themselves in the hands of the expanding private sector, while resisting SOEs dwindle into insignificance in terms of assets and output. At a certain point, there will be little else to sell and political clout will not save most of them from bankruptcy. Remaining valuable assets will be sold, again to private entrepreneurs [on this paradox, see Winiecki, 1993b].

Again, an experienced analyst will object here that bankruptcy is not always the most efficient way of reallocating resources - and will undoubtedly be right. The sale of a restructured (and slimmed down!) enterprise as a going concern is quite often more efficient since it allows the retention of a large part of human capital created in the old firm. This more efficient solution is, however, not always a feasible solution in the case of politically-strong state mastodons that resist privatization (or attempts at restructuring by the state before privatization). A more costly solution is simultaneously a more feasible one - and one in accordance with the recommended tactics of avoiding head-on collision with politically strong but economically weak economic agents.(...)

REFERENCES

Balcerowicz, L., 1992, 800 Dni (800 Days), BGW Publishing House, Warsaw, in Polish.

Balcerowicz, L., 1993, 'Common fallacies in the debate on the economic transition in Central and East European countries', EBRD, London, mimeo.

Beksiak, J., *et al.*, 1989, 'Zarys programu stabilizacji i zmian systemowych', Warsaw, September, mimeo (English edition: 'Outline of a programme of stabilization and systemic changes', in: The Polish Transformation: Programme and Progress, CRCE, London, July 1990, pp. 21-59).

Beksiak, J., and J. Winiecki, 1990, 'A comparative analysis of our programme and the Polish government programme', in: The Polish Transformation: Programme and Progress, CRCE, London, July 1990, pp. 9-18.

Blanchard, O., *et al.*, 1991, Reform in Eastern Europe, The MIT Press, Cambridge, Mass.

Bruno, M., 1992, 'Stabilization and reform in Eastern Europe: a preliminary evaluation', IMF Staff Papers, Vol. 39, No. 4.

DeMuth, C., 1990, 'Is perestroika possible? Advice from a U.S. deregulator', paper prepared for the Karl Brunner Symposium on Analysis and Ideology, Interlaken, June 4-8, 1990, mimeo.

Dornbusch, R., 1990, 'Priorities of economic reform in Eastern Europe and the Soviet Union', Cambridge, Mass., December 29, mimeo.

Douglas, R., 1989, 'The politics of successful structural reform', paper delivered to the Mont Pelerin Society meeting, Christchurch, November 28, mimeo.

Douglas, R, 1990, 'The politics of successful structural reform', The Wall Street Journal, January 26-27.

Giersch, H., 1991, 'Some general lessons from West Germany's postwar experiences', in: Towards a Market Economy in Central and Eastern Europe (ed. by H. Giersch), Springer, Heidelberg, pp. 1-21.

Gruszecki, T., and J. Winiecki, 1991 'Privatization in East-Central Europe: a comparative perspective', Außenwirtschaft, Nr. 1, pp. 67-100.

Haggard, S., and S.B. Webb, 1993, 'What do we know about the political economy of economic policy reform?', The World Bank Research Observer, Vol. 8, No. 2, pp. 143-168.

Hirschman, A.O., 1963, Journeys toward Progress: Studies in Economic Policy-making in Latin America, Twentieth Century Fund, New York.

Klaus, V., 1990, 'A perspective on economic transition in Czechoslovakia and Eastern Europe', in: Proceedings of the World Bank Conference on Development Economics, 1990, pp. 13-18.

Klaus, V. (an interview in Zemedelske Noviny, February 13), 1991a, 'The economic reform', Czechoslovak Economic Digest, No. 1, pp. 21-22.

Klaus, V., 1991b, 'Main obstacles to rapid economic transformation of Eastern Europe: the Czechoslovak view', in: Towards a Market Economy in Central and Eastern Europe (ed. by H. Giersch), Springer, Heidelberg, pp. 77-91.

Klaus, V. (an interview with), 1992, 'Jestem optymista (I am an optimist, Rzeczpospolita, February 2.

Kornai, J., 1990, The Road to a Free Economy. Shifting from a Socialist System: The Example of Hungary, Norton, New York.

Kornai, J., 1992, 'The post-Socialist transition and the State: reflections in the light of Hungarian fiscal problems', American Economic Review, Vol. 82, No. 2, pp. 1-21.

Levy, B., 1993, 'An institutional analysis of the design and sequence of trade and investment policy reform', The World Bank Economic Review, Vol. 7, No. 2, pp. 247-262.

Lipton, D., and J. Sachs, 1990, 'Privatization in Eastern Europe: the case of Poland', Brookings Papers on Economic Activity, No. 2, pp. 293-341.

North, D.C., 1979, 'A framework for analyzing the state in economic history', Explorations in Economic History, Vol. 16, July, pp. 249-259.

Olson, M., 1982, The Rise and Decline of Nations. Economic Growth, Stagflation and Social Rigidities, Yale University Press, New Haven.

Olson, M., 1987, 'Diseconomies of scale and development', The Cato Journal, Vol. 7, No. 1, pp. 77-97.

Schrettl, W., 1991, 'Structural conditions for a stable monetary regime and efficient allocation of investment: Soviet country study', in: Transformation of Planned Economies: Property Rights Reform and Macroeconomic Stability (ed. by H. Blommestein and M. Marrese), OECD, Paris.

Siebert, H., 1991, 'The transformation in Eastern Europe', Kieler Diskussionsbeiträge 163, Kiel, January.

Waterbury, J., 1989, 'The political management of economic adjustment and reform', in: J. Nelson and contributors, Fragile Coalitions: The Politics of Economic Adjustment, Transaction Books, New Brunswick.

Winiecki, J., 1984, 'The overgrown industrial sector in STEs: explanations, evidence, consequences', Warsaw, mimeo.

Winiecki, J., 1986, 'Are Soviet-type economies entering an era of long-term decline?', Soviet Studies, Vol. 38, No. 3, pp. 325-348.

Winiecki, J., 1987, Economic Prospects: East and West, CRCE, London.

Winiecki, J., 1989a, 'How to get the ball rolling', The Financial Times, January 13.

Winiecki, J., 1989b, 'Wie die Nomenklatura privatisiert', Frankfurter Allgemeine Zeitung, November 28.

Winiecki, J., 1990, 'Political and economic reform in Eastern Europe: the case of Poland,' paper prepared for the Mont Peletin Society General Meeting: 'Europe in an Open World Order', Munich, September 2-8, mimeo.

Winiecki, J., 1991, 'How it all began: sources of the recent breakdown of the Soviet economic system', in: Towards a Market Economy in Central and Eastern Europe (ed. by H. Giersch), Springer, Heidelberg, pp. 55-76.

Winiecki, J., 1992a, 'Shaping the institutional infrastructure', in: The Transformation of Socialist Economies. Symposium 1991 (ed. by H. Siebert), J.C.B. Mohr (Paul Siebeck), Tübingen, pp. 3-19.

Winiecki, J., 1992b, 'The transition of post-Soviet-type economies: expected and unexpected developments', in this Review, No. 181, June, pp. 171-190.

Winiecki, J., 1992c, 'The political economy of privatization', in: Privatization. Symposium in Honor of Herbert Giersch (ed. by H. Siebert), J.C.B. Mohr (Paul Siebeck), Tübingen, pp. 71-90.

Winiecki, J., 1992d, Privatization in Poland. A Comparative Perspective, J.C.B. Mohr (Paul Siebeck), Tübingen.

Winiecki, J., 1992e, 'The Polish transition programme: underpinnings, results, interpretations', Soviet Studies, Vol. 44, No. 5, pp. 809-835.

Winiecki, J., 1993a, Post-Soviet-Type Economies in Transition, Avebury, Aldershot, Hants.

Winiecki, J., 1993b, 'Co dalej z prywatyzacja?' (What to do with privatization?) Rzeczpospolita, March 24.

Winiecki, J., 1993c, 'Knowledge of Soviet-type economy and "heterodox" stabilization-based outcomes in Eastern Europe', Weltwirtschaftliches Archiv, Vol. 129, No. 2, pp. 384-410.

Wyplosz, C., 1992, 'Hard times in Eastern Europe: the economics and politics', paper presented at the 7th Congress of the European Economic Association, Dublin, August 29-31, 1992, mimeo.

CHAPTER 11

PRIVATIZATION: AVOIDING MAJOR MISTAKES*

Economic theory tells us that of the various forms of ownership, private ownership is the most efficient. But theory tells little about how to get from where East-Central Europe is at present to an economy with predominantly private ownership. The ongoing privatization debates reflect uncertainty regarding the proper paths to privatization, as well as conflicting goals and interests. Goals, paths and interests are, in fact, interrelated, adding to the complexity of the problem.

In recognition of this complexity, this [author] will not offer yet another allegedly guaranteed formula for success. It is, rather, **a (probably non-comprehensive) list of major mistakes that can be made with respect to privatization coupled with recommendations on how to avoid them.** The existence of some trade-offs among potential mistakes, however, implies that not all of them can be completely avoided.

The relative success of the East-Central European countries in avoiding these mistakes will be evaluated. The chapter deals only with the post-communist economies of the region. East Germany is excluded from

comparative evaluation for obvious reasons, while Yugoslavia is included (even if it does not fit exactly the 'post-communist' formula at the federal level).

---

* *This is an article published originally as:* Privatization in East-Central Europe: Avoiding Major Mistakes, in: The Emergence of Market Economies in Eastern Europe. *Ed. by Ch. Clague and G. Rauscher,* **Blackwell,** *Oxford, 1992.*

AVOIDING CAPITALISM WITHOUT CAPITALISTS

One of the pitfalls on the path to a capitalist market economy is associated with the muddle over the relationship between private property and the market. The muddle is ideological in its origins. The democratic left is now read to accept the market [see Le Grand and Estrin, 1989]. In fact, after the collapse of state planning, it has little choice! However, a corollary of the market economy is private ownership [for critiques of market socialism, see Baechler 1990 and de Jasay 1990]. But **left-leaning economists, not being able to accept both market and private ownership at the same time, have been busy for some time devising various schemes aimed at the creation of 'capitalism without capitalists'** [Winiecki 1990a].

Although these ideas originate mostly in the West, some of their protagonists have found adherents within East-Central European governments and major political groups. The most fashionable of these illusion-spinning schemes are state holdings, or state investment banks, or 'state-somethings' that are to be allocated a majority of shares in state enterprises turned into joint-stock companies [see Gomulka 1989; Nuti 1988 and 1989; Iwanek and Swiecicki 1987; and Swiecicki 1988]. Bureaucratically appointed managers of such institutions would, then, be expected to simulate the behavior of managers in privately-owned firms in the stock market. They would be given the same rights as shareholders, except that they would not benefit from capital gains or pay the price of capital losses.

At the level of interaction between the state bureaucracy and state enterprise managers, these schemes can be criticized in terms of public choice theory. Politicians and bureaucrats are not impartial umpires deciding on the issues in a disinterested manner. They have their own interests (re-election for the former, empire-building and/or leisure on the job for the latter) which influence their relations with state enterprise managers.

It is an illusion to expect that 'playing at the stock market game' may be more important for both sides of the interaction than these other interests. Monsen and Walters [1983] concluded in their study of West European state enterprises that they had 'not been able to discover a single case of a top executive of a European nationalized company who was replaced for failing to earn a required rate of financial return. By contrast, there are dozens of cases of managers who have resigned in protest, been fired, or were not reappointed because of a major disagreement with their governments over policy'.

At the level of conflict of interest between owner (the state) and manager, illusions of 'capitalism without capitalists' can be criticized in terms of property rights and agency theory. Private ownership links investment decisions to capital gains and losses and is thus more efficient than state ownership, which has much more room for opportunistic behavior on the part of managers. **There is a world of difference between the shareholder who uses his own knowledge or hires a specialist to play the stock market with his own money and a bureaucrat who risks the state's (i.e. taxpayer's) money.** As Kornai [1990] aptly points out, 'simulated joint-stock companies, the simulated capital market, and the simulated stock-exchange' all 'add up to...Wall Street - all made of plastic'.

All of the East-Central European post-communist countries have resisted the temptation to go for a fake rather than a genuine article. In this resistance they have shown greater maturity than some of their Western advisers. Not all of them, however, have avoided another ideological trap. Namely that of a 'third road' in the form of self-managed (or labor-managed) firms and their more recent successor, employee share ownership (see the critique in Gruszecki and Winiecki [1991]).

These illusions have been - not surprisingly - strongest in Yugoslavia, where it is planned to sell up to 60 percent of share value to employees in each enterprise. The non-transferability of shares is to be introduced for an unspecified period. Employee-owned firms of that sort are only marginally better in efficiency terms than labor-managed firms [Gruszecki and Winiecki 1991]. Their successes, alleged or real, should be seen in the context of the market dominance of privately-owned firms that force efficient behavior on employee-owned firms.

If employee-owned firms become the dominant form of ownership, however, their deficiencies, known from property rights and agency theory, will leave a strong imprint upon their performance - and on that of the economy as a whole. In Yugoslavia all 'third road' attempts stem also from the interest of the communist ruling elite to perpetuate themselves in power. They are also increasingly perceived as a vehicle of Serbian domination over the more capitalist-oriented northern republics: Slovenia and Croatia.

In Poland, however, a lobby in favor of self-management in the recent past and of employee share ownership currently is strongly linked to the victorious 'Solidarity', unfortunately giving these concepts enhanced credibility. The Polish government has wisely resisted attempts at making either of these ideas a dominant form of denationalization, but the pressure continues to be strong. Hungary is the country where these 'third road'" illusions are weakest.

THREE MOST DAMAGING MISTAKES

There are many ways in which privatization could go wrong, quite apart from opting for 'capitalism without capitalists' or some 'third road'. Three errors, in particular, are likely to be the most damaging for successful privatization, namely: (1) concentrating upon the means or methods of privatization before considering its goals; (2) neglecting the time factor; and (3) disregarding the politics of privatization.

Some countries, lured by the glamour of British-style privatization through public sale of shares of enterprises, have concentrated on this particular method to the detriment of **clear thinking of what they want to achieve**. If the goal has been 'people's capitalism' (with as wide a dispersion of ownership as possible), then British-style privatization would be a conceivable means to achieve it. But the United Kingdom already had a well-established capitalist class, while the East-Central European countries do not. **Since the kernel of the capitalist market system is, not surprisingly, capitalists - people who take capital risk - the transition to the capitalist market economy should entail measures that support the emergence of capitalists.**

A sale of small lots of shares to the general public is not helpful in this respect. At least some other means, such as sale of small and medium-sized enterprises to private individuals or small groups of individuals, or sale to foreigners of some enterprises or controlling blocks of shares, should also be considered.

The first Polish non-communist government gave its highest priority to designing the rules for British-style privatization. But the rather not unexpected result was that it had continuously to scale down its public-sale-based privatization plans, from 150 privatized enterprises in 1990 to 50 and, finally, to 5 enterprises privatized by January, 1991. At that rate privatization would last several hundred years. Privatization of commercial real property (shops, restaurants, pharmacies, etc.) is proceeding at varying speed in different areas, while the sale of small state-owned enterprises has not really even begun.

Hungary did not completely avoid the lure of the tried and tested British-style privatization. However, the government has understood well the need to foster a domestic capitalist class, and has, therefore, been more active in selling small and medium-sized enterprises to domestic entrepreneurs. At the same time, it also has understood the need for ownership control over management and is generally concerned about finding buyers of a controlling block of shares.

Czechoslovakia, a late starter, has followed a markedly different privatization path, particularly with regard to larger state-owned enterprises. It began the process of selling off small state enterprises and commercial property in early 1991. Yugoslavia, with its unfinished political change and communist influence, has in its privatization program given a high priority only to the conversion from labor-managed firms to employee share ownership.

The second major mistake is to forget that various methods of privatization require differing time spans for implementation - and time is a scarce commodity for countries in transition to the market system. A propensity for state enterprise managers to overinvest and generally use more resources in times of expansionary macroeconomic policy is well known. An economy with a predominantly state ownership is unbalanced by definition and is also inflation prone. (Recent Polish experience showed that in times of restrictive macroeconomic policy, such an economy is unbalanced and recession prone [see Winiecki 1990b]).

Accordingly, privatization should proceed rapidly to change the highly unsatisfactory ownership structure in favor of privately-owned firms. It is here that the British-style privatization reveals its major weakness in the East-Central European context. Asset valuation, preparation of prospectuses for would-be buyers, advertising campaigns, and, finally, public subscription all require time. The privatization of one or two dozen enterprises in the United Kingdom took more than a decade.

Could the East-Central European countries with their thousands of state enterprises, not to mention their rudimentary financial markets, follow that pattern? After persisting in this illusion for some time, the Polish government (both the previous Mazowiecki and the present Bielecki one) began to search for more rapid means of privatization that could be applied in parallel with public sales of shares. Czechoslovakia recognized from the start that public sales could last for decades, if not centuries, and opted for a free (or almost free - there are nominal charges only) distribution of a large part of state industrial assets to its citizens according to a voucher scheme entitling them to receive shares in enterprises of their own choice up to the value of the voucher. Only Hungary has stuck to the idea of the 'businesslike' (i.e., sales only) privatization that may last for decades.

Kornai [1990] has cautioned that *embourgeoisement* is a long process and has warned against 'instituting private property by a cavalry attack'. However, an acceleration of this process should not be regarded as impossible [see Beksiak, et al. 1989; see also Gruszecki and Winiecki 1991]. If the alternative is half a century to a century of privatization, shortcut privatization is not only possible but also highly desirable. **The costs of decades of dominance of state ownership will certainly be higher than those resulting from unavoidable problems associated with the free distribution of state assets to citizenry.** Quite a few analysts in East-Central Europe and elsewhere have agreed with this conclusion.

The last major mistake to be considered concerns the neglect of building a constituency for privatization. After all, **it is a major political change and, as such, coalitions supporting the change are needed.** 'People's capitalism', the wide distribution of the ownership of financial assets, is an approach that may under proper circumstances (as in the United Kingdom, for example) receive wide acceptance. However, the impoverished populations of the post-communist countries are clearly unable to buy, even at discounted prices, the bulk of state industrial assets.

Therefore, free distribution to the population is preferable for reasons of both political efficacy and equity. **Free distribution would generate more political support than sale, which would give too large a share to the hated communist *nomenklatura*.** Political efficacy considerations suggest yet another rationale for free distribution of state assets to the population. The population at large may be the only constituency that can be organized to resist the claims of a less numerous but already better organized constituency: employees of large state-owned enterprises who prefer the free distribution of assets to employees over distribution to the population at large.

The previous Polish government failed to recognize the importance of building a political constituency, although its single-minded pursuit of British-style privatization did not give it much of a chance to find one. Hungary fares better only because employee ownership is not so popular there, but the insistence on the sale of assets rather than free distribution limits grass roots support for privatization.

Czechoslovakia, with its free distribution scheme, seems to have generated greater popular support for privatization. In Yugoslavia, the idea of selling rather than giving shares in enterprises to their employees did not win much enthusiasm. Workers are already receiving the benefits of ownership without having to pay for the shares.

Summing up, when it comes to avoiding the most damaging mistakes Czechoslovakia is clearly in the lead, with Hungary next, Poland coming in a poor third, and Yugoslavia bringing up the rear. Not only has Yugoslavia made all three mistakes discussed here (as has Poland to some extent), but it is on an altogether wrong track - an as yet incompletely defined "third road".

One *caveat* is necessary at this point. It is not possible to avoid all mistakes, simultaneously. For example, if Czechoslovakia decides to speed up the privatization process by the free distribution of a large part of state industrial assets (through the voucher scheme), then it will privatize sooner than other post-communist countries of East-Central Europe. Most probably, the privatization will also be smoother due to greater political support. But this choice entails costs as well as benefits. Free distribution leads to large dispersion of ownership with all the attendant costs of weaker control by owners over managers. Although it is expected that the process of reconcentration would start soon, the *interim* period would be one of weaker performance than under traditional capitalist control with clearly identifiable owners of the controlling block of shares. To lower these unavoidable costs somewhat, the privatization should envisage a mix of methods. A combination of free distribution of assets to citizens could be combined, for example, with a small scale (10-20 percent) free distribution of shares to employees. This combination would create the clearly identifiable group of owners right from the start. Of course, there are disadvantages to even temporary employee control: shares would not be concentrated in the hands of a group willing to effect radical change in the organization.

THE INSURANCE PRINCIPLE

The last issue to be considered is the choice of the one and only versus that of many methods of privatization. **Given the fact that the road to success is unknown, a simultaneous application of a broad array of privatization approaches is another insurance against failure.** Sale of small and middle-sized enterprises to individuals, sale of some larger firms to foreigners, free distribution of shares in most larger firms to citizens - all these are complementary rather than competing solutions.

Those countries employing simultaneously a variety of approaches stand a better chance of success. Hungary appears to be in the lead in this respect, with Poland ahead of Czechoslovakia (perhaps due to the head start of the transition in Poland). While considering a broad array of privatization approaches as an insurance against failure under high uncertainty, yet another issue should be noted. The analysis here has focused on what Gruszecki [1990] and Gruszecki and Winiecki [1991] call 'privatization from above', or the reassignment of property rights of the formerly state-owned enterprises. On the other hand, the success of the change in the ownership structure of post-communist economies depends also on the 'privatization from below', that is, on the unfettered establishment and expansion of private firms.

These considerations of **not putting all eggs in one basket** would be incomplete without mentioning the demand for the creation of a network of market institutions attuned to the needs of the expanding private sector (at this stage, composed almost exclusively of small businesses). Small business development banks, agricultural development banks, small business-oriented insurance companies, innovation centers, and venture capital institutions are urgently needed as ingredients for success.

There is a bias in governments' efforts in favor of the more glamorous aspects of institution-building: establishment of the two-tier banking system, privatization of large state enterprises, and the establishment of a stock market. But small businesses, whether privatized or built by their owners from scratch all critically depend for their expansion on a network of institutions that in no post-communist economy are yet in place, even in a rudimentary state. The deficiencies of these institutions are so great in all of the countries in question that no ranking of nations is even possible.

But regardless of ranking, difficulties are enormous everywhere, and many things may happen in East-Central Europe on the way to the future. We do not know all the answers and paths leading from here to there. And let us not forget that 'there', meaning the West, is a moving - not a static - target.

REFERENCES

Beksiak, J., *et al.*, 1990, *The Polish Transformation: Programme and Progress*, Centre for Research into Communist Economies, London.

Gomulka, S., 1989, How to Create Capital Market in a Socialist Country and How to Use It for the Purpose of Changing the System of Ownership. Prepared for the LSE Financial Markets Group Conference on New Financial Markets: Economic Reform in Eastern Europe, mimeo

Gruszecki, T., 1990, Privatization in Poland in 1990. Paper for the Conference on 'Implementation of the Polish Economic Programme', Warsaw, mimeo.

Gruszecki, T., and J. Winiecki, 1991, Privatization in East-Central Europe: A Comparative Perspective, *Aussenwirtschaft*, Vol.46, No.1.

Kornai, J., 1990, *The Road to Free Economy*, Norton, New York.

Le Grand, J., and S. Estrin, Eds.,, 1989, *Market Socialism*, Clarendon Press, Oxford.

Monsen, R.J., and K.D. Walters, 1983, Managing the Nationalized Company, *California Management Review*, Vol.25, No.4.

Nuti, D.M., 1988, Competitive Evaluation and Efficiency of Capital Investment in the Socialist Economy, *European Economic Review*, Vol.32.

- , 1989, Remonetization and Capital Markets in the Reform of Centrally Planned Economies. Prepared for the LSE Financial Markets Group Conference on New Financial Markets: Economic Reform in Eastern Europe, mimeo

Iwanek, M., and Swiecicki, M., 1987, Handlowac kapitalem w socjalizmie (How to trade with capital under socialism), *Polityka*, June 16, in Polish.

Swiecicki, M., 1988, Reforma wlasnosciowa (Ownership Reform). A paper for the seminar on 'Transformation Proposals for Polish Economy, Warsaw, Main School of Planning and Statistics.

Winiecki, J., 1990a, No Capitalism Minus Capitalists, *Financial Times*, June 20.

Winiecki, J., 1990b, Post-Soviet-Type Economies in Transition: What Have We Learned from Polish Transition Programme in Its First Year, *Weltwirtschaftliches Archiv*,Vol.126.

CHAPTER 12

BALANCING THE ECONOMICS AND POLITICAL ECONOMY OF PRIVATIZATION·

Freeing people from the fetters of the economic system of the past will create the opportunity for spontaneous, broadly conceived development of market relations. Yet **this does not relieve the authorities of the need for purposive development of institutions to facilitate and accelerate this process.** (...)

Privatization is an essential element in the whole programme of systemic changes leading to the creation of an efficient market economy. At the same time, we know that privatization of state property - if only in view of the extent and complexity of this undertaking - cannot be regarded as a once-for-all action, but must be a process. Yet this process can be accelerated by a policy of privatisation from above by the state, the creation of economic incentives for privatization, institutions serving the process, etc. For many reasons **there is an urgent need for the government to carry out just such a policy of accelerating privatization.**

For this purpose it is necessary to adopt a privatization programme or, as a minimum, **a [declaration] of guiding principles.** The team sets out proposals in this respect below. But it must be remembered that this is not an autonomous programme. Privatization can be successful only if the

---

* These excerpts are from the Program of Stabilization and Systemic Change, that was prepared in September 1989 by a team of Polish experts [J. Beksiak, T. Gruszecki, A.

economy is liberalized in advance or in parallel with it (...). Stabilization of the Polish economy is also essential, so as to reduce the exceptionally high degree of uncertainty which paralyses the operations of entrepreneurs.

On the basis of analysis of the social discussion about the aims of privatization in the Polish economy and the discussion of the team itself, our team adopted the principle that the main aim of privatization is the creation, in the shortest possible time, of the conditions for the free movement of capital, with a preference for individual private ownership (physical persons and private entrepreneurs) rather than institutional and collective owners. The preferred model of privatization is thus to lead to a rapid increase in the extent and strength of the private sector, the diffusion of ownership and an increasing [numbers] of private entrepreneurs in the economy. In this way the aim of clear identification of the roles of owner and entrepreneur is achieved to some degree automatically. (...)

We draw attention here to **the essential political, psychological and propaganda effect of the proper start to the privatization process.** The conduct of this operation must begin with a political declaration (e.g. a resolution of the Sejm and the Senate) that Poland is setting out irreversibly on the road of development of an economy based on the private sector. Confirmation of the inviolability of private property, e.g. in a change in the Constitution in 1990, would also be expedient.

No less important is that **the declaration of intent should be quickly followed by concrete, broadly conceived measures.** This would be a signal both for Polish society and for abroad (including international financial institutions) that the government intends to carry out real changes in the economic system, rather than - like previous governments - another stage in trying to reform what cannot be reformed.

The team therefore suggests, as the first radical step, a proclamation, say on 1 November 1989 (together with a series of measures in the stabilization programme), that 20% of the shares in each state enterprise employing more than 250 persons on the day of the proclamation and trans-

---

Jedraszczyk, and J. Winiecki] for the parliamentary club of victorious 'Solidarity' movement (an English version, see Beksiak et al., [1990]).

formed into a joint stock company on 1 January 1990 will become the property of the workforce, including management, of these enterprises. These shares will carry the right to vote in elections to the supervisory council (the remaining 80% of the shares, being the property of the State Treasury, would be deprived of these rights until they are sold or possibly transferred to citizens). Whether or not this measure fulfilled, at least indirectly, one of the most important aims of privatization, i.e. broadening the stratum of owners bearing capital risk, it would further the achievement of several other important aims of privatization. Giving the workforce a share in ownership in the way proposed above would:

- lead to the desired diffusion of ownership, hitherto concentrated in the hands of the state, among a significant part of the population;

- transform (...) undefined 'general national property' into unequivocally defined private property;

- facilitate the flow of capital through the stock exchange into the most efficient uses, thanks to guaranteed transferability of shares.

Finally, beside traditional aims of privatization, which are important for privatization in every country, the above measures would solve a problem of fundamental importance for a Soviet-type economy, namely, they would radically shorten the transition period from abolition of the founding organs [respective ministries and agencies] and the *nomenklatura* system to full privatization of enterprises. The transfer of shares carrying the right to vote in elections to supervisory boards to the employees of these enterprises identifies private owners who, until the sale of the remaining 80% of the shares, are - through the supervisory council - the sole decision makers on the affairs of the enterprise.

The team is conscious that **this is not an ideal solution, since identity of shareholders and employees shortens the time horizon for investment** (which is considerably longer in the case of the entrepreneur owners who bear an incomparably greater measure of capital risk). Yet the alternative to the above measure would be to begin what is essentially a long-term process of selling whole enterprises and the shares in enterprises into private hands, without obtaining any speedy and widespread results. **The authors choice is in favour of achieving moderate progress in the efficiency of operation of all enterprises in the short term.**

The formula for the start of the privatization process which we have adopted does not create barriers to the transfer of the remaining part of the enterprises (the 80% of the shares in each of them) into private hands by other methods; such barriers would arise if alternative solutions were adopted for the transition period, e.g. collective ownership (self-management). Thus privatization in the form of sale of the remaining shares to individual private buyers (investors) can be the next step in the process of privatization, fulfilling the aim of identification of owners bearing capital risk.

CHAPTER 13

LESSONS FROM PRIVATIZATION*

To begin with, privatization everywhere started almost immediately after the political change, but what is interesting in almost every country the preference was given to different methods of privatization. So, in Hungary they put most stress on attracting foreign investors as buyers of Hungarian state enterprises, and succeeded in having quite a few major companies sold to key foreign investors, usually large multinational companies.

Poland chose a different path. There, preference of the government was the public sale of shares, that is, the so-called 'classical British-style privatization'. However, *de facto* developments made the actual composition of privatization methods look different because, on the one hand, in Poland there was stronger political resistance to privatization, while on the other, given the strength of Polish trade unions, privatization has shifted much more in the direction of the employee-ownership type of privatization, that is the only one type preferred by union activitists. So, among some 750 state enterprises privatized in Poland (out of about 8,000 existing at the start of transition), about 150 was privatized by either public sale or direct sale to major foreign investors, while the remaining 600 were turned into the so-called 'leasing employee-owned companies', that is, companies that were leased to employees and later, once the lease installments were paid, are to be owned by these employees.

In the Czech Republic, they chose yet another form of privatization, which I am fond of calling "citizens' privatization". There, the government

* This is a section of the written version of my speech in Tokyo about privatization in Eastern Europe, given in October 1995, and later issued in mimeographed form by the hosts, that is Japanese International Cooperation Agency (JICA).

offered vouchers to all citizens willing to buy them, at a token payment, and with those vouchers citizens were able to bid for shares of privatized companies. They could do it directly, or, more often as it turned out, also indirectly *via* mushrooming investment funds.

For a change, in Russia, they took yet another approach. There, not very numerous free marketeers were afraid that they would not be able to overcome the resistance of the old communist *nomenklatura* managers. And therefore, they chose the kind of insiders' privatization, that is, in the case of most enterprises, the majority of shares were distributed to managers and employees of each company, while the minority only was spread across the population at large or sold to foreign investors.

Thus, what concerns privatization lessons, I would venture an opinion that **the first lesson drawn from privatization in the region I am concerned with is that local socio-political conditions determine not only outcomes of the privatization process but also the choice of preferred methods of privatization.** This, in my opinion, would be the first lesson.

The second lesson, and an extremely important one at that, **is that it is necessary to build political support for a major socio-economic change, such as privatization.** And here, as evidence in support of this thesis I would juxtapose the Czech Republic and Poland.

In the Czech Republic the understanding of the need to gain popular support for privatization was clearly understood from very early days of the Czech 'Velvet Revolution'. It started in November 1989, as some of you may remember, and already n e x t   m o n t h Vaclav Klaus, the then Minister of Finance in the Czechoslovak Federal Government, announced the major citizens' privatization scheme. This early promise was very well received by the population, because it was presented as the case of remedying to some extent the wrongdoings of the communist system that, i.a., deprived people of the right to own productive assets. Therefore, the argument run, to compensate people, to some extent at least, so that every citizen will have the right to get the possibility to buy shares of privatized Czechoslovak (later only Czech) enterprises, and, in this way, to become an owner of productive assets.

This 'compensation for communist wrongdoings' approach has been so widely accepted that when left-leaning economists of the 1968 'Socialism with human face' generation offered an alternative solution of employee ownership and ESOP-type firms, they did not fire the imagination of the people who continued their strong support for the early introduced citizens' privatization scheme. Actually, **this privatization scheme, introduced so early and in a way that was so appealing to the sense of justice, contributed importantly to a better reception of the hardships that transition necessarily brings about**, especially in the early stages of the process of moving to a capitalist market economy. For it was seen as a kind of compensation.

Unfortunately, in my own country different ideas prevailed at the early stage. In Poland, there was a very strong trade union with very high political ambitions, I mean 'Solidarity', and therein the Utopian left wing was pressing strongly for their preferred employee ownership method as the dominant method of privatization of state enterprises. However, the government, very much intent on moving toward the capitalist market economy in a well proven manner, did not embrace the idea of the citizens' privatization as an antidote to employee ownership, known from property rights theory as a rather inefficient solution. They preferred a method that has already been proven, meaning the British style public sale of shares, a method that is relatively clear and transparent in the sense that those pursuing it cannot be accused of corrupt deals.

Government decision makers thought that in this way they would protect themselves against attacks of the Utopian wing of 'Solidarity'. However, what they did not realize was that it is not enough to prove that they were honest, but that they should also win people's minds. And this is what they could not achieve with the public sale of shares, and small packages of shares at that, by those willing to bid for those shares. Obviously, this is not the stuff that fires the imagination of the people. And, therefore, privatization in Poland, thanks to the vitriolic campaign of the left-wingers in the 'Solidarity' on the one hand and the nationalists and ex-communists on the other, became a symbol of something shady, suspect, almost an archetype of a swindle. And, therefore, instead of becoming a factor of facilitating transition, it became just the opposite: an albatross around the neck of transition. In consequence not only Polish privatization but also Polish transition has encountered greater resistance than it could have encountered, had privatization choices been different.

So, rephrasing the lesson already formulated above, I would state the following: **Never forget that it is not enough to prove that you are right. You should also try to build a coalition that will allow you to succeed in implementing what you think is right.**

I would now move to yet another issue that also carries an important lesson. Namely, privatization almost everywhere brought about many surprises, both for privatizing authorities and politicians in general. Thus, for example, in Hungary, the conservative government was very distrustful of the old communist *nomenklatura*, and in order to prevent shady deals by which *nomenklatura* could enrich itself, it strongly centralized the privatization process, that is the sale of enterprises. But centralizing the sale, whether the sale of underwear or of enterprises, never works. And therefore, apart from major deals with multinationals that could be relatively easily arranged in a centralized way, there hasn't been much progress in privatization in Hungary. So, as you see, in Hungary actual developments were partly different from government's intentions.

Now, in the Czech Republic, a country probably most successful in privatization of all post-communist economies (this is at least my personal opinion), the guiding idea was also somewhat erroneous because they imagined the Czechs as a society of shareholders. Their main idea was that people who get vouchers all would bid for shares of state enterprises and all would retain and/or trade in those shares.

However, in Czech Republic the distribution of willingness to take risk is not different from that in other countries. Consequently, only a minority could be classified as risk takers, while all the rest have been, as everywhere, more risk averse. Therefore, there has been a room for expansion of various investment funds that took vouchers from people in return for the promise of a steady flow of income to the voucher owners, who entrusted their vouchers to investment funds.

So, in the end, about 75 percent of all vouchers was placed with the mushrooming investment funds, in Czechoslovakia first, and in Czech Republic later. About 25 percent of those who got vouchers decided to bid for shares themselves, which is, I would say, still a strikingly high ratio. It compares favorably with the ratios for Great Britain and the United States, where about 20 percent of the population owns shares, but nonetheless the outcome was different from the ideas held at the start of transition.

In Poland I already signaled the divergence between governmental preferences and the reality. The government preferred the public sale. However, at the enterprise level, trade unionists & employees pressed usually with success for the employee ownership, and as a result, about three-fourths of enterprises were privatized that way. In terms of employment and output the shares are not as unfavorable, because the largest enterprises were sold *via* public sale of shares or sold directly to major foreign investors. Once again, the outcomes were different from those expected.

So, **the third lesson of privatization is, in my opinion, a lesson of humility, a reminder of the fundamental unplannability of social processes.** It follows from the above that the privatization process, given all the possible surprises that we cannot imagine at the start, should allow for as wide a spectrum of privatization methods as possible, which means that there should not be the one and only method applicable in all situations. The range of methods available should be very wide because we never know what socio-political preferences would emerge, what legal obstacles would be encountered, etc.

Yet another lesson concerns linkages between the components of the 'Holy Trinity' I mentioned at the start. There is a need of progressing in all areas developments, in all areas important for transition (even if progress as of necessity not identical). Because if a given country lags in some areas then, unsolved problems in one area become a drag on another. A case of Russia is very illuminating in this respect. In Russia, for political reasons, reformers were unable to pursue consistently macroeconomic stabilization. At the same time, however, privatization team of Russian government succeeded in the first phase of privatization, that is, in making enterprises privately-owned (as I already signaled, largely by 'insiders').

The idea of privatizers was that this should be only the first phase to be followed by further phases of the ownership changes. Only then the structure of ownership would move toward a more efficient one, namely, toward the one in which a core outside investor emerges in most cases. This has been historically proven as the most efficient way of enterprise management, because ownership by insiders distorts enterprise opportunities for the expansion and is even less efficient in the contraction or even stagnation phase.

However, very little happened afterwards because, as I signaled already, the unsolved problems in other areas became a drag on Russian privatization. Foreign investors or domestic private investors are much more ready to invest their financial resources, their time and effort, when certain preconditions are fulfilled in a given country: where there is political stability, macroeconomic stability, stability of rules, and uniformity of implementation of these rules.

The last two variables are most difficult to obtain any time soon everywhere, but the first two certainly have not been present in Russia, either. And, therefore, because of the lack of political and macroeconomic stabilization, with a very arbitrary way, in which government officials were behaving, there have been very little willingness by foreigners and by domestic entrepreneurs to buy into those freshly privatized companies, to buy shares from either managers, or employees, or both. And, therefore, Russian privatized sector at the moment seems to be stuck in the form of private ownership that is known in theory of property rights as maybe the least efficient form of private ownership. It is, maybe, somewhat more efficient than state ownership, but certainly of the forms of private ownership, it should be regarded as the least efficient one.

So, another important lesson of privatization in Eastern Europe is, again, a lesson that **you should not be lagging behind too much in any major area of transition**, because at a certain point it becomes a drag on other areas, as in the case of Russian privatization.

CHAPTER 14

HAYEKIAN LESSON OF
POLISH TRANSITION*

During the whole period of transformation, i.e since the memorable 'Autumn of Nations' in 1989, politicians, analysts and societies in general have concentrated their attention, energy, and resources on privatization, that is the transformation of state ownership into private ownership. Privatization, understood in a manner defined above has been largely seen as a cornerstone of transition to a capitalist market economy in the longer run (please note that the terms: 'transition', 'transformation' and 'systemic change' are used here interchangeably). Private ownership is best performing within the framework of the institutions of the market. There has been a near *consensus* on the latter view (a few utopian strands of economic thinking notwithstanding).

Since this essay concerns Poland more than any other post-communist economy in transition - as a case study for ideas developed here - it is worth mentioning that in Poland the term 'ownership changes' has been used at the start as **a substitute for privatization** (even the ministry that transforms state-owned enterprises into privately-owned ones is called the Ministry of Ownership Changes and not, as is the case with other countries in East-Central Europe, the ministry, or agency, or office of privatization).

This has not been a linguistic slip-up but a **conscious political economy decision** on the side of the team shifting Polish economy onto a path

---

* *This is an abbreviated version of an article that appeared, under the title* The Superiority of Eliminating Barriers to Entrepreneurship over Privatization Activism of the State, *in* **Banca Nazionale del Lavoro Quarterly Review,** *December 1996, No.196.*

of a capitalist market system. For in Poland the resistance to privatization has been stronger than in the other countries in the region. The main source of this stronger resistance have been the *de facto* collectivistic ideological origins of the 'Solidarity' movement under communism and its later activity, consisting of a marriage of a trade union and a *quasi*-political party. I have already discussed this problem elsewhere [Winiecki, 1992 and 1993]. In every post-communist country there have been social-istic opponents of privatization on the left and nationalistic ones on the right. But the uniqueness of the Polish situation consisted of the fact that they were also overrepresented in the systemic change-oriented centre.

Unsurprisingly, stronger resistance to privatization has been translated into a very slow (and fiercely contested) privatization process, as well as meagre privatization effects. Privatization in Poland markedly lags behind that in the Czech Republic, Hungary, and a number of other countries in transition, even those that are not noted for their successes in other areas of systemic change.

At the same time, however, Poland is widely regarded as one the lead-ers in the shift to a capitalist market economy among the countries of the region. Moreover, the share of the private sector in GDP and employment is in Poland about as large as in the countries regarded as success stories with respect to privatizing their economies. What happened? **There is yet another, generally underappreciated, process. It is the development of the generic private sector,** contributing to the growth of the size of the private sector in the national economy. And it is the relative role of the former *vis-à-vis* that of the latter in post-communist transition - and les-sons drawn therefrom - that will come under scrutiny in this article. Poland is taken as the case study, but the Reader will see that the potential for such success exists, under certain conditions, elsewhere as well.

INSIGNIFICANT CONTRIBUTION OF PRIVATIZATION

Privatization does not consist merely of the ownership changes in state-owned enterprises, that is of the privatization activism of the state, but also of the creation of new private enterprises and expansion of those, which already exist and have been privately-owned from the start. This is what the present writer calls the generic private sector. The final objective of privatization is, after all, **the creation of an economy with the ownership structure similar to that of Western countries (that is, at a minimum 85-90% of output of the enterprise sector generated by private firms).**

The foregoing objective can be reached by foregoing two complementary routes. One of these routes attracts everybody's attention; this situation hardly changed since 1989. It is the activism of the state, or the **privatization 'from above'**. Another route may be called, using parallel terminology, **the privatization 'from below'** [for more on this distinction, see Gruszecki and Winiecki, 1991].

With over six years of political system transformation already behind us, it is worth taking a calm look at both these routes. One thing which can be said at the outset is that **in the whole area of public activity - from political conflicts to the allocation of funds - privatization 'from above' has definitely dominated over privatization 'from below'**

It is hardly surprising, though. At the very beginning of the transformation process, politicians, trade union activists and even analysts in Poland and elsewhere noticed almost exclusively the privatization 'from above'. The public sector - in reality, the s t a t e sector - dwarfed the private sector, outside agriculture, with respect to its size. Consequently, **people tied any hope of a successful radical systemic change with the transformation of state-owned enterprises into privately-owned ones.** Or, in accordance with the utopian beliefs still common in Poland in 1989-90, transformation into independent enterprises managed by the workers collectivities. It should be noted that in other countries in the region (except Hungary) the generic private sector had at the start even smaller shares than in Poland.

A legitimate question to ask is the following: to what extent did Polish privatization 'from above' live up to those great expectations? The correct answer, surprising to those who fought - and are still fighting - heroic battles for or against privatization, is that this extent was **very small**. I will support the statement by quoting some numbers. I begin with quoting some independent studies on the subject for one cannot take respective bureaucracies official statements' for granted.

Bobinska [1994] tried to calculate how many state enterprises (SOEs for short) have been privatized and got numbers sharply different from the officials ones. According to official figures of the then latest privatization report of the ministry, 52% of SOEs underwent 'ownership transformation'. However, 'ownership transformation' may mean different things to different people.

A thorough calculation by Bobinska reveals the following: 'Out of a total of 8,441 state-owned enterprises in 1990, 1,595 (18.9%) have been transferred to the State Treasury Agricultural Ownership Agency, i.e. a **state-owned institution**. 263 enterprises (3.1%) were communalized, i.e. taken over by **local governments** and 2,521 (29.9%) were transformed on the basis on the above-mentioned law [of July 1990 - J.W.]. The remaining enterprises have not undergone a n y transformation.' Going below the surface, Bobinska also established that among those enterprises officially described as 'having undergone transformation' only 98 (1.2%) have been transformed into joint-stock companies and have had at least 50% of their stock sold, i.e. have a c t u a l l y been privatized; 424 (5%) have been **transformed but not privatized**; 707 (8.7%) have been liquidated under the terms of Art. 37 of the privatization law of 1990, including 85 enterprises (0.5%) that have been sold. In most of the enterprises, the assets are merely leased and therefore true privatization will have occurred only when they have been paid for in over 50%; 172 enterprises (2%) have also been liquidated according to Art. 19 of the old law on state-owned enterprises; and there are 1,220 enterprises (13.2%) undergoing transformation. At the same time 4,062 enterprises or **nearly half of the total** (48.2% to be exact), have not undergone a n y sort of transformation.

Bobinska concluded that **'over the past four years privatization has been carried out fully and completely in only 1.7% of the enterprises according to the terms of the privatization law'** [of 1990 - J.W.]. Thus, official statements do not present the real picture of Polish privatization.

Barely two percent of enterprises being really privatized, means surprisingly little but one might ask whether the percentage of the enterprises is not a misleading indicator. For it does not take into account the fact that in a communist (Soviet-type) economy - from which Polish post-communist economy emerged - most state-owned enterprises are large and very large, and consequently 1.7% may account for a much higher share of employment and production.

Helpful in answering this query is a study on the growth of the private sector in Poland [Chmiel and Pawlowska, 1996], which estimates the changing shares of the individual types of privatization in the economy as a whole (privatization, referred to by us as privatization 'from above'; re-classification of the cooperative sector from public to private sector, i.e. purely statistical operation; and what we call privatization 'from below'). A very detailed analysis of the quoted pair of authors shows that, quality of the official data notwithstanding, the share of privatization 'from above' in the share of the private sector in GDP and employment is nonetheless very small. It varies from 'imperceptible' (below 1%) to 'perceptible' with the latter term still signifying relatively small shares (that is small relative to the share of privatization 'from below').

In two out of the four branches of the economy which the study examined - transport and trade - the contribution of this type of privatization to total employment stood at significantly less than 1%, and in the two sectors where the authors assessed the share as 'perceptible', i.e. in industry and construction, these shares at the end of 1994 stood at, respectively, 4.4% and 11.3%. The shares in production were not significantly different from the shares in employment. By contrast, the contribution of the generic private sector to total employment stood at 33.2% in industry and 60.7% in construction (shares in aggregate output were respectively over 26% and 73%). The details are shown in Table 1.

Thus, a more detailed analysis confirms the initial assessment that privatization 'from above' does not play any significant role in changing the structure of ownership in the productive sector in Polish transition from socialism to capitalism (furthermore, nothing at all happened in what is called in Western Europe the public sector: from physical infrastructure to health and education).

Table 1. The Share of Private Ownership in Output of Selected Sectors of the Polish Economy, 1989 and 1993 (in %)

Sector Year	Public Sector	Private Sector	of which: Generic Private Sector	of which: Reclassified Co-op Sector b	of which: Privatized Sector
Industry					
1989	84.8	15.2	9.6	7.7	0
1994a	60.6	39.4	30.6	3.5	5.3
Construction					
1989	67.3	32.7	30.0	2.7	0
1994a	13.5	86.5	73.5	0.6	12.4
Transport					
1989	91.0	9.0	6.3	2.7	0
1993	54.8	45.2	44.3	0.8	0.1
Retail Trade					
1989	40.5	59.5	4.8	54.7	0
1994	9.2	90.8	81.5	9.3	0

a Data calculated according to new, slightly different statistical classification of the European Union

b Under the communist system co-operatives were classified as a part of the 'Socialized Sector'. After systemic change it was reclassified as a part of the private sector.

Source: J.Chmiel & Z. Pawlowska, "Sektor prywatny w Polsce, 1990-1994 (Private Sector in Poland, 1990-1994), Zeszyty Centrum im. Adama Smitha, 1996

Given the foregoing, it is all the more important to explain **why in Poland the share of the private sector in the economy as a whole is not much - if at all - lower than in other countries undergoing the transition process,** including those which have had much greater successes in privatization 'from above'. Here I am referring especially to Hungary, which has attracted more of the foreign capital than any other country in the region and the Czech Republic, which has privatized most of the state-owned enterprises through its innovative 'coupon privatization'. The lesson(s) to be learned may be important not only for Poland but also for other transition economies.

CRUCIAL ROLE OF DISMANTLING BARRIERS

At the outset it seems worthwhile to stress what factors, apart from failed privatization 'from above', did n o t decisively contribute to Poland's success. Thus, the reasons for our success surely do not include a particularly stable macroeconomic framework of the privatization process. Although Poland has been relatively successful in managing its stabilization programme, compared to countries of the former Soviet Union or Romania or Bulgaria, it was far from the iron-willed consistency showed in this area by the government of Vaclav Klaus, first in Czechoslovakia and now in the Czech Republic.

Poland was even less notable for the stability of its political situation. Again, compared to post-communist countries with incomplete political change that - in this writer's opinion - is a prerequisite of economic change [see, *i.a.*, Winiecki, 1991] , Poland may be regarded almost as a paragon of political stability. However, political stability is also a relative term. To illustrate the point, the first non-communist Hungarian government, headed by the late Prime Minister Antall from 1990 to 1994, dealt with five Polish prime ministers.

Therefore, we have to look elsewhere for the reasons of our success. I find the reason, first of all, in **a more decisive policy of liberalization and deregulation compared with other countries of the region**. Poland has gone farther than nearly all other countries undergoing transformation in creating conditions allowing private companies an almost unrestricted access to all sectors of the economy and areas of activity (such as, e.g., foreign trade).

The elimination of most restrictions to private entrepreneurship actually went into effect as early as the beginning of 1989. One might try to argue, as certain defenders of the pre-1989 era in Poland do, that the foundations for the change of the system were, then, in fact laid down by communist reformers. This, however, would be a perversion of the reality. The communist system was unable to change; it was only able to reform, that is to try (unsuccessfully) to improve the unimprovable [see my earlier writings, especially Winiecki, 1986, 1990 and 1991]. It was only the political change of 1989, which ensured that the right to unfettered entrepreneurship did not remain only on paper, as it was the case with all the earlier reforms of the socialist economy.

To begin with, the comparison of the **unrestricted right of establishment** in Poland with the various territorial, sectoral, and other limitations, which still exist in other countries makes it easier to understand the causes for the exceptionally dynamic growth of the generic private sector in our economy. With all the complaints about the bureaucratic slowness (and not inconsiderable corruption), Polish rules for the registration of private companies are incomparably more liberal, even when contrasted with, for instance, the requirement to obtain licenses from district or county government offices existing in the otherwise very liberal Czech Republic [Benacek, 1993].

While analyzing the mechanisms of liberalization and deregulation to somewhat greater extent, we note the particular significance of the **extension of the liberal rule of establishment to both wholesale trade and foreign trade** [see Gomulka, 1992]. Smaller private wholesalers were much quicker than the state-owned mastodons in identifying the products for which there is a large and unsatisfied demand and signal consumers' preferences to producers. This faster identification of changes in the structure of demand by private wholesalers creates positive stimuli for producers to changes in the structure of supply. At the same time, the liberalization of foreign trade makes it possible for private wholesalers to import higher quality goods. In addition to the positive stimuli (signaling consumers' preferences) wholesalers therefore convey potential threats. The most serious of the latter is obviously the possibility of bankruptcy in the event of not adapting to the new, more exacting requirements.

These twofold adaptive pressures affect not only private producers, but also those among the state-owned producers who have become convinced about need to adapt, first of all because they realized that the emerging market system is there to stay and temporizing means endangering one's prospects of success (or even survival). In this manner, the linkage of private wholesaling with the liberalization of foreign trade becomes a powerful factor contributing to the growth of innovativeness in the whole economy.

From the vantage point of the market process/evolutionary economics perspective the foregoing developments create the necessary conditions for **the spontaneous, trial-and-error-type search for efficient outcomes** within the framework of the Hayekian 'general rules' of open, competitive economy. In line with Schumpeter the spontaneous developments may be decomposed into 'destruction' (elimination of errors) and 'innovation' (generation of new trials).

In the case of a radically liberalized, deregulated Polish economy of early 1990s elimination of errors manifested itself through the exit of many large state-owned wholesale enterprises and generation of trials by the takeover of markets by smaller but better motivated and generally more efficient private wholesalers. In the case of producers, the trial-and-error searches have been more complex, given the slower emergence of viable competitors of manufacturing SOEs due to higher capital threshold. Therefore, error elimination to a greater extent consisted of a loss of market share to private Polish producers or to imports rather than exit by manufacturing SOEs, while trial generation was seen through product, technological and/or organizational innovation in SOEs, as well as emergence of successful private competitors. Of course, an often limited adaptation of manufacturing SOEs has largely been the result of the political clout of large industrial firms that both created a climate of indulgence for loss-making (and economic failure in general), as well as effective resistance to exit of loss-makers.

Let us stress again the importance of twofold impact of unrestricted entry of both firms and goods under competitive conditions of an open economy for the industrial sector. It should be noted that **in industry (mining, manufacturing, utilities) the share of private sector's employment and output barely reached half of the total by the end 1994,** that is after more than five years of Polish transition. By contrast, in those sectors where that threshold is not so high, more and more often almost the only players left in the game, except for some large firms, are private companies as, for example, in construction, commerce, and non-infrastructural services (except for some largest firms).

Lagging privatization 'from above' means that state monopolies, especially in the physical infrastructure sector (energy, railways, telecommunications, etc.) continue to be costly and painful 'humps' on the body of the fast growing Polish private sector-based economy. However, these humps, as well other state-made monopolies and near-monopolies in coal mining, oil refining and distribution, etc., did not, at least for the time being, unduly hinder the rapid expansion of the generic private sector. The period of a relatively low-cost existence of completely unprivatized industries is, however, coming slowly to an end (more on this in the last section of this article).

Now, I would like to restate the reasons of Poland's success in changing the ownership structure of its economy, in terms of the ongoing economists' debate of the relative merits of 'big bang' versus gradual change. I would submit that **Poland's successes are due to those particular features of its transition strategy that have been most strongly criticized by the believers in procrastination as the best strategy of change**.

Not a few of them, let it be noted, belong to the 'reformers of the unreformable' (or 'improvers of the unimprovable') from the past. Contrary to all the complaints about 'ruining everything' (meaning the state enterprises...) and 'excessive openness to imports', **it is precisely these features that forced adjustment upon the largely unwilling state-owned producers**. To put it in yet another way, the **most successful were those developments where economic processes were largely left to the spontaneous market forces**.

The view formulated in the preceding paragraph calls for reflection. For wherever the successes depended on the spontaneous market forces, the outcomes were a success. On the other hand, wherever lasting, consistent political involvement a n d administrative efficiency of the state apparatus were required, the effects have been by-and-large unsatisfying. What makes the view even more worth of reflection, this has often been the case also in countries with a somewhat more efficient administration than Polish one *viz.* (Hungary, the Czech Republic). Considerations of the problem in question are presented in the following section of this essay.

TRANSFORMING STATE PROPERTY AND
ORGANIZATIONAL CAPABILITY OF THE STATE

As stressed already, the overwhelmingly dominant role of the state sector at the start of the post-communist economy concentrated expectations on the privatization 'from above'. But the reliance on the state went much further than that. The establishment of the institutional framework of a market economy, accomplishment of the macroeconomic stability, to say nothing of a social safety net appropriate to free-market conditions - all these measures were supposed to be designed and, much more importantly, implemented quickly and efficiently by agencies of the state.

By contrast expectations were much more limited with respect to the privatization 'from below'. Of course, nearly everybody expected generic private firms to emerge and grow but somehow they were often perceived as a necessary but auxiliary component of the size structure of the firms dominated at the upper end and at the middle by privatized ex-SOEs. At the same time, very little thought, resources and organizational effort has been expended on the creation of the conducive environment for the expansion of the generic private sector.

But in spite of everything, it is the latter that expanded very rapidly, and not only in Poland. Also in countries where privatization 'from above' has been regarded as very successful (Czech Republic) or relatively successful (Hungary). The generic private sector has been performing quite well and its shares in the total output and employment, *vis-à-vis* that of the privatized ex-SOEs may not necessarily be smaller.

There is, obviously, no such lopsided relationship as in Poland due to greater successes of privatization 'from above', but the shares in question are impressive. In the Czech Republic it is the enterprises with employment up to 25 persons that have been increasing production by leaps and bounds. Since the small business sector has been almost the same as the generic private sector in post-communist world, almost 30% of all employed in the national economy in the small business sector translates into 30% share of the generic private sector. Furthermore, Zemplinerova & Benacek [1995] estimate that adding those employed o n l y in the 'grey', or unregistered, economy may increase the total by another ten percentage points to some 40% of the total employment (the term 'only' means that part of the 'grey' economy consists of those already counted who are also working in the registered economy).

The estimates of the relative strength of the generic private sector and privatized ex-SOE sector for Hungary are more difficult for many reasons: unsatisfactory data due to the near-collapse of Hungarian statistical services, relative incomparability of statistical categories concerning small business sector, the unclear ownership structure in many Hungarian quasi-privatized enterprises, etc. Nonetheless, output of small firms employing up to 20 or 25 persons have been for years the only growing part of the national economy. Its share, however, may be smaller than in the Czech Republic. By contrast, though, the share of the unregistered private sector, that by definition is small business sector, is thought to be larger in Hungary than in the Czech Republic.

Great expectations apart, early considerations of the systemic change rarely included more elaborated thoughts about the effectiveness of the state in carrying out the many tasks demanded from the state concerning the transition process. The exceptions are articles, like the one written by Brian Levy [1993], who approached this much underappreciated question in a systematic manner [*see text no.10*]. (...)

Levy's approach makes it easier to understand the relative success of the privatization 'from below' in comparison with privatization 'from above'. The elimination of barriers to entrepreneurship is markedly easier than privatization of the state property. For the latter requires a rather elaborated legal framework, well designed administrative procedures and a network of public and private institutions partaking in the process in varying roles. It is worth noting that **even privatization 'short-cuts'**, such as the well known and highly appreciated Czech *coupon privatization*, although markedly speed up the privatization process, **are organizationally more intensive than the simple removal of barriers** to the generic private sector.

SUPERIORITY OF SPONTANEOUS ORDER

However convincing, the preceding considerations are based on certain unstated assumptions. The present writer asserts that the elimination of fundamental barriers to entrepreneurship ('the freedom of enterprise' - to put in economic philosophy terms) is easier than privatizing the state property and links the success of the former with the dynamic growth of the private sector in Poland. Thus, he assumes that **there are reasons why planned actions of thousands of officials yield less satisfactory results than spontaneous developments of the generic private sector.**

At this point we need to refer to Friedrich von Hayek and his theory of spontaneous order. Over the past 20-30 years the superiority of spontaneous order, not planned by anybody but created by the process of evolution of the economic, political, and social order, created through the trial-and-error process, was enormously strengthened by the argumentation from the philosophy of science, known as **growth-of-knowledge theory**, that emerged from works of the said Friedrich Hayek, but also Michael Polanyi and Thomas Kuhn. In a nutshell, it is based on the well argued thesis that the **possibilities of articulating knowledge are limited.** The knowledge we are able to articulate is only a fraction of the knowledge we possess. However, **we are able to use the inarticulate part of our knowledge in our own actions**.

These seemingly abstract concepts have extremely important consequences for economic theory and policy. For it is precisely the consequences of the existence of the inarticulate, *tacit* knowledge that result in the relatively much worse outcomes of the privatization 'from above' *vis-à-vis* the privatization 'from below'. And such outcome may happen regardless of the competence and diligence of officials involved in the former. In the light of the growth-of-knowledge theory, **officials**, no matter how knowledgeable, **are at a very serious disadvantage due to the very limited ability to use the inarticulate knowledge** that other participants in the economy possess. While private producers use both their articulate and inarticulate knowledge in their everyday market endeavors, officials have to depend primarily on the articulate knowledge passed on through bureaucratic channels. If they use inarticulate knowledge, it is only their own and their closest collaborators. In comparison with the inarticulate knowledge encapsulated in market decisions of thousands and often hundreds of thousands of private participants, their decisions of necessity are based on a dramatically smaller pool of knowledge [the point is best explained in Lavoie, 1985].

It should be kept in mind, though, that Hayek's theory of the spontaneous order is a g e n e r a l explanation, holding true for e v e r y country and its officials who are condemned, for the above-explained reasons, to the relatively ineffective economic decisions *vis-à-vis* those taken by market participants.

And, let me add yet another argument. They not only apply more limited knowledge than dispersed market participants but also undertake decisions for which they bear no financial responsibility. This latter argument from the property rights theory points to the fact that those who bear financial responsibility for their actions not only use knowledge more efficiently but also do it in a more responsible manner, in a sense that they are constrained by a threat of a loss. By contrast, politicians and bureaucrats, whose actions - in case of a loss - shift its costs on the taxpayers of their country, are much more prone to follow their whims or ideological preferences, regardless of the economic sense.

But the foregoing Hayekian and property rights considerations may be used to explain the variety of state actions around the globe: the superiority of the privatization 'from below' over that 'from above' in post-communist countries in transition, as well as, say, high probability of failure of 'sophisticated' industrial policies in mature Western economies. It says nothing about consequences of the **particular weaknesses of a post-communist state**.

The generally recognized low organizational capability of the inherited state, its inefficient and corrupt administration, all this should be taken into consideration in the design and implementation of transition programs. The several dozen years of communist centralism has to a large extent extinguished in the people any feeling of responsibility. At the same time, the arbitrariness in the decision-making, as well as the lack of any really observed 'rules of the game' by the ruling stratum, have gravely damaged ethical standards (not only among administrators [see Szymanderski and Winiecki, 1996]). Under such circumstances political liberalization must have resulted in increased corruption. For **the fear of the secret police disappeared, while the *bourgeois* ethics, this cornerstone of the capitalist economy, has not been restored** [Krasznai and Winiecki, 1993 and 1995].

In his excellent essay about the state in the process of transition, Janos Kornai [1992] pointed out numerous weaknesses of the post-communist state. Apart from those already stressed, Kornai enumerated also the lack of political *consensus,* normally serving as the beacon of orientation, the feeling of uncertainty among the old bureaucracy and resultant servility, as well as the drain of the best people by the business sector. Another important determinant of the weakness of the state is the lack of experience of the judicial system in handling its new duties in the capitalist market economy (weak property rights' enforcement).

Kornai stressed **the inconsistency between the weak, overloaded and corrupt state on the one hand and ever growing demands on the state** to solve (and solve quickly) all the problems associated with the systemic change. The latter demands are **far in excess of the state (meaning: its administration) capacity to fulfill**. It was not without some irritation that the said author asks all those demanding the state to intervene, whenever they do not like some developments, that regardless of the merits or demerits of the particular case they should be aware that it is precisely 'that sort of the state on which they would devolve [all those] functions - and that **for quite some time it would remain that sort of the state'.** In other words, rabid interventionists not only ignore the relative disadvantage of the state in taking decisions concerning economy that have been stressed for some decades by Hayek and other neo-Austrian thinkers and by property rights theorists. They also seem to be unaware that they demand action from the state that is not only disadvantaged in general, but also **they demand it from the post-communist state that is at a much more severe disadvantage due to the legacy of communism.**

From the foregoing analysis of weaknesses of the post-communist states (and lasting weaknesses at that) stem important conclusions concerning the role of the spontaneous order in transition to the capitalist market economy. The Hayekian approach suggests that economic processes regulated by the market should be given the largest possible extent of freedom in the post-communist transition. The Polish experience, where privatization has been stalled, while at the same time private sector has been growing at impressive rates, gives strong empirical support to the recommendation formulated in the preceding paragraph. The experience of other countries in the forefront of the transition to the capitalist market economy, where privatization 'from above' fared better, is also supportive of this recommendation.

Furthermore, wherever the state cannot renounce its obligations in the design (and sometimes also in implementation) of the exit strategy from the economic scene, its rules should allow the widest room for spontaneous developments within the newly established rules, so that decentralized decisions of the private agents, characterized by the superior knowledge base, supersede bureaucratic ones. This is, by the way, the principle followed by the Czech leadership with good results.

One *caveat* is in order here. The greatest possible room for spontaneous economic processes should not be seen as an encouragement for anarchy. **The spontaneous economic processes should be given room within the broad, liberal institutional framework** (the already mentioned Hayekian 'general rules') that mean a modicum of political stability, relatively stable money and macroeconomic framework, strongly protected property rights, relatively efficient law enforcement, etc.

All those who think that the near-disappearance of the basic functions of the state in some post-communist countries such as Russia augurs the emergence of the much desired limited state and will bring about great economic prosperity as a result [see, e.g., Bell, 1996] seriously misunderstand the nature of the problem. **The state should be limited in its functions but these functions should be implemented swiftly and efficiently.** The efficiency of such a small state is dependent on the existence of certain preconditions such as political acceptance of the system, proper attitudes toward law and law enforcement, a moral order supportive of the free economy. Only then the state can remain small (in terms of the share of resources it takes away from citizens in the form of taxes) and at the same time efficient.

If these preconditions are not fulfilled even to a minimum degree, we see the Hobbesian anarchy that in the particular post-communist context is translated into mafia-like redistributive coalitions that instead of using the Olsonian 'logic of collective action' [Olson, 1995, 1980] use guns and explosives in their corruptive and extortive activities. The foregoing sharply reduces the incentives for normal citizens to exploit the opportunities given by economic freedom. The potential of the spontaneous order is employed to an extremely limited degree. (...)

REFERENCES

V. Benacek, 1993, "Toil and Trouble of an Indigenous Entrepreneur during Transition. The Case of the Czech Republic". CERGE, Prague, September 30, mimeo

K. Bobinska, 1994, "Sytuacja gospodarcza sektora przedsiebiorstw", in *Koniunktura Gospodarcza Polski*, Biuletyn Centrum Adama Smitha, No.2,

J. Chmiel and Z. Pawlowska, 1996, "Sektor prywatny w Polsce w latach 1990-1994" (Polish Private Sector in 1990-1994), Zeszyty Centrum im. Adama Smitha, Warsaw

S. Gomulka, 1992, "On the Design of Economic Policy: The Challenge of Eastern Europe", in *Debate on Transition, Acta Oeconomica*, Vol. 44, No. 3-4

T. Gruszecki and J. Winiecki, 1991, "Privatization in East-Central Europe: A comparative perspective", *Aussenwirtschaft*, No. 1

J. Kornai, 1992, "The Post-Socialist Transition and the State: Reflections in the Light of Hungarian Fiscal Problems", *American Economic Review*, Vol. 82, No. 2, May

Z. Krasznai and J. Winiecki, 1993, "Formal and Informal Constraints in Transition to the Market: Costs of Neo-Classical Utility Maximization". Paper prepared for the Symposium on *'Moral Foundations of a Free Society'* Madralin, 1-4 July, mimeo [see also, 1995, *Communist Economies and Economic Transformation*, Vol.7, No.2]

D. Lavoie, 1985, *National Economic Planning. What is Left?* Ballinger, Cambridge, Mass.

B. Levy, 1993, "An Institutional Analysis of the Design and Sequence of Trade and Investment Policy Reform", *The World Bank Economic Review*, Vol. 7, No. 2

Mickiewicz, T., 1995, "Nierównowaga praw i obowiazków pracy i kapitału: Polska okresu transformacji systemowej"(The Imbalance between Labour and Capital in Polish systemic transformation), Zeszyty Centrum im. Adama Smitha, Warsaw

D.C. North, 1979, "A Framework for Analyzing the State in Economic History," *Explorations in Economic History*

M. Olson, 1965, *The Logic of Collective Action,* Harvard University Press, Cambridge, Mass.

M. Olson, 1980, The Rise and Decline of Nations, Yale University Press, New Haven,

J. Szymanderski and J. Winiecki, 1996, Property Rights, Private Sector, and Public Attitudes, in: J. Winiecki, Ed., 1996 (see below)

J. Winiecki, 1986, 'Why Economic Reforms Fail in the Soviet System. A Property Rights-Based Approach", Seminar Paper No.374, Institute for International Economic Studies, Stockholm, mimeo [same, 1990 *Economic Inquiry*, Vol.28, No.2]

J. Winiecki, 1991, *Resistance to Change in the Soviet Economic System,* Routledge, London

J. Winiecki, 1992, *Privatization in Poland. A Comparative Perspective,* J.C.B. Mohr (Paul Siebeck) Tubingen

J. Winiecki, 1993, "Kleska wyborcza obozu reform: Przyczyny spoleczne i polityczne", *Rzeczpospolita*, October 9-10

J. Winiecki, Ed., 1996, Institutional Barriers to Economic Growth: Polish Incomplete Transition, Adam Smith Research Centre, Warsaw

A. Zemplinerova and V. Benacek, 1995, New Private Sector in the Czech Republic. *Reform Round Table Working Paper No.18*, Institute of Economic Studies, Prague University, January, mimeo

CHAPTER 15

COMMUNIST LEGACY IMPACT OF MORAL CORROSION ON TRANSITION*

The paper looks at the transition to a capitalist market economy from a very specific vantage point. The authors look in the first section of the paper at transition costs that result from time profile of the transition process and resultant problems of incomplete rules and weak enforcement of these rules (weakness of **formal constraints**). They posit that although these costs will be rather high, the difference of speed between liberalization and institution-building does not answer the question how high these costs will be.

The answer to the last question lies in the strength of **informal constraints**, i.e. in a moral order prevailing in societies under consideration. The authors of the paper formulate a hypothesis that these costs will be *particularly high* in post-socialist economies in transition because of the corrosive influence of communism upon moral order prevailing there at the time of communist takeover. The role of informal constraints and their influence on the costs of economic activity are considered in the second section, while arguments explaining reasons for the particularly great depth of moral decay under communism and its impact on transition costs are considered in the third section.

---

* *This is the text of a paper presented by this author (together with Zoltan Krasznai) at a Liberty Fund-sponsored conference 'Moral Foundations of a Free Society', held in July 1993 in Madralin (Poland). It was later published under the title:* Formal and Informal Constraints in Transition to the Market: Costs of Neoclassical Utility Maximization, *in:* **Communist Economies and Economic Transformation** *(vol.7, no.2, 1995).*

With the main conclusion already formulated in the third section of the paper, the present writers turn in concluding words to a related issue of universality of high costs of dual transition to democracy and market. With weakened moral order under the preceding despotic regime and increased opportunities under liberalization the increase in unlawful/immoral (or simply utility maximizing) behaviour is inevitable. What sets post-socialist transition apart is the intensity of the phenomenon.

INCOMPLETE RULES, LEARNING, AND WEAK ENFORCEMENT RAISE TRANSITION COSTS

Transition from socialist, centrally administered economy to capitalist, market economy consists of two parallel developments: getting the prices right (liberalization) and getting institutions right (institutional change). Although both are needed to obtain a **workable market economy**, the speed of two developments is markedly different. The process of shaping institutional infrastructure, even if necessary from the start, is a much longer - and more complex - process and its length *vis-à-vis* other changes, i.e. **time profile of transition, results in higher transaction costs and/or lower value added produced from the same resources than is normal for capitalist, market economy.**

Thus, although systemic transition means that the old high-cost institutional framework (socialism) is abolished and a far more superior, low-cost framework (capitalism) is introduced [see, e.g., Schmieding, 1991], the time profile of transition temporarily raises transaction costs or reduces value added or does both at the same time. These losses of one sort or another stem largely from the initial incompleteness of the rules, the time-consuming need for familiarity with the newly established rules (learning costs), and weak enforcement of these rules.

The best understood source of high transaction costs is certainly relatively slow introduction of new rules of the game. For no matter how strenuously authorities try to establish a minimum of rules to get the system going, what they supply is less than demanded by the requirements of a workable market economy. (...)

It has been repeatedly stressed that the new interim arrangements for control by the state over state-owned enterprises (SOEs for short) weakened constraints on managers of these enterprises. They may adopt a wait and see attitude to transition in the hope that the thrust of transition will weaken or even be reversed. For that reason they may avoid difficult choices such as cutting cost rather than output [see, e.g., Winiecki, 1990; Schmieding, 1991] or they may use an increased freedom of manoeuvre (due weakened constraint) to decapitalise the enterprise or sell it cheaply to a third party, usually foreign one, in return for hefty pay-off [see, e.g., Frydman and Rapaczynski, 1991]. Consequently, until proper owners' control is established, i.e. until SOE is privatized, an economically inefficient behaviour may reduce value added created by at least some - if not most - SOEs.

Privatization is the most complex and time-consuming of institutional changes but other, apparently simpler changes have been known to be also a source a variety of losses. With incomplete rules, certain transactions (e.g. foreign investments) simply do not take place, thus depriving the national economy in question of possibilities to increase capacity to add value to their economies. Or, in those cases where the decision to go ahead prevailed, the transaction costs involved would reduce the price obtained by the Treasury.

However, **not only incomplete institutional change but also the unavoidable learning process imposes high transaction costs on the economy in transition.** Even if the rules are there, the accumulation of knowledge about the new institutional framework and the emergence of routines in the application of new rules take time. In the interim the trial-and-error process adds costs to a variety of transactions and simultaneously becomes a deterrent for others who would become discouraged from transacting by these high costs. Let it be noted that here, too, just as in the case of incomplete institutional change, inefficient outcomes may also involve corrupt practices. For ambiguous and untried laws give the opportunity to unscrupulous administrators to extract bribes for interpreting the law in favour of parties where there is no clear legal base to do so. However, the authors leave for consideration in the next section of the paper other, probably more frequent cases of attempts to extract bribes just for doing what should be done anyway and doing it speedily.

Weak law enforcement is yet another source of additional transaction costs in economies in transition. Uncertainty as to whether and how the judicial system will enforce private contracts will force economic agents to reduce the variety of transactions, by reducing them to simpler ones (cash only transactions, simultaneous exchanges, transactions based on accepted standards of value, i.e. tied to the US$ or D-Mark), and to reduce the range of contracting parties to those, who will be constrained in their actions by the benefits of repeated transactions with the party in question. Errors and procrastinations will have exactly the same effect. And it should be noted that just as in the case of the learning process the window of opportunity for corruption will be opened wider under such circumstances.

But higher transaction costs due to the weak law enforcement mean much more in the economy in transition from the Soviet system than inefficient - and possibly corrupt - judiciary. Weak law enforcement means first of all **weakened basic law and order**, an easily observable phenomenon in economies in transition. Therefrom result higher costs of security measures at plants and offices, higher insurance costs, etc. As some businesses also resort to underhanded methods, costs of competing for those who do not also rise.

Any improvement in law and order will also be costly as the number of law enforcers will have to increase, they will have to be better paid, better trained, and better equipped. All this will have to be paid by taxes thus increasing indirectly transaction costs. However, let it be noted that weak moral order impinges upon the performance of the law enforcement apparatus itself; thus, any significant improvement may take considerable time.

The present writers conclude this section with the thesis that time profile of the transition inevitably imposes costs on the economies undergoing the process in question. But the extent of these costs is only partly dependent upon the slower speed of institution-building and resultant problems of incomplete rules, learning process, and weak enforcement of the rules. A substantial, if not actually decisive, part of these costs stem from the weak moral order that increases the probability of cost-increasing behaviour.

CORRODED MORAL ORDER RAISES
TRANSITION COSTS EVEN MORE

Incomplete rules, learning how to apply them, as well as weak enforcement of these rules are f o r m a l constraints on behaviour of economic actors. Even under normal circumstances rules are not perfectly consistent and are not fully enforced (or even not fully enforceable). This is, as neo-institutional economics tells us, due to the costliness of measurement of economic activity and different interests of principals and agents [a useful overview of the literature see Eggertsson, 1990]. For reasons of weakness of formal constraints in economies in transition, costs of inconsistency and weak enforcement are sharply higher than in mature capitalist, market economies [they were higher still in Soviet-type economies, see Szymanderski and Winiecki, 1989; Winiecki, 1987, 1991].

But incompleteness of rules, slow learning of their application, and weak enforcement are not in themselves decisive for the s i z e of losses due to transaction costs. This is the hypothesis, which we advanced toward the end of the preceding section of the paper. These losses may be higher or lower depending on the moral order operating in societies, in this case in societies that were subject to communist regimes for the life-span of a generation or more (the latter in the case of the former USSR).

To explain the influence of moral order upon the transition from socialist, centrally administered to capitalist, market economy we have to try first to define the phenomenon itself. Following North [1986, 1990] we may define it broadly as i n f o r m a l constraints (in contrast to rules and their enforcement that are formal constraints). A particular moral order is a set (an evolving set, to be a little more precise) of social norms such as codes of conduct, standards of behaviour, taboos, etc., that are either externally enforced by societal approval or disapproval of particular behaviour or internally enforced, inherited through upbringing. They often tend to be reinforced or modified by accepted comprehensive view of the world at large (*Weltanschauung* in an appropriate German term) that in the modern jargon is often called **ideology**. An alternative instrument of reshaping a moral order is experience that leads to reinforcement, refinement or in some cases also rejection of a norm from the set constituting a particular moral order.

What we wrote above stands in contrast to the basic tenets of mainstream, i.e. neoclassical, economics whose economic agents are pure rational utility maximizers. They view each opportunity in the light of the utility maximization principle. It means that if economic agent can, e.g., steal with impunity, he rationally does so. But such approach to economic agents' behaviour stands in sharp contrast to the reality. People cling, often tenaciously and at a substantial cost to themselves, to their moral codes. Very definitely individuals not always steal when stealing can be done with impunity, neither cheat if cheating pays under given circumstances, nor shirk or engage in opportunistic behaviour [alternatively Alchian and Demsetz, 1972, or Olivier Williamson, 1975, terminology] if it is costlessly possible to do so.

The broadly observable phenomenon is that they quite often refrain from such rational behaviour because their individual moral codes tell them otherwise. At any moment of time, as North [1986] rightly stresses, these standards of behaviour play a critical role in constraining their choice set. To the extent that they feel constrained, just because they believe in their moral codes, they tend to obey the rules, live up to the letter and spirit of contracts freely entered into, will uphold private property rights, etc.

Of course, morally underpinned behaviour of economic actors, and of the people in general, is neither universal nor transcendental. At any moment of time there are individuals whose norms of behaviour are closer to that neoclassical neoclassical abstraction of rational utility maximizer. Also, their share in the society is not frozen forever. To quote an excellent saying of a Polish pre-war satirist, since time immemorial in every society there always were thieves, policemen and victims of theft; what matters for law and order in a given society are proportions between these categories.

These proportions tend to change over time, sometimes drastically, as we shall stress in the following section of the paper. And with changing proportions change also transaction costs. The more individuals perceive the rules as being unjust, the more they see that those who established the rules behave in an arbitrary manner, the more often or more heavily they lose as a result of acting in accordance with the rules and their moral codes, the less many of them will respect the rules and the weaker will be their resolve to follow prescriptions of the inherited code. In such societies pure utility maximization will increasingly prevail and with it costs of transacting will sharply go up. We posit that **this is what happened under the communist rule and what explains high costs of transition at present - and for the years to come.**

EROSION OF MORAL ORDER UNDER COMMUNISM: CAUSES AND CONSEQUENCES

Erosion of a moral order is not a purely communist phenomenon. Some of the economic problems of the Western world that surfaced in the last quarter of a century stem from the same sources. Increased transaction costs are the result of pervasive (and corrosive) influence of state intervention and deformed welfare system (with perverse incentives). Resultant growing discrepancy between effort and reward weakened the respect law, undermined work ethics, and weakened capitalist economic order. Some reversal has taken place in the last ten years or so due to better perception of the threats to the well-being of respective societies resulting therefrom and political changes this perception brought about in many Western nations.

However, if Western world has gone through the era of s o m e adverse changes in the moral order, **the communist world underwent dramatically greater adverse changes since 1917 in the former Soviet Union and since 1945 in communist dominated Soviet satellites.** The extent of moral degradation had to be lived through to be believed.

Rules of the game have been generally believed to be either unfair or not respected by the communist ruling stratum. No bureaucracy in the normal sense, i.e. operating according to certain well established routines, existed in communist regimes. Arbitrariness has been reigning supreme [see, e.g., Szymanderski, 1978; Brenner, 1990]. Advancement was purely dependent on links with the local party chieftains (or bosses of other segments of the ruling stratum) and pure opportunism of those wanting to make a career. This, coupled with the privileged access to goods and services by the ruling stratum as the primary distribution rule, undermined whatever moral codes, pre-capitalist and capitalist alike, survived the Bolshevik revolution of 1917 or Soviet subjugation of 1945.

First, in everyday life, an old Russian custom of corruption (this 'salutary relief from the pressure of absolutism' according to Lord Acton) has reached new heights. It also afflicted countries whose industrial tradition and associated *bourgeois* morality have been well established for centuries. To give a comparative example, cheating in state shops by the personnel became a norm rather than the exception. According to the then Chairman of the State Price Commission in Czechoslovakia in mid-1970s shopkeepers were cheated - according to the check-ups made by price inspectors - about 40% of cases. A decade later similar check-ups in groceries and butchers' shops revealed cheating by shopkeepers to have been present in respectively 45% and 65% of cases. And if these figures seem to the readers shockingly high, we hasten to add that similar check-ups in Poland and the Soviet Union found that cheating was even more dominant, effecting 60 to 80% of cases [see sources in Winiecki, 1989].

Not only dishonesty pure and simple became closer to a norm than to an exception but, worse still, the human bonds that survived various adversities in human history began to crumble, particularly in the Soviet Union, where moral order was much longer under pressure and the old regime and its moral underpinning were persecuted much more severely. Again, an example helps to grasp the extent of moral degradation. The Soviet economic weekly revealed not long ago that in large Russian cities almost 30% of newborn babies are not taken from maternity hospitals by their parents but are left to be cared for by state foster moms. To that mind-numbing figure one should also add that of other children whose parents were deprived of the right to care for them, to see the enormity of the scale of family decay [*Ekonomicheskaya Gazeta*, 1987, No.52].

Human bonds were obviously breaking up. The problem of informers (that, like a ghost, haunts post-socialist societies) belongs to the same category. Informing on your family members, friends or colleagues became for quite a few an accepted (even if not advertized!) way of getting ahead in life under communism. As a Polish philosopher, Rev. Jozef Tischner, aptly stated in a larger context, **communism inculcated in people's minds the ease of betrayal** [*Rzeczpospolita*, April 4-5, 1992].

It is no surprise, then, that many, in the words of Alexander Zinoviev [1984], became conditioned not by a (seriously weakened) moral order but by 'technical rules of survival'. This being the case, the impact upon performance must have been uniformly bad. Arbitrariness of the ruling stratum's advancement decisions generated a Gresham law of selection. 'In organisations where fundamental laws of human behaviour and development are ignored, egoists, conformists, cowards and unscrupulous people begin to play more important roles than individuals who are brave, honest, responsible and concerned with everybody's welfare. Under such conditions bad characters drive out good characters' [Kozielecki, 1985]. Incidentally, the present writers regard this factor as one of less well recognized factors contributing to the collapse of the communist system.

However, for the subject in question another consequence is of crucial importance, namely society's attitude to advancement in public life and success in general. With such selection rules and such people getting more often than not an upper hand in every walk of life (even literature or hard science were not excluded!), the consequence has been suspicion, distrust, malice and ill-will toward a n y success [see Brenner, 1990; Tischner, 1991]. How harmful such attitudes become under the transition to the system based *inter alia* on the principle of competition need not be dwelled upon here.

Such has been, then, the heritage of the past that post-socialist societies are trying to cope with in the process of transition. It should not be surprising that the size of losses due to both transaction costs of those transactions that take place and due to the unrealized value added in unconsummated transactions must have been particularly large

The size of these losses under weak formal and informal constraints has been also influenced by two additional factors. First, the general shift from the economy run basically on the principle that what is not expressly allowed is prohibited to the one based largely on the opposite principle extended the area of economic activity both lawful and unlawful. Thus, also cheating and stealing could be extended over the much wider area and it duly did, as proved, e.g., by the string of banking swindles in Poland. The opening up of economies in transition to capitalist market economy opened them also to cross-border crimes, such as, for example, car stealing by internationally connected gangs.(...)

Second factor influencing the size of the losses concerns the disappearance of fear. In economies that genuinely turned to democracy and market, the fear of the ubiquitous secret police has evaporated and, however welcome, the change brought about also a wave of unlawful and activities. Many of those whose moral codes have been severely weakened did not cheat, steal or engage in other unlawful activities in the past out of fear of repression (that was excessively repressive by any standard of the civilized society). Now, with the fear evaporating, and the moral order not yet restored, they feel free to demand bribes, swindle their compatriots, etc. The emerging private sector is afflicted by such attitudes as well, since business ethics has also been absent from the considerations of many [see, e.g., Morgan, 1991].

A question may be posed if and when all this change for the better. (...) Although there are reasons for optimism because capitalism is the only system that contains economic incentives for improving the moral order, the present writers expect the progress to be slow. Economic policies may change almost overnight. Changing laws may take months. Changes in economic structure may take years. But changes in informal constraints ruling individuals' behaviour are measured in terms of decades. And in the meantime today's economies in transition and tomorrow's capitalist market economies will continue to operate at lower levels of generated value added and higher levels of transaction costs than mature capitalist market economies.

Let it be noted, however, that the authors are optimistic in a sense that they assume continuing, albeit slow, strengthening of the moral order (*bourgeois* ethics) under the stated earlier conditions of a genuine shift to democracy and market. And it is this criterion, i.e. change in b o t h political and economic system, that differentiates between various countries of Eastern Europe. For in the opinion of the present writers in the countries where political change has been incomplete or largely engineered by the old communist regime, the strengthening of a weakened or non-existent moral order will not take place. It may not even be possible to establish a workable market economy.

It is stressed rightly that individual's behaviour was shaped under the communist regime by lawlessness and arbitrariness. Therefore, a prerequisite of change is a reestablishment of the rule of law. 'Only when people realize that some laws cannot be changed, that advancing in rank and acquiring wealth has become more often a matter of talent, of entrepreneurial insight and of chance, can one expect to slowly extirpate these attitudes' [Brenner, 1990]. The foregoing not only needs time, as stressed earlier in the section, but also raises the question of trust in and ability of members of the old communist ruling stratum to consistently act in accordance with this prescription.

Thus, if people see the same perpetrators of lawlessness and arbitrariness at the helm of the transition, they will interpret it in one way only. They will suspect that nothing changed in substance in spite of the new market form in which old substance has been packaged. They will not change their behaviour and the result will be little actual entrepreneurship and a lot of racketeering [predictions coming true in this respect, see Winiecki, 1989]. And even assuming partial changes and the introduction of a new set of rules by democratic leadership, the old apparatus will be interpreting them in a way it was accustomed to, i.e. arbitrarily, thus prolonging the distrust and postponing the beginning of the attitude change. Therefore we expect that under incomplete political change the costs of attempted transition will be much higher still, while effects - much lower. A goal of a workable (i.e. tolerably efficient) market economy may even be unattainable.

ARE OUR PROBLEMS UNIQUE?

Conclusions of our paper have already been formulated at the close of the preceding section. So, there seems to be no need to dwell upon them any further. Therefore the authors suggest to turn attention to another, related issue, namely the uniqueness vs. universality of transitional increase in unlawful/immoral (utility maximizing) behaviour. In other words, are our countries suffering from the unique malady or is it a more general phenomenon that affects all economies that democratize and liberalize at the same time. The present writers suggest on the basis of history of many such attempts that it is rather the latter than the former. Our earlier stress on the impact of communism tends to underline the d e p t h of moral decay rather than its uniqueness.

In all economies that suffered simultaneously from political despotism and economic mismanagement caused largely by state controls and inward orientation, the freedom - when it comes - is increasing the opportunities for moral and immoral, for scrupulous and unscrupulous. As stressed in the preceding section, the opening up increases the range of opportunities for both good and bad. And the disappearance of fear encourages utility maximizing behaviour exactly at the time when political change also weakened the position of traditional law enforcement apparatus (usually closely linked up with the fallen and discredited despotic regime). Thus, not only more individuals, uninhibited by informal constraints, stand ready to act in an unlawful/immoral manner but also those who could and should deter them are ill-prepared (and largely ill-motivated) to do so.

The foregoing has important consequences for the general public acceptance of transition to a capitalist market economy that in their eyes seems to be associated with the decline moral order and increase in criminality. (...) What the authors of this paper would like to stress is that it helps to generate in some segments of the population a memory deformation well known by psychologists known as idealization of the (otherwise repulsive) past.

Such developments happened in many developing countries that tried to shake off the dual shackles of political oppression and economic controls by the state. People, burdened with the inevitable costs of transition and aroused by various scandals made possible in the transitory period, in search of a change turned to their yesterday's oppressors. Fallen dictators were showered with affection, took part in presidential elections and gathered a sizable part of the vote or even were returned to power. (...)

REFERENCES

Alchian, Armen A., and Harold Demsetz, 1972, Production, Information Costs and Economic Organization, *American Economic Review*, Vol.62, 1972, No.5

Brenner, Reuven, 1990, 1990, The Long Road from Serfdom and How to Shorten It, *The Canadian Business Law Journal*, Vol. 17, No.2

Eggertsson, Thrainn, 1990, *Economic Behaviour and Institutions*, Cambridge University Press ·

Frydman, Roman, and Andrzej Rapaczynski, 1991, Markets and Institutions in Large-Scale Privatization: An Approach to Economic and Social Transformation in Eastern Europe,, in: *Reforming Central and Eastern European Economies*. A World Bank Symposium ed. by Victorio Corbo, Fabrizio Coricelli and Jan Bossak, Washington D.C.

Kozielecki, Jozef, 1985, *Zycie Gospodarcze*, Nos. 51/52 (in Polish)

Morgan, James, 1991, Poland Wakes to the Day of the Deal, *Financial Times*, April 13-14, 1991

North, Douglass, C., 1986, Institutions, Economic Growth and Freedom: An Historical Introduction, Washington University, School of Business and Center in Political Economy. Working Paper. September (mimeo)

North, Douglass C., 1990, *Institutions, Institutional Change and Economic Performance*, Cambridge University Press

Schmieding, Holger, 1991, From Socialism to an Institutional Void: Notes on the Nature of Transformation Crisis, Kiel Working Paper No.480, Kiel Institute for World Economics, July (mimeo)

Szymanderski, Jacek, 1978, Determinants of the Centralisation of Power, Institute of History, Polish Academy of Sciences, (in Polish), mimeo

Szymanderski, Jacek, and Jan Winiecki, 1989, Dissipation de la rente, managers et travailleurs dans le systeme sovietique: les implications pour un changement du systeme, *Revue d'Etudes comparatives Est-Ouest*, Vol.20, No.1

Williamson, Olivier H., 1975, *Markets and Hierarchies*, Basil Blackwell, New York

Winiecki, Jan, 1987, Why Economic Reforms Fail in the Soviet System. A Property Rights-Based Approach. Seminar Paper No.374, Institute for International Economic Studies, Stockholm, (mimeo)

Winiecki, Jan, 1989, Ethics and Politics to the Rescue of Neo-Classical Economics? *Economic Affairs*, April-May

Winiecki, Jan, 1990, Post-Soviet-Type Economies in Transition: What Have We Learned from the Polish Transition Programme in Its First Year? *Weltwirtschaftliches Archiv*, Vol. 126, No.4

Winiecki, Jan, 1991, *Resistance to Change in the Soviet Economic System*, Routledge, London

Winiecki, Jan, 1992, Shaping the Institutional Infrastructure, in: *The Transformation of Socialist Economies*. Ed. by H.Siebert, J.C.B. Mohr (Paul Siebeck), Tuebingen

Zinoviev, Alexander, 1984, *The Glittering Future* (quoted from Polish underground edition of 1984)

CHAPTER 16

PROPERTY RIGHTS, PRIVATE SECTOR AND PUBLIC ATTITUDES TOWARD INSTITUTIONAL CHANGE˙

On economic theory grounds, especially neo-institutional economic theory grounds, there has never been any doubt as to the crucial role of the private sector - in fact: of the dominance of the private sector - for the market economy. Nor there have been any doubts harboured about the need for the well designed and secure property rights. [On these points, see, e.g., Pejovich, 1990]. Nor there were any doubts on historical grounds. No society ever succeeded in building a capitalist market economy (and there has never been any other than capitalist market economy) without the dominant private sector. To use the expression of this author, **there is no capitalism without capitalists** [Winiecki, 1990].

However obvious, these conclusions were clear only for a minority of the systemic change-oriented elite that came to power in 1989. The government programme of October 1989, very specific on the need for stabilization and liberalization, stressed also, on the institutional side, the need for making Polish economy similar to that of Western economies in institutional respects as well. Quite obviously for the minority in question, it also entailed privatization and, consequently, bringing the share of the pri-

---

* This is an abbreviated version of Chapter 7, written jointly with Jacek Szymanderski, of the report: 'Institutional Barriers to Economic Development: Poland's Incomplete Transition'. Report's Editor: Jan Winiecki. **Adam Smith Research Center**, Warsaw, 1996.

vate sector in GDP and employment up to Western levels (70-80% share at a minimum).

The privatization consequences were not, however, as clearly spelled out as were other parts of the programme. Even the institution that was designed to accomplish the change has been euphemistically called Office (later: Ministry) of Ownership Transformation, without clearly spelling out what kind of ownership changes it was to accomplish.

There have been reasons for this circumspection. A large part of the victorious political 'Solidarity' camp was for quite some time attracted by the self-management idea, in spite of the decisive theoretical criticism of self-management and disastrous historical experience of the former Yugoslavia. In 1989 they still saw in self-management their beloved 'Third Way' to the future (and even succeeded in writing their belief into the 'Round Table' recommendations!).

Apart from this specifically Polish problem, there were other more general grounds on which to expect the support for systemic change involving large scale privatization to be rather shallow. After all, the generally criticised features of the state-owned enterprises (SOEs) were at the same time sources of additional material and non-material benefits for those who worked there. Thus, privatization, based on rightly assumed greater efficiency of privately-owned enterprises, would undoubtedly bring higher wages and salaries in the future but in the present would eliminate redundant labour, increase work discipline, reveal incompetence of many, scrap the welfarism at the enterprise level, and eliminate theft and corruption.

Although it was perceived that there existed a general support for systemic change that promises to make Polish economy more like any Western economy, **it was rather obvious that the general support would not translate automatically into case-by-case support if and when a given enterprise was to be privatized**. In this manner, the general reasons for resistance to change mixes with the specifically Polish reasons. The **probability of success** of this resistance has been made stronger in Poland by the tradition of workers' militancy (since 1980 under the banner of 'Solidarity')

In the end not only parties of the communist *ancient regime* and the utopian left wing of 'Solidarity' but also of the nationalist and fundamentalist-catholic right turned out to be hostile to privatization. Given such an unholy alliance, privatization proceeded very slowly.

At that time such outcome was regarded as a disaster. It is hardly surprising, though. At the very beginning of the transition process politicians, trade union activists, analysts and the general public concentrated their attention almost exclusively. After all, the state sector dwarfed the private sector outside agriculture, and many sensible people tied hopes for radical change for the better with the transformation of SOEs into privately-owned ones (those less sensible did so with the transformation of SOEs into self-management units).

However, the much resisted Polish privatization did not live up to those expectations. **The contribution of privatization to the creation of the dominant private sector has been very small** [*see text no.14*].

Nonetheless, in spite of the failures of privatization, the share of the private sector in GDP exceeded at the same time 50% of the total, while that of employment exceeded 60% - and since then shares of the private sector increased again, given the disparity in output growth rates. Thus, in the aggregate, Poland does not differ much from other success stories of transition.

This has been the case because privatization does not consist only of transformation of SOEs into privately-owned enterprises, but also of the establishment of new private enterprises and expansion of the existing ones. Using the terminology applied elsewhere [see Gruszecki and Winiecki, 1991] we may distinguish the privatization 'from above', that is the one attracting most attention, and privatization 'from below', the growth of the *generic* private sector from the ground up. Both ways contribute to the creation of an economy with the ownership structure similar to that of Western countries.

In Poland privatization 'from below' more than made up for the weakness of privatization 'from above'. Polish generic private sector outside agriculture produces almost 45% of GDP with over 35% of aggregate employment. And these shares increased 3-4 times since the beginning of transition.[*See the preceding text*]. (...)

If I now wanted to restate the reasons of Poland's success in changing the ownership structure of its economy, I would stress that **we owe the successes to those particular features of the transition strategy, which have been most strongly criticized** by the believers in procrastination as the best strategy of systemic change. Most of them, let it be noted, belong to the 'reformers of the unreformable' (or 'improvers of the unimprovable') from Polish communist past. Contrary to all the complaints about 'ruining everything' (meaning the state enterprises...) and 'excessive openness to import', it is precisely these features that forced adjustment upon often unwilling producers. To put it in yet another way, the **most successful were those developments where economic processes were left to the spontaneous market forces**.

Incidentally, herein lies the explanation of the earlier and faster recovery from the 'transformational depression' at the start of transition. Property rights are more secure in the generic private firms. Proper work habits are instilled from the very start. Industrial relations in general are healthy. All this contrasts sharply with the behavioural patterns carried over from the communist past in privatized SOEs. Therefore, efficiency of resource use and production factors employed is generally higher in former. So is the financial soundness of *generic* private firms. In consequence, **the higher is the share of the** *generic* **private firms in the aggregate output of the private sector and the smaller is the share of the privatized firms, the stronger, more dynamic the recovery**. The question is, however, whether the foregoing thesis applies to the whole process of transition from Soviet-type centrally administered to capitalist market economy.

It has been a fortuitous coincidence that in Poland strong resistance to privatization 'from above' has been coupled with more decisive removal of the fetters constraining the generic private sector. But in the opinion of this author **the institutional barriers we stress in the report will increasingly circumscribe the growth and diversification opportunities of the private sector**.

The still buoyant private sector will increasingly be adversely affected by twofold institutional and policy developments. The spate of regulations intent on controlling a variety of aspects of business activities through licensing, quality and other controls, concessions, ill-regulated environmental standards, etc. - all these increase output costs directly and indirectly. Directly through compliance costs and indirectly through corruption costs. These are topped by ever more costly labour regulations that strongly discourage compliance and result in shifting a part of business activities from the registered to the unregistered ('grey') economy, by the capriciousness of the tax regulations and decisions, as well as by the disadvantaged position of the private sector *vis-à-vis* other public authorities (with respect to public procurement, etc.).

While regulation throttles the private sector's vitality and increases its cost, the continuous existence of the substantial - and in some sectors still dominant - public sector limits the opportunities for expansion of the private sector in a more roundabout manner. There are a few layers of this roundabout effect on the prospects of the private sector.

The first layer is the political imbalance between the economically dominant and more efficient private sector and economically less efficient, largely unreconstructed public sector. The very size of the latter and its inability and/or sheer unwillingness to adjust to the requirements of the market economy creates demand for financial resources to support the loss-makers. These resources are more often than not granted to the loss-makers as **the public sector is politically over represented. The two dominant political camps, ex-communists and 'Solidarity', as stressed earlier, draw their strength from the same segments of the economy: large state enterprises and budget-financed public services** (health, education, etc.). Given the fact that the economically more efficient private sector is politically underrepresented, economic rationale for more efficiency-based allocation criteria often gives ground to political expediency of support for own political supporters.

This political expediency results in a variety of more or less overt forms of support:

1. Direct budget subsidies. These, given their high visibility, are rather small and not used very often;

2. Indirect grant- or loan-type support from a variety of state agencies. As these are more difficult to track by the opposition and even more by the interested public, they play an increasing role in maintaining the inefficiency of the public sector;

3. Indirect budget subsidies in the form of government guarantees. The budgetary allocations for the purpose have been rapidly increasing of late and their allocation among recipients shows a strong bias in favour of large heavy industry SOEs having political clout;

4. Indirect tax concessions through tolerated non-payment of taxes and social security contributions by many large SOEs or outright forgiveness of the unpaid taxes, contributions and accrued interests.

5. Pressure on state-owned banks to support politically important state-owned loss-makers directly, through new loans, or indirectly, through partial forgiveness of past loans within the framework of the debt restructuring loans.

All these measures of support substantially soften the budget constraint of state mastodons and make them even less willing to undergo the necessary adjustment (including closures of some SOEs that do not give any hope of leaving the list of persistent loss-makers). **However, their adverse impact is much wider than on mastodons themselves.**

They create an economic equivalent of the cosmic b l a c k h o l e, gluttonizing the financial resources necessary elsewhere in the economy. Firstly, they are needed by the expanding private sector for which the continuous existence of the black hole reduces even further the opportunity to benefit from the services of the banking sector ('even further' because small and medium-sized firms are generally disadvantaged *vis-à-vis* large ones in their relations with banks and most financial institutions). Secondly, they might be used for the inevitable institutional changes in the social security, first of all the pension system (see the previous section of the report).

Over time, the still rapidly expanding private sector may at best slow down considerably and at worst decline under the twofold impact of the increasingly costly burden of regulation and continuing existence of the unprivatized, highly subsidized state enterprise sector. The question is how such adverse trends are to be avoided. To answer it, we are forced to move from economics of transition to political economy of transition.

A look at the post-1989 history is not at all encouraging, especially with respect to the necessary drastic reduction of the state enterprise sector through privatization and the imposition of the market rules of the game on the remaining unprivatized public enterprises. Given the political overrepresentation of SOEs, neither non-communist governments formed by the 'Solidarity' camp, nor subsequent post-communist governments have exerted strong pressure on state enterprises to adjust. In fact, **post-communists, devoid of any serious ideological preferences and intent only on remaining in power and using the state for personal gain, made political favouritism the cornerstone of their politics of postponing or avoiding institutional change.** For it is the political favouritism that gains votes and it is the *conditio sine qua non* of being able to live off the state.

Such policy, if it is going to be successful, assumes that further institution-building in the transition process is unwelcome by a sufficiently large body of the electorate. Public opinion surveys in the last few years largely support such assumption. As quoted already in the overview, a quite recent survey showed that liberal capitalist order is criticized by 70% of the electorate od post-communist SLD, by 73% of the backward-looking peasant party electorate (PSL) and by almost 80% of the "Solidarity' electorate! Thus, it is criticized from b o t h ends of political spectrum. The foregoing leads us to the conclusion that **the spectrum of economic philosophies is U-shaped, like Hannah Arendt spectrum of political philosophies.** Therefore, the distance between left wing views on the economy and their lack of acceptance of capitalism and right wing views and their lack of acceptance of capitalism is much smaller than the distance between both and the centre that actively promotes or at least acquiesces to capitalism. This, however, may be the general rule. A typically post-communist country problem is that both wings are usually relatively strong *vis-à-vis* the centre (that in Western societies gets some 70-90% of the vote).

It is worthwhile to identify main determinants of such criticism of and resistance to capitalist market order to evaluate probability of a shift of opinion that will allow a resumption of systemic change in the future. **The source of the strong support of parties and groupings that criticize post-1989 systemic change lies first of all, in the opinion of the present**

writer, in the erosion of a moral order brought about by half a century of communism.

Large state enterprises were the monuments of waste. The distance between what was trumpeted as achievements by propaganda and reported to higher levels of hierarchy and what was there in reality was greater than elsewhere in communist economies. At the same time better rewards than elsewhere for more fiction than elsewhere added to cynicism and demoralization. Xymena Gliszczynska [1994], labour psychologist, wrote about the shift of the locus of *lumpenproletariat* from the margin of the society to large state enterprises.

By the same token, we may use the term *lumpenintelligentsia* with respect to a substantial part of professionals and 'white collars' in general educated under communism. Thus, in Western societies and in East European ones before the advent of communism, those who acquired formal education and began professional career entered at the same time a given professional group that maintained its own professional standards and moral codes. The assault of communism very quickly liquidated autonomous professional associations and later eroded codes themselves.

The greater the passage of time from the normal world, its standards and codes, the greater was demoralization of *lumpenintelligentsia* that never knew any other world than that of communism. The same was the case of workers from large state enterprises (the new *lumpenproletariat*). In a rather large number of cases people learned to do without standards and codes, especially as they turned out to be an obstacle rather than help in obtaining higher pay and promotion.

The systemic change brought these habits to an end or at the very least threatened to do so in the not too distant future. Demoralized professionals and 'white collars' faced not only demands for better work from their new superiors but also a prospect that their juniors, who did not have enough time to become demoralized by the Soviet system, will soon replace them in their rather badly paid but also undemanding jobs. And in the medium term there has been the prospect of thousands of talented and diligent youngsters finishing better schools than those they attended themselves (often paying in private schools for their education!) and working with skills and enthusiasm in the environment that rewarded talent, skills, risk-taking, and hard work.

Those demoralized by the old regime soon after the start of transition began looking for a political representation that would promise them the return to the past or at least the substantial slowdown of the transition process. We are reminded by Douglass North [1979], a recent Nobel laureate in economics, that there are winners and losers in the economic activity and that those who lose in the market often do not adjust but turn to politics to regain what they lost.

It is not necessary that they actually lose. It is enough that they feel the threat of a loss or even have a feeling of uncertainty. Thus, people may talk of crisis even in the face of increasing living standards, as was the case of a majority of households in Poland in transition, not because they were worse off but because we live through times when 'the future appears most uncertain and can hardly be ascertained by extrapolating past trends' [Giersch, 1995].

This feeling of uncertainty has been reinforced by the perceptions of capitalism people held at the start of transition. As stressed by Szymanderski [1996] in the already quoted paper, the perceptions of capitalism have been formed by the ever dimmer intergenerational transmission of the images of the past normality and by, largely superficial, encounters with the West. The promise of the return to the mainstream or to 'normal economic standards of the West' was largely understood as the promise of a dramatic improvement in living standards, given what people saw at Western shops (without seeing Western factories and offices...).

The fact that such an improvement has been predicated upon preceding structural changes, associated redundancies and even enterprise closures, on the productivity increases, reduction of resource costs, elimination of sloppiness, shirking, and theft, as well as many other determinants of success, has hardly been taken into account. The fact that there have been identifiable losers or that the improvement in living standards (although significant) was not dramatic, added to frustration, disorientation, and reinforced search for alternatives - even phony or fraudulent ones. It is not surprising, for example, that almost 90% of those who in 1990 presidential elections voted for an economic charlatan (Tyminski) voted in 1995 for Kwasniewski.

The completion of the transition to a capitalist market economy is, however, necessary if Poland is not to end up in the middle of nowhere. Overregulated, overcentralized, and arbitrarily managed economy will not perform even with tolerable levels of efficiency (to say nothing about catching up with the community of countries we aspire to join). The institutional barriers analyzed in the report, if not removed, are going to exert an ever greater adverse influence on Polish economic performance.

To quote North [1979] again, in predatory economic systems there are two determinants of institutional (property rights) structure: interests of the ruling stratum and the cost reduction of maintaining the economic system, necessary for its survival. The inefficient institutions may survive for quite some time if they are benefiting the ruling stratum. But over time the pressure for their change is going to build up as efficiency deteriorates and the well-being declines. Let us add: especially, if the free elections are maintained. Changes in the voting pattern may then result.

Thus, the logic of the foregoing analysis suggests that things will get worse before they get better. Once they get worse, the well known *dictum* of George Shultz, an American businessman and politician, applies: 'If situation gets bad enough, people will do even the most obvious and sensible things'. Thus, there is room for medium term optimism.

REFERENCES

Giersch, H., 1995, Economic Dynamism: Lessons from German Experience. Prepared for the First International Hayek Memorial Conference, Vienna, March 15-17, mimeo.

Gliszczynska, X., 1994, Psychologiczne bariery pozytywnych efektów prywatyzacji (Psychological Barriers to Positive Effects of Privatization), w: Monitoring procesów prywatyzacyjnych 1992-1994, Centrum im. Adama Smitha, mimeo, in Polish.

Gruszecki, T., and J. Winiecki, 1991, Privatization in East-Central Europe: A Comparative Perspective, *Aussenwirtschaft*, No.1

North, D.C., 1979, A Framework for Analyzing the State in Economic History, *Explorations in Economic History*, Vol.16, July.

Pejovich, S., 1990, *The Economics of Property Rights: Towards a Theory of Comparative Systems*, Kluwer, Dordrecht.

Szymanderski, J., 1996, Stosunek opinii publicznej do zmian instytucjon-alnych w Polsce (Attitudes of Public Opinion to Institutional Changes in Poland). Zeszyty Centrum im. Adama Smitha, No.23, in Polish.

Winiecki, J., 1990, No Capitalism Minus Capitalists, *Financial Times*, June 20.

INDEX

For Product Safety Concerns and Information please contact our EU
representative GPSR@taylorandfrancis.com Taylor & Francis Verlag GmbH,
Kaufingerstraße 24, 80331 München, Germany

Printed and bound by CPI Group (UK) Ltd, Croydon, CR0 4YY

11/04/2025

01843992-0018